U.S. Environmental Protection Agency
Office of Enforcement and Compliance Monitoring

National Enforcement Investigations Center

Multi-Media Compliance Inspection Manual

Fourth Edition

For enforcement programs in:

Air
Water
RCRA
CERCLA
TSCA
FIFRA

Government Institutes, Inc.

PUBLISHER'S NOTE

This handbook was prepared by the U.S. Environmental Protection Agency's National Enforcement Investigations Center for use within the agency. Government Institutes determined that it contained information of interest to parties outside EPA so we undertook on our own to reproduce this material in order to serve those interested.

This publication is designed to provide accurate and authoritative information with regard to the subject matter covered. It is sold with the understanding that the publisher is not engaged in rendering legal, accounting or other professional service. If legal advice or other expert assistance is required, the services of a competent professional person should be sought.— From a Declaration of Principles jointly adopted by a Committee of the American Bar Association and a Committee of Publishers.

Publication of this book does not signify that the contents necessarily reflect the views or policies of Government Institutes, Inc.

July 1989

Published by

Government Institutes, Inc.
966 Hungerford Drive, #24
Rockville, MD 20850
U.S.A.

ISBN: 0-86587-779-3

Printed and bound in the United States of America

CONTENTS

CONTENTS (cont.)

TABLES

INTRODUCTION

PURPOSE

This manual is intended as a guide for investigators who conduct multi-media compliance audits of facilities that discharge, emit, prepare, manage, store, or dispose of pollutants controlled by Federal, State or local environmental laws and regulations. Investigative methods are presented that integrate the enforcement programs for air, water, solid waste, pesticides, and toxic substances. This manual describes general activities and functions and focuses on special features of specific media and associated statutes.

The purposes of a facility multi-media compliance audit are to:

- Review a facility's pollution control practices
- Evaluate operation, safety, and waste management equipment
- Determine status of compliance with applicable laws and regulations.

The environmental laws which EPA administers and enforces are summarized in Appendix A. Emphasis is given to identifying violations of regulations, permits, approvals, orders and consent decrees, and the underlying causes of such violations. Due to the complexity of laws and regulations, a comprehensive, in-depth review is not always possible. Investigators should conduct a thorough review so that violations and problems that have an existing or potential effect on the environment are identified and properly documented.

Pollution sources may vary in complexity depending on facility size, process operations and extent and efficiency of existing pollution controls. Time and personnel resources required to conduct compliance audits will vary. A large industrial facility with multiple process operations may require evaluation under several environmental statutes, such as the Clean Water Act (CWA), Clean Air Act (CAA), Resource Conservation and Recovery Act (RCRA), Toxic Substances Control Act (TSCA), Comprehensive Environmental Response, Compensation and Liability Act (CERCLA), and the Federal Insecticide,

Fungicide and Rodenticide Act (FIFRA). A multi-media compliance audit of this magnitude requires an audit team with combined experience in the various environmental media to effectively determine the pollution potential and/or compliance of the facility.

OBJECTIVES

This guide provides protocols for multi-media compliance audits. Specific objectives of such audits are to:

- Document facility noncompliance with environmental laws, regulations, orders, permits, consent decrees, and approvals

- Determine ability of a facility to maintain "continuous compliance" across all environmental areas

- Identify need for remedial measures and enforcement action(s) to correct the causes of violations

SCOPE

The multi-media compliance audit approach is designed to minimize the number of visits to a single facility. This manual addresses audit team activities before, during, and following the on-site audit.

In performing compliance audits, investigators should follow established Agency policies and procedures for:

- Chain-of-custody and document control
- Receipt and handling of confidential information
- Employee conduct, responsibilities, and ethics
- Quality assurance and quality control
- Safety rules

When established policies and procedures do not exist, common sense, professional judgment and experience should be applied. Investigators need to collect valid, factual information and supporting data which are adequately documented to ensure that these will be admissible as evidence in any subsequent enforcement action(s).

PLANNING THE AUDIT

The success of an audit depends on thorough, up-front planning. Coordination with all interested and knowledgeable parties (e.g., Region, State, audit team members, NEIC supervisory staff) is essential to ensure a smooth operation. All concerned parties should be identified and informed as soon as possible to ensure necessary coordination.

A comprehensive plan (project plan) provides a means for informing all involved parties of the upcoming activities and ensuring an effective compliance audit. The project plan describes the project objectives, tasks required to fulfill these objectives, methods and procedures to be followed, resources required and schedules. The plan generally addresses the following:

<u>Objectives</u> - The plan defines what the audit is to accomplish (e.g., to assess environmental compliance with the regulations that apply to the source--water, air, et al.).

<u>Tasks</u> - The plan defines tasks for accomplishing the objectives and spells out procedures for obtaining the necessary information and evaluating facility compliance. The tasks usually involve an evaluation of process operations, pollution control/treatment and disposal practices, operation and maintenance practices, self-monitoring, recordkeeping and reporting practices, and pollution abatement/control needs.

<u>Procedures</u> - The plan provides or references policies and procedures for document control, chain-of-custody, quality assurance, and handling and processing of confidential information. Specific instructions for the particular audit may be provided.

<u>Safety</u> - The plan includes the written safety procedures which the EPA audit team must follow [Appendix B]. Additional safety procedures may be considered for extensive or prolonged investigations.

<u>Resources</u> - The plan describes personnel needs and equipment requirements. Experienced and knowledgeable personnel shall compose the compliance audit team.

<u>Schedules</u> - The plan provides schedules for the audit activities. This information is important to the participants as well as the Headquarters, Regional and/or State officials who requested the project. The dates for (a) starting and finishing the field activities, (b) analytical work, and (c) draft and final reports should be established and agreed upon by the participants.

THE AUDIT TEAM

KNOWLEDGE AND SKILLS REQUIRED

The audit team should possess a good working knowledge of the various environmental pollution control statutes. Team members should understand the rules, regulations and other provisions, including permits, registrations, authorizations, limitations, monitoring requirements, etc., as they pertain to the facility. The investigators should have knowledge of Agency policies and procedures, inspection authority, manufacturing and production processes, applicable pollution control technology and the nature of pollution problems and possible solutions, including available treatment and controls.

Individual team members may have more specific knowledge of a process, monitoring system, control equipment, environmental media, regulation, etc. than others. The team, as a whole, however, should have collective knowledge and background to efficiently and effectively conduct all aspects of a facility audit. They should also understand the techniques for evidence gathering and possess skill in collecting information and in interviewing officials of the public and regulated communities.

INVESTIGATOR RESPONSIBILITIES

Investigators represent the Agency when they deal with the regulated community and the public. They should conduct themselves in a professional manner and maintain their composure and credibility at all times. Cooperation and good working relations with facility personnel should be established and maintained. EPA investigators must adhere to the provisions described in the EPA handbook "Responsibilities and Conduct for EPA Employees."

Safety plans must be prepared in advance for audits where field sampling is conducted or where potential exists for exposure to hazardous substances or conditions [Appendix B]. Applicable safety provisions and precautions are to be followed throughout the audit. EPA field certification at basic, intermediate or advanced levels is required by Agency Order 1440.2, Health and Safety Requirements for Employees Engaged in Field Activities. If work at hazardous waste sites is involved, training and other requirements of the OSHA Hazardous Waste Site Worker Rule (29 CFR 1910.120) may also apply.

Audit team members will dress appropriately, including wearing protective clothing or equipment. Safety requirements must be identified before the on-site audit so that no delays occur. Investigators should provide their own safety equipment and should not rely on the facility, except in unique situations where special equipment is required. Required respirator "fit" testing, field certifications, and medical monitoring physicals must be completed in advance. In general, company safety requirements must be met in addition to the appropriate EPA requirements and guidelines addressed in the following documents:

Agency Safety Manual - Chapters 1 through 10

Agency Orders
- 1000.18 Transportation of Hazardous Materials
- 1440.2 Health and Safety Requirements for Employees Engaged in Field Activities
- 1440.3 Respiratory Protection
- 1440.4 Health and Safety Training Requirements for Mine Safety
- 1440.6 Motor Vehicle Occupant Restraint Systems
- 1440.7 Hazard Communication
- 3100.1 Uniforms, Protective Clothing and Protective Equipment
- 3100.3 Authorization of Performance of Hazardous Duty

Agency Guidelines
- Standard Operating Safety Guides
- Eye Protection Program Guideline
- Respiratory Protection Program Guideline
- Selection Guide for Chemical Protective Clothing

- Interim Health and Safety Guidelines for EPA Asbestos Inspectors

- Occupational Safety and Health Guidance Manual for Hazardous Waste Site Activities

Information which is claimed or requested to be held confidential must be handled properly to prevent disclosure to unauthorized persons. Investigators must have specific authorization for accessing and handling TSCA Confidential Business Information (TSCA Section 14). Other environmental media have confidentiality provisions and the inspector is referred to these statutes and regulations. Inspectors must be familiar with the confidentiality regulations to ensure that information is handled properly.

AUDIT PREPARATION

COMPILATION AND REVIEW OF BACKGROUND INFORMATION

Collection and analysis of background information on the facility to be inspected are essential to the effective planning and overall success of a compliance audit. Information can be obtained from the files of Federal, State and local agencies, technical libraries, EPA databases and other sources. The background review will enable investigators to become familiar with facility operations; clarify technical and legal issues before entry; and develop a sound, factual audit report.

During a properly conducted background review, the investigator should identify both the technical and legal information needed and available. The types of information which may be acquired and reviewed are discussed below.

Technical Information

Facility Background

- Maps showing facility location and environmental and geographic features (stacks, discharge pipes, and solid waste disposal sites)
- Geology/hydrogeology of the area
- Aerial photographs
- Names, titles, phone numbers of responsible facility officials
- Process description, process flow charts and major production areas
- Records reflecting changes in facility conditions since previous audit/permit application
- Production levels - past, present and future

Audit Reports, Records and Files

- Federal and State compliance files

- Correspondence between the facility and the local, State and Federal agencies
- Citizens' complaints and reports, follow-up studies, findings
- Audit records, reports, correspondence on past incidents or violations
- Emissions inventory
- Self-monitoring data and reports
- EPA, State, and consultant studies and reports
- Annual reports by the facility (e.g., PCB annual documents and inventories, Securities Exchange Commission §10K reports)
- Records, applications, reports, manifest files, etc. (e.g., RCRA reports, CERCLA submittals)
- Laboratory audit reports, QA/QC activities
- Records of previous hazardous substances spills

<u>Pollutant and Waste Generation, Control, Treatment, and Disposal Systems</u>

- Description and design data for pollution control systems and process operations
- Sources and characterization of wastewater discharges, hazardous wastes, emissions, types of treatment, and disposal operations
- Type and amount of waste generated which is discharged, emitted, stored, treated, and disposed
- Waste storage, treatment, and disposal areas
- Waste/spill contingency plans
- Available bypasses, diversions, and spill containment facilities
- Industrial process, pollution control, treatment and disposal methods, monitoring systems

Legal Information

Requirements, Regulations, and Limitations

- Permit applications, draft or existing permits, registrations, approvals, and applicable Federal, State and local regulations and requirements
- Application certificates, EPA identification numbers
- Information on draft permits which is different from current conditions
- Exemptions and waivers
- Receiving stream water quality standards, ambient air standards, State Implementation Plans, protected uses
- RCRA notification and Part A and Part B applications
- Pesticide labels
- Grant applications for publicly owned treatment works, research and development demonstration projects and progress reports on these projects
- Federal and State classification of facility (e.g., Interim Status, Small Quantity Generator)

Enforcement History

- Status of current and pending litigation against the facility*
- Deficiency notices issued to facility and responses by the facility
- Status of administrative orders, consent decrees and other regulatory corrective actions, if any, and compliance by the facility
- Penalties imposed against the company

---

* *Coordination should occur prior to the audit (in conjunction with the EPA Regional Office) with the local Assistant United States Attorney or Justice Department attorney responsible for the civil or criminal case and any consent decree.*

Information Sources

Laws and Regulations - Federal laws and regulations establish procedures, controls and other requirements applicable to a facility [Table 1]. In addition, State laws and regulations and sometimes even local ordinances may be applicable, or take precedence.

Permits and Permit Applications - Permits provide information on the limitations, requirements, and restrictions applicable to discharges, emissions and disposal practices; compliance schedules; and monitoring, analytical, and reporting requirements. Applications provide technical information on facility size, layout, and location of pollution sources; waste and pollutant generation, treatment, control and disposal practices; contingency plans and emergency procedures; and pollutant characterization - types, amounts, and locations of discharge, emissions or disposal.

Regional and State Files - These files often contain grant records, applications, facility self-monitoring data, and audit reports, as well as permits and permit applications pertaining to individual facilities. These information sources can provide compliance, enforcement, and litigation history; special exemptions and waivers applied for and granted or denied; citizen complaints and action taken; process operating problems/solutions; pollution problems/solutions; and laboratory capabilities. Consultant reports can provide design and operating data and recommendations for processes; pollutant sources; treatment, control, and disposal systems; and remedial measures.

Technical Reports, Documents, and References - These sources provide information on industrial process operations, data on available treatment, control and disposal techniques, such as their advantages or drawbacks, limits of application, etc. Such sources include Effluent Guideline and New Source Performance Standard development documents and EPA's Treatability Manual. Similar guidance documents on hazardous waste generation, treatment/disposal are also available.

Table 1

FEDERAL STATUTES/REGULATIONS FOR MULTI-MEDIA COMPLIANCE AUDITS

	Air CAA	Water CWA	Superfund CERCLA and EPCRTKA	Pesticides FIFRA	Solid Waste RCRA	Drinking Water SDWA	Toxics TSCA
Inspection Authority	114,[a] 211[a] [80, 86[b]]	308, 402 [122.41]	104	8, 9 [160.15, 169.3]	3007, 9005 [270.30]	1445 [142.34, 144,51]	11 [717.17, 792.15]
Recordkeeping Authority	114, 208 [51, 57, 58, 60, 61, 79, 85, 86]	308, 402 [122.41, 122.48]	103 372.10	4, 8 [160.63, 169, 160.185-195]	3001, 3002, 3003, 3004, 9003 [262.40, 263.22, 264.74, 264.279, 264.309, 265.74, 264.309, 270.30]	1445 [141.31-33, 144.51, 144.54]	8 [704, 710, 717.15, 720.78, 761.180, 762.80, 763.114, 792.185-195]
Confidential Information	208, 307 [2.201-2.215, 2.301, 53, 57, 80]	308 [2.201-2.215, 2.302, 122.7]	104 [2.201-2.215] 322 [350]	7, 10 [2.201-2.215 2.307]	3007, 9005 [2.201-2.215, 2.305, 260.2, 270.12]	1445 [2.201-2.215, 2.304, 144.5]	14 [2.201-2.215, 2.306, 704.7, 707.75, 710.7, 712.15, 717.19, 720.80-95, 750.16, 750.36, 762.60, 763.74]
Emergency Authority	303	504	104, 106 [300.53, 300.65]	27 [164.166]	7003	1431	7
Employee Protection	322	507	110		7001	1450	23
Permits Basic requirements include applications, standard permit conditions, monitoring, reporting		[122, 125]			[270]	[144, 147]	
EPA procedures for permit issuance	[124]	124]			[124]	[124]	
Technical requirements	[52]	[129, 133, 136, 302[c]] BMP[d] [125] SPCC[e] [112] Waivers [125, 130]			[260-266]	[146, 264]	
Specific References	NSPS[f] NESHAP[g] [61] CEM[h] [60] SIP[j] [52] PSD[k] [50]	Effluent guidelines [400-460] BMP [125], SPCC [112], Pretreatment [125, 403], Toxic [129]			Generators [262], Transporters [263], TSD[i] [265], Stds. for TSD Permits [264], Interim Stds [265], Storage <90 days [262], Exemptions [261]		PCBs [761] Dioxin [775]

a Statute (e.g., Clean Air Act, Section 114 or 211)
b [80, 86] - 40 CFR, Parts 80 and 86; CFR refers to Code of Federal Regulations
c Reportable quantities
d BMP - Best Management Practices
e SPCC - Spill Prevention Control and Countermeasures Plan
f NSPS - New Source Performance Standards
g NESHAP - National Emission Standards for Hazardous Air Pollutants
h CEM - Continuous Emission Monitoring
i TSD - Treatment, Storage and Disposal
j SIP- State Implementation Plan
k PSD - Prevention of Significant Deterioration

The background information sources for overall program areas and those that apply specifically to the water, air, solid waste, pesticides, and toxic substances programs are listed in Table 2.

NOTIFYING THE FACILITY

In most cases, notification for routine audits is given to the facility, but are not required. In cases where there is concern that physical conditions may be altered prior to the audit or that records may be destroyed, an unannounced audit should be conducted. The initial contact is usually by phone with follow-up written confirmation of the anticipated audit period. The notification letter specifies the authority for the audit and outlines the areas to be covered during the audit and the information to be provided. This approach improves the chances that responsible facility officials will be present and that necessary information will be readily available.

Typical information requested in a notification letter for availability during the audit may include the following:

- Raw materials, imports, intermediates, products, byproducts, production levels
- Facility maps identifying process areas, discharge and emission points, waste disposal sites
- Flow diagrams or descriptions of processes and waste control, treatment and disposal systems showing where wastewater, air emission, and solid waste sources are located
- Description and design of pollution control and treatment systems and normal operating parameters
- Operations and maintenance procedures and problems
- Appropriate packaging and shipping labels
- Self-monitoring reports and inventories of discharges and emissions
- Self-monitoring equipment in use, normal operating levels, and available data
- Required plans and records

Table 2

BACKGROUND REVIEW INFORMATION SOURCES

Overall Program Areas	Water Pollution CWA	Air Pollution CAA	Solid Wastes Pollution RCRA	Toxic Substances Pollution TSCA	FIFRA/CERCLA
NEIC Information Retrieval System data on corporate structure, financial conditions, pollution control history, environmental and health impacts of pollutants of interest.	NPDES permits/permit applications/draft permits	Air permits and permit applications (Federal/State/local)	Part A of permit application (TSDs only) to designate type and volume of wastes handled, type and design capacity of treatment, storage and/or disposal processes	Available information on chemical substances produced by facility	FIFRA
EPA grants (R&D, constructing, planning)	Applicable effluent guidelines	Self-monitoring requirements and self-reported data	Part B of permit application, if available	Applicable regulations regarding manufacture, identification, self-reporting requirements, concerning toxic materials (e.g., PCB rules)	Establishment numbers, Certified Applicator numbers
Information available on process operations; pollutants of interest; existing treatment, control and disposal practices; raw material	Compliance inspection reports (Federal/State/local)	Compliance inspection reports (Federal/State/local)	Draft/final RCRA permit	Inspection reports (Federal/State/local)	Applicable labels
Administrative Orders issued for environmental noncompliance	Laboratory performance reports	Applicable NESHAP	Applicable regulations for source designations	Technical manuals and references on applicable treatment/control and disposal technology, inspection and monitoring procedures and techniques	Inspection reports (Federal/State)
Applicable local ordinances on environmental control	Self-monitoring requirements and self-reporting data	Applicable NSPS	Groundwater monitoring plans/data		EPA Pesticide Inspection Manual
Compliance history and present compliance status	Best Management Practices Plan	Applicable air quality standards	UIC permit and present status		State Facility Permits for procedures, bulk storage
Available correspondence between regulating officer and facility officials	Spill Prevention Control and Countermeasure Plan	State Implementation Plan	Hydrogeologic reports on local area relative to UIC permit		CERCLA
Available contractor/consultant report on facility environmental control matters	Pretreatment requirements if facility discharges to POTW	Ambient air quality reports for AQCR	Self-monitoring requirements and self-reported data		Preliminary Assessment (PA) reports
Environmental compliance schedules and present status	Applicable Federal/State regulations related to water pollution control at facility	Stack test reports	Applicable regulation on manifest requirements		Site Inspection (SI) reports
Available aerial photography	Technical manuals and references on pollution treatment/control technology, process operation, monitoring inspection procedures	Air pollutants emission inventories	Inspection reports (Federal/State/local)		Remedial Investigation/Feasibility Study (RI/FS) reports
	Interstate Commission water quality data (Ohio River Sanitary Commission, Delaware River Basin Commission, Interstate Commission on the Potomac River	Continuous monitoring practices and facility and applicable performance inspections	Technical manual and references on applicable treatment/control and disposal technology, inspection and monitoring procedures and techniques		Records of Decision (RODs)
		Available contractor/consultant reports			Remedial Design (RD) reports
		Technical manuals and references on applicable pollution treatment/control technology, process operators, air pollution monitoring, inspection procedures			Removal Action reports

CONDUCTING THE AUDIT

The compliance audit will consist of the following phases:

- Entry
- Opening conference
- The on-site inspection
- Closing conference

ENTRY

The team should arrive at the facility during normal working hours, unless special circumstances, such as suspected illegal activity at night, are being investigated. The investigators shall identify themselves to the owner, agent in charge, or other responsible facility official; present their official Agency credentials to the facility official, whether requested or not; and explain the purpose of the audit. Tables 3 and 4 outline the various Federal environmental statutes which give Agency employees the authority to enter facilities, review records, and collect samples.

If the audit is conducted at a Federal facility that has national security information, restricted or classified areas, special procedures may be required for entry. For example, a military installation regulation may stipulate that investigators shall provide proof of appropriate security clearance before entry is approved into restricted areas. When this occurs, the investigators should refer such special cases to their appropriate legal staff (e.g., Office of Regional Counsel).

When the facility provides a blank sign-in sheet, log or visitor register, it is acceptable for investigators to sign it. Note, however, that EPA employees must not sign any type of "waiver" or "visitor release" that would relieve the facility of responsibility for injury or which would limit the rights of the Agency to use data obtained from the facility. When such a waiver or release is presented, team members should politely explain they cannot sign such a document and request a blank sign-in sheet. If they are refused entry because they do not sign such a release, the team should immediately report all pertinent facts to the appropriate

Table 3

INSPECTION AUTHORITY UNDER THE MAJOR ENVIRONMENTAL ACTS

CAA - § 114(a)(2)

". . .the Administrator or his authorized representative, upon presentation of his credentials - shall have a right of entry to, upon, or through any premises of such person or in which any records required to be maintained. . .are located, and may at reasonable times have access to and copy any records, inspect any monitoring equipment and method. . .and sample any emissions. . .."

CWA - § 308(a)(4)(B)

". . .the Administrator or his authorized representative. . .upon presentation of his credentials - (i) shall have a right of entry to, upon, or through any premises in which an effluent source is located or in which any records required to be maintained. . .are located, and (ii) may at reasonable times have access to and copy any records, inspect any monitoring equipment or method. . . any sample any effluents which the owner or operator of such source is required to sample. . .."

RCRA - § 3007(a)

". . .any such person who generates, stores, treats, transports, disposes of or otherwise handles or has handled hazardous wastes shall upon request of any. . .employee or representative of the Environmental Protection Agency. . .furnish information relating to such wastes and permit such person at all reasonable times to have access to, and to copy all records relating to such wastes."

". . .such employees or representatives are authorized. . .to enter at reasonable times any establishment or other place where hazardous wastes are or have been generated, stored, treated or disposed of or transported from; to inspect and obtain samples from any person of any such wastes and samples of any containers or labeling for such wastes."

- § 9005(a)(1)

". . .representatives are authorized. . .to enter. . .inspect and obtain samples. . .

TSCA - § 11(a)(b)

". . .any duly designated representative of the Administrator, may inspect any establishment. . .in which chemical substances or mixtures are manufactured, processed, stored or held before or after their distribution in commerce and any conveyance being used to transport chemical substances, mixtures or such articles in connection with distribution in commerce. Such an inspection may only be made upon the presentation of appropriate credentials and of a written notice to the owner, co-operator or agent in charge of the premises or conveyance to be inspected."

FIFRA - § 8 and 9

". . .any person who sells or offers for sale, delivers or offers for delivery any pesticide. . .shall, upon request of any officer or employee of the Environmental Protection Agency. . .furnish or permit such person at all reasonable times to have access to, and to copy: (1) all records showing the delivery, movement or holding of such pesticide or device, including the quantity, the date of shipment and receipt, and the name of the consignor and consignee. . .."

". . .officers or employees duly designated by the Administrator are authorized to enter at reasonable times, any establishment or other place where pesticides or devices are held for distribution or sale for the purpose of inspecting and obtaining samples of any pesticides or devices, packaged, labeled and released for shipment and samples of any containers or labeling for such pesticides or devices."

"Before undertaking such inspection, the officers or employees must present to the owner, operator or agent in charge of the establishment. . . appropriate credentials and a written statement as to the reason for the inspection, including a statement as to whether a violation of the law is suspected."

". . .employees duly designated by the Administrator are empowered to obtain and to execute warrants authorizing entry. . .inspection and reproduction of all records. . .and the seizure of any pesticide or device which is in violation of this Act."

SDWA - §1445

". . .the Administrator, or representatives of the Administrator. . .upon presenting appropriate credentials and a written notice to any. . .person subject to. . .any requirement. . .is authorized to enter any establishment, facility or other property. . .in order to determine. . .compliance with this title, including for this purpose, inspection, at reasonable times, of records, files, papers, processes, controls and facilities or in order to test any feature of a public water system, including its raw water source."

CERCLA (Superfund) - § 104(e)

"Any officer, employee or representative of the President. . .is authorized to. . .

require any person. . .to furnish. . .information or documents relating to. . .identification, nature and quantity of material. . .generated, treated, stored, or disposed. . .or transported. . .nature or extent of a release. . .ability of a person to pay. . ."

". . .access. . .to inspect and copy all documents or records. . ."

". . .to enter. . .place or property where any hazardous substance or pollutant or contaminant may be or has been generated, stored, treated, disposed of, or transported from. . .needed to determine the need for response. . ."

". . .to inspect and obtain samples. . ."

Table 4

SUMMARY OF FEDERAL ENVIRONMENTAL ACTS REGARDING RIGHT OF ENTRY, INSPECTIONS, SAMPLING, TESTING, ETC.

Act/Section	Designated Representative	Presentation of Credentials	Notice of Inspection	Sampling Permitted	Inspection of Records	Sample Splits	Receipt for Agency's Samples	Return of Analytical Results
Clean Water Act - § 308(a)	Yes, auth. by Administrator	Required	Not required	Yes (effluents which the owner is required to sample)	Yes	Not required	Not required	Not required
FIFRA - § 8(b) (Books and Records)	Yes, designated by Administrator	Required	Written notice required with reason and suspected violation note	Access and copy records	Yes	N/A	N/A	N/A
FIFRA - § 9(a) (Inspections of Establishments)	Yes, designated by Administrator	Required	Written notice required with reasons for for inspection	Yes	See § 8	Required, if requested	Required	Required, promptly
Clean Air Act - § 114(a)	Yes, auth. by Administrator	Required	Not required except notify State for SIP sources	Yes	Yes	Not required	Not required	Not required
RCRA - § 3007(a) § 9005(a)	Yes, designated by Administrator	Not required	Not required	Yes	Yes	Required, if requested	Required	Required, promptly
SDWA - §1445(b)	Yes, designated by Administrator	Required	Written notice required, must also notify State with reasons for entry if State has primary enforcement responsibility	Yes	Yes	Not required	Not required	Not required
TSCA - § 11(a, b)	Yes, designated by Administrator	Required	Written notice required	(The Act does not mention samples or sampling in this section. It does state an inspection shall extend to all things within the premise of conveyance.)	Yes	N/A		N/A
CERCLA - §104(e)	Yes, designated by President	Not required	Upon reasonable notice for information	Yes	Yes	Required, if requested	Required	Required, promptly

supervisory and legal staff, and leave the facility if the matter cannot be resolved. All events surrounding the refused entry should be fully documented, including the name of the person refusing entry.

Various Federal environmental statutes give Agency investigators the authority to enter facilities, review records and collect environmental samples [Tables 3 and 4]. The audit should be made with the consent of the facility owner and/or authorized person, unless the audit is conducted under a warrant. When the investigator is allowed to enter, entry is considered voluntary and consensual by the facility operator or owner, unless the investigator is expressly told to leave the premises. Consent to enter can, however, be revoked at any time during the audit. If this occurs, all information collected during the consensual phase remains in possession of the investigators. When withdrawal of consent takes place, the same procedures apply as for denial of entry.

Because audits may be considered adversary proceedings, investigators may be challenged as to their legal authority, techniques and competency. Facility personnel may also display antagonism to Agency personnel. In all cases, the investigators must courteously explain the authorities and the reasons for the protocols followed. If explanations are not satisfactory or disagreements cannot be resolved, the team should leave and obtain further direction from the appropriate Agency supervisory or legal staff.

In certain circumstances, audits will be conducted under authority of search warrants. A warrant is a judicial authorization for appropriate persons to enter specifically described locations and to perform certain audit functions. It is possible that a pre-audit warrant could be obtained when there is reason to believe that entry will be denied or when violations are expected which could be hidden during the time a search warrant was obtained. When authorized by a judge or magistrate, administrative search warrants can be served by a team member. Criminal search warrants, once obtained, are to be served by designated Federal law enforcement officials (e.g., EPA OCI Special Agents) and not by an audit team member.

OPENING CONFERENCE

At the opening conference with facility officials, the project coordinator presents his or her credentials; provides names and credentials of the other team members, purpose of the audit and laws under which the audit is being conducted; and outlines procedures and proposed schedule to be followed. If not previously done, any required notices should also be presented to facility representatives at this time.* A cooperative working relationship is encouraged between the investigators and the facility officials; this arrangement will simplify assignments and contribute to the success of the compliance audit.

Major topics discussed at the opening conference should include: audit objectives, processes and areas to be inspected, anticipated audit schedules within various areas of the facility, types of records to be reviewed, safety requirements, handling of confidential data (which should be obtained only if absolutely necessary), manner of handling questions during the course of the audit and the closing conference. Facility officials should be informed of their right, under RCRA, CERCLA/Superfund and FIFRA, to receive duplicates, replicates, or splits of any samples taken and receive the results of analyses. If team members desire to take photographs or copies of records during the audit, this should also be discussed in the opening conference.

Photographs are used to prepare a thorough and accurate investigation report, as evidence in enforcement proceedings and to explain conditions found at the plant. The facility, however, may object to the use of cameras in their facility and on their property. If a mutually acceptable solution cannot be reached and photographs are considered essential to the audit, Agency supervisory and legal staff should be contacted for advice.

Facility personnel may also request that photographs taken during the visitation be considered confidential, and the Agency is obliged to comply, pending further legal determination. Self-developing film, although often of less

---

* *Under FIFRA, TSCA, and SDWA, written notification is required before entry. For "unannounced audits," this notification can be provided at the time of entry. Under TSCA, the investigator presents a TSCA Inspection Confidentiality Notice which informs the facility of their right to claim certain materials as Confidential Business Information (CBI).*

satisfactory quality, is useful in these situations. A facility may refuse permission to take photographs unless they can see the finished print. Duplicate photographs (one for the investigator and the other for the facility) should satisfy this need. When taking photographs considered TSCA Confidential Business Information (CBI), self-developing film eliminates processing problems, otherwise, the film processor must also have TSCA CBI clearance. Note, however, that some self-developing film may contain disposable negatives which must also be handled in accordance with the TSCA CBI requirements. Giving the facility the option of developing the film may resolve problems when self-developing film is not satisfactory.

Photographs must be fully documented, following procedures for handling evidentiary materials [Appendix C].

GENERAL AUDIT PROCEDURES

The general elements that are common to all environmental compliance areas which are process operations, pollution control, treatment and disposal, and operation and maintenance are discussed below. Specific guidelines that complement the general elements are contained in the following section, organized by environmental media - air, water, solid/hazardous wastes, and toxic substances, pesticides, etc. Checklists, although not necessarily comprehensive can be helpful, and several are provided in the appendices.

On-site audit activities include reviewing records, reports, and data; observing and evaluating equipment, monitors, devices and operations; and interviewing facility personnel. Therefore, it is important to have a knowledgeable facility representative(s) accompany the investigators during the audit.

Process Operations

Collectively, the audit team must have a basic understanding of the physical plant under investigation and the general processes used at the facility. This knowledge is necessary to aid in determining the substances (e.g., raw materials, products, byproducts, and waste materials) and how these are managed, including release as pollutants into the environment. The compliance audit team is not required to have an in-depth understanding of the industrial processes, but investigators should have sufficient understanding to conduct a thorough and efficient audit.

The compliance audit team may perform the following:

- Determine if changes have occurred since the last audit, permit issuance, etc. in process units, their operation and flow diagrams by comparison with available information. Determine the present production level and rate of product, byproduct, and waste generation. Determine the rate of raw material usage. Determine production process unit mode (e.g., continuous or batch). Information on production is essential if pollution control limits are based on production rates or products. Process modifications may have changed the types and loads of pollutants emitted, discharged or disposed. Different production levels could cause higher emission mass loadings or gas flow rates. Varying operating conditions can cause pollutant collection and control problems.

- Identify those processes or physical elements of the facility which contribute to sources of pollution (air, water, solid/hazardous waste). Identify the sources, characterization, flow rates, etc. at points where wastewater, gaseous emissions, and solid wastes are generated. Determine fate of byproducts (e.g., do they discharge or emit directly to the environment or to storage facilities or to a treatment facility). Determine types and amounts of pollutants being discharged.

- Determine the variability of process controls and production rates and their relationship to pollutant emission discharges. Determine if production upsets are tied to pollution incidents, exceedences, etc., and the facility response to these upsets.

- Determine if process or facility modifications are proposed or planned. Obtain information on these modifications, including schedules, and certainty of the modifications (e.g., is the change proposed or planned, have funds been reserved). Obtain documentation or facility estimates on wastes generated and discharged.

Pollution Control, Treatment and Disposal

After investigators have determined which processes generate wastes and how much, they should determine how the waste materials are handled and ultimately released, treated, or disposed. This includes tracking the waste from generation to final disposition, using process flow diagrams, physical audits, and facility records.

The compliance audit team may perform the following:

- Determine which waste streams are regulated by Federal, State or local regulations, licenses and approvals. In doing so, the investigators will be able to tailor their audit activities to the handling, disposal and treatment requirements of the appropriate regulations. Identify the various items regulated under the established Federal regulations as shown in Table 1. Although it is desirable to obtain information on all waste streams generated (both those that are and those that are not specifically regulated), the emphasis must be placed on the handling of regulated wastes. This will ensure that the audit team accomplishes the major objective of determining compliance with applicable regulations in a reasonable period.

- Obtain updated descriptions and schematics of major pollution control equipment and waste storage/treatment/disposal areas. Visually inspect equipment and storage/treatment/disposal areas. Locate points of pollutant emission or discharge and waste disposal or storage, including alternative locations, such as diversions, bypasses and overflows.

- Obtain design information and startup dates for pollution control/ treatment devices and waste disposal areas. Observe disposal areas and equipment during operation. Locate and observe indicating and recording instrumentation for monitoring control/treatment devices; compare operating levels to design specifications to determine if devices are operating normally. Review operations maintenance and inspection records. Identify any operating problems and their probable causes.

- Evaluate sampling techniques, equipment, and locations used for collection of representative samples. Identify recycle and dilution streams and other flow characteristics and relate to the sampling locations. Determine if samples are being collected consistently with permit/regulation requirements (e.g., grab vs. composite) and frequency of sample collection. Observe monitoring procedures such as flow measurement, sample collection and preservation, calibration procedures, in-stack monitors, etc. Determine if proper parameters are being monitored, if the methods and records are consistent with permits and regulations, and if results are properly calculated and reported. Evaluate quality assurance/quality control procedures followed by the company.

- Determine facility plans to expand existing treatment facilities and install new treatment units. Obtain copies of design criteria, consultants' reports, etc. Based on these data and first-hand observations, determine what additional treatment may be required to meet existing permit limits, regulations, and other requirements.

- Evaluate compliance with schedules, including status of engineering plans and equipment design, procurement, fabrication, installation and testing and startup of equipment. Determine if the final requirements can be achieved on time, and verify if structures are in place. Identify any delays associated with particular construction schedule and possible violations. If schedules are not being met, determine if the facility has rescheduled activities (e.g., corporate resolutions, financing agreements, contracts, equipment orders and engineering services documents). Verify dates when documents were completed. Determine if recruitment and training of new personnel (and potential new hires) for new pollution control activities have been initiated.

- Review laboratory analytical methods, procedures, recordkeeping, and quality control measures. Determine if the methods conform to permit and regulatory requirements. Determine if laboratory quality assurance and quality control are sufficient to evaluate data (e.g., proper and timely calibration, fresh chemical reagents, and scheduled equipment maintenance). In some cases, laboratory evaluations may involve off-site (company or contract) laboratories. In these cases, determine if the off-site labs have already been evaluated by EPA as part of the contract laboratory program, other compliance, etc.

Operation and Maintenance (O&M)

Knowledge of the operation and maintenance practices for the process and control facilities provides the investigator insight into plant management and problems including frequency of breakdowns, malfunctions, upsets, outages, diversions, spills and leaks, bypasses, and waste variability. It is important to determine the causes of these incidents and if they can be corrected. O&M review includes preventive, routine, and remedial maintenance programs; spare parts inventory; emergency operating and response programs; training and certification of plant personnel; alarm systems for power and equipment failures; backup systems; and housekeeping practices throughout the plant. The O&M review also includes review of facility and corporate policies and protocols and schedules for such items as reading and calibrating instrumentation, examining recording charts and logs, and updating O&M manuals, engineering drawings and specifications, supplier manuals, and equipment data cards.

The compliance audit team may determine major factors which affect process discharge, emissions, disposal, controls and changes in operation. O&M practices should be evaluated as to whether they are adequate for the proper management of pollution control equipment. Abnormal releases can be due to progressive equipment deterioration or lack of repair. Also, as equipment ages, efficiency drops and original removal rates may not be achieved. Startup and shutdown of process and control facilities can create problems of surge waste releases which may be alleviated by improved plant management.

AUDIT PROCEDURES FOR SPECIFIC MEDIA OR SPECIAL AREAS

Air

Air pollution audit items are divided into four groups:

- Operating conditions
- Control equipment
- Continuous monitoring
- Compliance records and testing.

The team should be prepared to observe, review, and document these audit items so that factual information can later be evaluated and compliance determined.

Before the audit, State air pollution control regulations that are part of the approved State Implementation Plan (SIP) and State operating permits should be reviewed. In addition, the checklists in Appendix D, which address the New Source Performance Standards (40 CFR Part 60) and the National Emission Standards for Hazardous Air Pollutants (40 CFR Part 61) including asbestos, should be compared to an updated emissions inventory to determine if the facility has any sources subject to these Standards. An updated emissions inventory will also provide a list of regulated point sources within the facility.

Operating Conditions

- Determine if construction and operating permits are current.

- Review records to determine if facility is operating within the limitations of the permit.

- Review records for abnormal operations, shutdowns, malfunctions. Determine cause, frequency, and potential impact on emissions.

- Determine if any operational changes (feedstock, fuel flow rate, temperature changes, etc.) have been made that could potentially affect emissions.

- Observe evidence of air pollution effects on premises, especially over surrounding areas (e.g., odors, dusting, deposits on cars, vegetation damage). Fugitive emissions may require special attention. Odor problems may best be characterized outside the plant because of olfactory fatigue inside the plant.

Control Equipment

- Compare observed operating conditions with baseline values obtained from compliance stack tests or from manufacturer's specifications.

- Compare control equipment monitoring values (pressure drop, flow rates, primary and secondary currents, etc.) with permit and/or regulatory requirements.

- Conduct control system evaluation. Review instrumentation, design and operational flow rates, temperatures, pressure drops, and emission monitors. From these data, the investigator should be able to determine if the plant is achieving compliance under normal operating conditions.

- Review control equipment maintenance procedures, malfunctions and corrective actions taken.

- Check number of emissions violations and any complaints filed since the last audit.

Continuous Emission Monitoring (CEM)

- Review operational (calibration, span, checks, etc.) and maintenance practices.

- Review records for excess emission reports (EERs) and determine cause.

- Review Performance Specification Tests and compare with 40 CFR 60, Appendix B requirements.

- Correlate the opacity monitor readings with VEOs.

Compliance Records and Testing

- Check source records for compliance with applicable regulations, including NESHAP, NSPS.

- Review source test reports. For most large sources (potential emissions of any pollutant greater than 100 tons per year) the facility should have a source test that shows compliance with regulated limits. The test method should be one specified in the SIP - usually an EPA reference test method (40 CFR Part 60, Appendix A). The test report should contain process conditions at the time of the test and enough data to determine if the test was conducted properly.

- Determine if on-site visible emission observations are warranted; an investigator doing CAA audits must be certified for visible emissions observations; otherwise, the readings will not be enforceable.

Water

Water pollution audit components can be categorized into five groups:

- Control and treatment systems
- Self-monitoring systems (including both field and laboratory measurements)
- Operation and maintenance
- Best Management Practices (BMP)
- Spill Prevention Control and Countermeasure (SPCC) Plan

Before the audit, the investigators should review the checklists in Appendix E, and obtain and review copies of the discharge permit, permit application, discharge monitoring reports (DMRs), and any additional required plans (Spill Prevention Control and Countermeasure Plan, etc.).

Control and Treatment Systems

Determine if all wastewaters generated by the facility are adequately controlled, recycled, directed to the wastewater treatment plant (on or offsite), discharged through an outfall regulated by a National Pollutant Discharge Elimination System (NPDES) permit, etc. Identify any wastewater discharges directly to a receiving waterbody that are not included in a facility NPDES permit.

If the facility discharges to an off-site treatment plant, determine if the discharge is required to meet pretreatment standards. Review these standards and appropriate wastewater characterization data, as necessary.

If the facility has an on-site wastewater treatment plant (WWTP), determine if the plant has the appropriate unit processes and is properly sized to effectively treat the quality and quantity of wastewater generated by the facility. Review operations records and DMRs and visually inspect the facility. Assess the ability of the WWTP to withstand low temperatures, excess storm flows, peak process flows, shock loads, and infiltration. If past or proposed process modifications have/will result in changed wastewater characteristics, determine what has/will be undertaken to ensure that this wastewater is adequately treated.

Self-monitoring Systems

Self-monitoring consists of flow and water quality measurements and sampling by the facility in addition to the laboratory which analyzes water samples required by the NPDES permit program.

Field - Confirm that acceptable sampling and flow measurement, as specified by the NPDES permit, are conducted at the correct locations, with the proper frequency, and by acceptable methods. Determine if all necessary calibrations and O&M are performed. Samples must be collected at prescribed locations. Flow rating and calibration must use standardized techniques. Clean and properly prepared containers must be used in sampling. Approved procedures are to be used in the handling, preserving, and transporting of samples [Appendix E].

Laboratory - Evaluate procedures affecting final reported results including:

- Sample preservation methods and holding times
- Chain-of-Custody
- Use of approved procedures (40 CFR 136 or approved alternatives)
- Adequacy of personnel, equipment, and other components of laboratory operations
- Adequacy of quality assurance/quality control program
- Recordkeeping and calculations

Evaluate how the data are entered into lab notebooks; the sign-off procedures used; analysis of spikes, blanks and reference samples; how the lab data are transposed onto the official, self-monitoring report forms sent to the enforcement agency; and the extent and capability of outside contract laboratories, if used.

Operation and Maintenance

Determine if wastewater treatment processes are operated properly. Observe the presence of solids, scum, grease, and floating oils or suspended materials (pinpoint floc, etc.), odors, and weed growth in the treatment units. Note appearance of wastewater in all units. Identify all out-of-service processes and determine cause. Determine level of maintenance by observing condition of equipment (pumps, basins, etc.) and reviewing records (outstanding work orders, spare parts inventories). Assess handling, treatment and disposal of sludges and other residues generated from processes and wastewater treatment system.

Best Management Practices (BMP) Plan

Determine if the facility handles toxic materials and if a BMP Plan is required (40 CFR 125, Subpart K or by NPDES permit). If applicable, review facility BMP Plan or BMP Permit requirements. Determine if facility is following required provisions. Review any records required by the plan for adequacy.

SPCC Plan

Determine if the facility is required to develop and implement an SPCC Plan (40 CFR 112). Obtain a copy of the plan and required records to assess compliance with the plan provisions. Visually inspect containment and run-off control systems and procedures. Investigate any evidence of spilled materials.

Solid/Hazardous Waste

The compliance evaluation for solid/hazardous wastes managed at a facility generally includes:

- Obtaining, reviewing, and evaluating information from Federal, State, and local regulatory agency files

- Interviewing facility personnel

- Examining facility records, including any internal waste tracking/storage/disposal logs and audit records

- Visually inspecting the waste management units.

An integral part of any evaluation is compiling facility background information including facility size, operating unit dimensions (area, depth, volume, etc.) and construction methods (presence/absence of liners, special compacting, etc.).

The investigator must determine how extensive a records review must be to meet the audit objectives. Factors such as the number of documents available, resource allocation, and time constraints determine whether the objectives are realistic and can be achieved; however, in all cases, the records review must be sufficient to demonstrate facility compliance or noncompliance. Often, because of time constraints, documents may be copied (either microfilm or photocopies) for future off-site review and evaluation. To ensure effective use of resources, documents reviewed/copied while onsite should be limited to those containing information within the audit scope.

A RCRA Inspection Manual (OSWER 9938.2A - March 1988) is available to assist investigators evaluating hazardous waste generators, transporters, and treatment, storage, and disposal (TSD) facilities. Investigators may also use the various RCRA evaluation checklists in Appendix F during the audit to supplement their knowledge of the RCRA regulations and ensure that all items are adequately addressed. RCRA Land Disposal Restrictions evaluation checklists are given in Appendix G.

The investigator should also be aware of the requirements of CERCLA, including a owner/operator's responsibilities to notify the proper regulatory authorities of former hazardous substance releases and sites (non-interim status) where hazardous substances have been stored, treated, or disposed

[CERCLA, Section 103(a) and (c)]. Military installations are also responsible for conducting site assessments through remedial action programs to identify past hazardous substance releases and handling facilities [40 CFR 300.64-68]. The investigator should determine, through records review, interviews, etc., whether all RCRA and CERCLA [Appendix H] sites have been reported to the proper authorities. The investigator should also evaluate assessment and response programs at a facility, if this objective is within the scope of the audit.

Additionally, the facility should be evaluated concerning State and local requirements controlling past and current disposal of municipal waste, nonhazardous industrial waste, and construction debris. The information concerning such past disposal activities may lead to unreported RCRA and CERCLA sites.

The initial step in evaluating compliance with solid/hazardous waste requirements is to identify all waste streams generated at the facility and determine which are regulated by Federal,* State** or local regulations, licenses and approvals. Preferably, this determination is initiated during background document review before the on-site facility audit and supplemented/modified using information obtained while onsite. All waste streams generated (even those that the generator claims are not regulated) must be evaluated for regulatory inclusion. This will allow the investigator to determine whether the generator has properly identified all regulated waste streams.

Once regulated waste is identified, the investigator can track the material from generation to final on-site disposition (on-site treatment/disposal) or storage and transport for off-site disposal and determine compliance with applicable regulations. Throughout the audit, the investigator must keep in mind that both past and present activities need to be evaluated for compliance with applicable regulations.

---

* *Definitions, identification, and listing of Federally regulated waste are given in 40 CFR 260 and 261 and CERCLA § 101.*

** *Nonhazardous solid waste is usually regulated by the State and these regulations must be obtained to evaluate applicable facility activity.*

Information obtained during the audit inspection will be used, with the applicable regulations, licenses, approvals, etc., to evaluate the waste handling activities and determine status of compliance, as outlined in the following sections. Areas of potential facility noncompliance must be documented as thoroughly as possible. Document copies and photographs should be included for future reference and evidence.

Facility Status Under RCRA

The investigator should determine if the facility has notified EPA of its hazardous waste handling activities (waste generation, transport, treatment, storage, or disposal) and if it has a required EPA identification number (40 CFR 262.12).

TSD facilities must apply for a RCRA permit [Section 2010(e) of RCRA]. Determine if RCRA Part A and B permit applications have been submitted (40 CFR 270), and whether the facility has been issued a RCRA permit. If a RCRA permit has been issued, the facility must comply with both specific permit provisions and 40 CFR Part 264. If no RCRA permit has been issued, the facility is subject to the interim status provisions of 40 CFR Part 265. In both cases, the facility may also be subject to requirements of State/local regulations, permits, licenses and/or approvals. Before the audit, the investigator should determine if State/local regulations apply. The investigator should have a copy of the current Part A application (with amendments), the Part B application (if available) and the RCRA permit (if applicable) during the audit so that the accuracy of the Part A and Part B applications can be verified and compliance with the permit determined.

Hazardous Waste Generators

Generators, as defined in 40 CFR 260.10, are subject to the requirements of 40 CFR 262 and any additional State/local regulations, licenses, and approvals. In general, determine if the waste is properly identified and the waste containers are properly marked, including the date when waste accumulation was initiated. Also, ensure that the generator has obtained an EPA identification number (40 CFR 262.12). Because generators are not authorized to accumulate waste longer than 90 days, or 180 or 270 days for conditionally exempt small quantity generators, the length of accumulation of all waste in storage should be determined.* Determine if the generator has maintained signed hazardous waste shipping manifests for waste shipped offsite for the last 3 years and evaluate if these manifests were completed/handled properly (40 CFR 262, Subpart B). The facility "Contingency Plan and Emergency Procedures," "Preparedness and Prevention Plans," and "Personnel Training Program" should also be evaluated (40 CFR 265, Subparts C and D and CFR 265.16).

The investigator should determine whether the facility is properly managing containers and tanks (40 CFR 264/265, Subparts I and J). All containers onsite during the audit should be inspected for general condition (leaks, corrosion, etc.) and proper packaging, labeling, and marking (40 CFR 262, Subpart C). The investigator should determine if all storage area inspections are performed regularly and documented. The investigator should review the checklists in Appendix F, Table F-6 before conducting an audit of hazardous waste tank systems and should follow the guidance provided in the Tank Systems Inspection Manual (OSWER 9938.4, September 1988).

The investigator should determine whether the facility is in compliance with technical requirements for underground storage tanks (40 CFR Part 280). Inspections conducted under these parts should assure that the following forms are completed and accurate:

- Notification for Underground Storage Tanks
- Description of Underground Storage Tanks (complete for each tank at each facility)
- Certification of Compliance (complete for all new tanks at each facility)

---

* *If a generator has stored waste for more than 90 days [262.34(a), (b), and (c)], waste management is subject to the Federal requirements of 40 CFR 264/265 and 40 CFR 270 or the comparable State requirements in authorized states. Small quantity generators are subject to different requirements [261.5, 262.34(d), (e), and (f)].*

Copies of these forms are reproduced in Appendix F, and appear in the Federal Register, Vol. 53, No. 185 dated September 23, 1988, pages 37208 through 37210.

The investigator should determine whether the owner/operator manages wastes that are burned for energy recovery, recycled, or disposed of in a manner such that they are subject to 40 CFR Part 266 (Standards for the Management of Specific Hazardous Wastes and Specific Types of Hazardous Waste Management Facilities). These regulations contain standards for generators, transporters, marketers, and users that recover energy from hazardous waste and used oil. The regulations also contain standards for lead-acid battery reclaimers, and recyclable materials used for precious metal recovery or in a manner constituting disposal. Table F-14 [Appendix F] is a checklist for evaluating compliance with Part 266 requirements.

The investigator should determine if the generator is managing a waste subject to the land disposal prohibitions of 40 CFR Part 268. If the waste is a restricted waste the investigator should determine whether the waste is restricted as a result of constituent concentrations and if one of several extensions or exemptions apply. Generators of restricted wastes are required to:

- Determine whether they generate restricted wastes
- Determine waste treatment standards
- Determine whether waste exceeds treatment standards
- Provide for appropriate treatment and/or disposal
- Satisfy documentation, recordkeeping, notification, certification, packaging, and manifesting requirements
- Meet applicable requirements if the generator is or becomes a TSDF

Appendix G contains checklists for specific land disposal requirements placed on generators.

Hazardous Waste Transporters

Hazardous waste transporters, as defined in 40 CFR 260.10, are required to comply with the Federal requirements of 40 CFR 263 and any State/local regulations, licenses, and approvals. The transporter must also meet applicable requirements of 49 CFR 171-179.

The investigator should ensure that the transporter has obtained an EPA identification number (40 CFR 263.11) and is completing and handling the waste shipping manifests properly, including maintaining a copy of each manifest for at least 3 years. If a transporter stores waste in a transfer facility (40 CFR 263.12), determine length of waste storage.* Any containers of waste in a storage facility should be inspected for proper condition and proper marking and labeling. If loaded trucks are present, proper placarding should be checked.

Treatment, Storage, and Disposal Facilities

The investigator should determine if present facility operations and types and quantities of waste handled are the same as those authorized by the original Part A permit application (and approved amendments) or the final RCRA permit, as applicable. Ensure that the TSD facility has obtained an EPA identification number (40 CFR 265.11/264.11). Operations at all TSD facilities must be evaluated for compliance with the general requirements of Subparts A through H of either 40 CFR 265 or 40 CFR 264. The investigator should determine which subparts are applicable to each facility. Compliance evaluation of general facility standards includes, but is not limited to evaluation of:

- Waste Analysis Procedures (40 CFR 265/264.13, Subpart B)

---

* *Under Federal regulations (40 CFR 263.12), transporters can only store waste at a transfer facility 10 days or less. State regulations may differ.*

  - Written waste analysis plan
  - Analytical/sampling procedures including laboratory evaluation
  - Recordkeeping

- Facility Security (40 CFR 265/264.14)

  - Access to the facility
  - Display of warning signs

- General Facility Audit Requirements (40 CFR 265/264.15)

  - Written audit plan
  - Remedial action
  - Recordkeeping

- Personnel Training (40 CFR 265/264.16)

  - Written training plan
  - Recordkeeping

- Facility Preparedness and Prevention (40 CFR 265/264, Subpart C)

  - General maintenance
  - Communications/alarm system
  - Fire control equipment
  - Arrangements with local authorities

- Contingency Plan and Emergency Procedures (40 CFR 265/264, Subpart D)

  - Written contingency plan
  - Availability of emergency coordinator

- Manifest System, Recordkeeping (40 CFR 265/264, Subpart E)

- Use, handling, and maintenance of shipping manifests
- Facility operating record (including waste characterization/ quantity, waste tracking, disposal and treatment location)

• Groundwater Protection (40 CFR 265/264, Subpart F)

  - Monitoring system (well location, design, operation)
  - Sampling and analysis including laboratory evaluation
  - Data recordkeeping
  - Characterization of site hydrogeology
  - Preparation, evaluation, and response
  - Waiver request (if any)
  - Detection vs. assessment monitoring
  - Corrective action plan(s)

• Closure and Post-Closure (40 CFR 265/264, Subpart G)

  - Written closure/post-closure plans

• Financial Requirements (40 CFR 265/264, Subpart H)

  - Financial assurance
  - Closure costs

All facility written plans (waste analysis, facility audits, contingency, training, closure), should be copied to allow for in-depth evaluation. By observing facility operations, such as self-inspection procedures, the investigator can determine whether the facility is actually following the plans. In many cases, a facility may have used several modifications of these plans, all with different effective dates. All current plans must be evaluated. Out-of-date plans should also be reviewed for compliance with applicable regulations in effect at the time those plans were in place.

The investigator must also evaluate facility records required to be maintained by the regulations (operating records, manifests, waste analysis results, etc.). The extent of the record review must be sufficient to determine patterns of compliance/noncompliance with the recordkeeping requirements. The investigators must decide on the minimum number of records necessary to identify patterns of compliance/noncompliance. Documentation (investigators' notes, copies of documents, and photographs) of noncompliance must be retained for future use and evidence.

The investigator should determine whether the TSD facility is handling a waste subject to the land disposal prohibitions of 40 CFR Part 268 and as set forth in the revisions to 40 CFR Parts 260 to 265 and 270 (51 Federal Register 40635 et seq). Appendix G contains a checklist that highlights the land disposal prohibitions for storage, treatment and disposal facilities. A review of the checklist before the inspection is recommended because the requirements are dependent upon the type of facility being inspected.

In addition to the general requirements specified above, the investigators must evaluate the facility for compliance with the specific requirements for each type of hazardous waste management activity. This includes, but is not limited to, an evaluation of:

- Use and Management of Containers (40 CFR 265/264, Subpart I)
  - General operation procedures
  - Condition of containers (leaks, corrosion, etc.)
  - Marking and labeling of containers
  - Compatibility of waste with containers
  - Management of containers
  - Inspection records
- Tanks (40 CFR 265/264, Subpart J)
  - General operating procedures
  - Compatibility of waste with tank construction material
  - Integrity of tanks
  - Corrosion rate of tank materials
  - Compatibility between waste treated/stored in tanks

- Inspection records
- Closure procedures

• Surface Impoundments (40 CFR 265/264, Subpart K)

  - General operating procedures
  - Freeboard levels
  - Protective coverings of dikes
  - Inspection records
  - Closure/post-closure provisions

• Waste Piles (40 CFR 265/264, Subpart L)

  - General operating procedures
  - Protection from wind dispersal of waste
  - Compatibility between various wastes within the pile
  - Run-on protection
  - Runoff characteristics, containment, and handling
  - Closure/post-closure provisions

• Land Treatment (40 CFR 265/264, Subpart M)

  - General operating procedures
  - Run-off/run-on control provisions
  - Waste analysis
  - Waste loading
  - Protection of food chain crops
  - Unsaturated zone (zone of aeration) monitoring
  - Recordkeeping
  - Closure/post-closure provisions

• Landfills (40 CFR 265/264, Subpart N)

  - General operating procedures
  - Run-on/run-off control and management
  - Protection from wind dispersal

- Recordkeeping
- Required treatment of ignitable/reactive waste and liquid material (prior to landfilling)
- Leachate collection/handling procedures
- Closure/post-closure provisions

• Incinerators (40 CFR 265/264, Subpart O)

- General operating procedures
- Waste analysis
- Startup/shutdown procedures
- Monitoring/control equipment and provisions (combustion and emission control)
- Monitoring and inspection records
- Closure procedures

• Thermal Treatment (40 CFR 265, Subpart P)

- General operating conditions
- Waste analysis
- Monitoring/control equipment and procedures (combustion and emission controls)
- Open burning/waste explosives procedures
- Monitoring and inspection records
- Closure

• Other Chemical/Physical Treatment (40 CFR 265, Subpart Q)

- General operating procedures
- Waste analysis
- Monitoring/control equipment
- Inspection records
- Closure

- Underground Injection (40 CFR Part 265, Subpart R)

    - Requirements of Part 265, Subparts A through E apply

- Miscellaneous units (40 CFR Part 264, Subpart X)

    - Performance standards
    - Monitoring, analysis, inspection, response, reporting, and corrective action
    - Post-closure care

Land Disposal Restrictions Program

The Land Disposal Restrictions program (40 CFR Part 268) is a Congressionally mandated series of regulatory deadlines imposed on EPA for restricting land disposal of hazardous wastes. If EPA does not propose treatment standards for hazardous wastes by the deadlines imposed by Congress, then the wastes are automatically banned from land disposal.

Land disposal is defined as the placement in or on the land and includes the following disposal techniques:

- Landfills
- Surface impoundments
- Waste piles
- Injection wells
- Land treatment facilities
- Salt domes
- Salt beds
- Underground mines or caves
- Concrete bunkers or vaults

The deadlines imposed are as follows:

- November 8, 1986

Spent solvents with waste codes of F001 through F005 and Dioxin wastes with waste codes F020 through F023 and F026 through F028

- July 8, 1987

  "California List" including wastes with a pH less than or equal to 2, hazardous waste liquids containing PCBs >50 ppm, liquid, and non-liquid halogenated organic carbons (HOCs), free cyanides, and some metals

- August 8, 1988

  First third of the listed hazardous wastes

- June 8, 1989

  Second third of the listed hazardous wastes

- May 8, 1990

  Third third of the listed hazardous wastes

Refer to Appendix G for an inspection checklist.

<u>CERCLA Off-Site Policy</u>

The inspector should determine whether the facility is accepting CERCLA response action wastes (CERCLA Sections 104 and 106) for treatment, storage, or disposal. If so, the facility must:*

- Have no relevant violations at or affecting the unit or units receiving CERCLA wastes [40 CFR 300.440(b)(1)].

---

* *See 40 CFR 300.440 on "Procedures For Planning and Implementing Off-site Response Actions" for the full text of EPA's Off-Site Policy.*

- Have no receiving units which are releasing any hazardous waste, hazardous constituent, or hazardous substance into the ground water, surface water, soil, or air (if facility is a RCRA Subtitle C facility and is receiving post-SARA decision document* CERCLA wastes).

- Have no non-receiving units releasing any hazardous waste, hazardous constituent, or hazardous substance into the ground water, surface water, soil, or air, unless the release is addressed by an enforceable agreement for corrective action under Subtitle C of RCRA or other applicable Federal or State authority (if a RCRA Subtitle C land disposal facility).

If the facility is a RCRA Subtitle C treatment, storage, and permit-by-rule facility, then releases of any hazardous waste, hazardous constituent, or hazardous substance from non-receiving units must be evaluated to determine if they pose a significant threat to public health or the environment.

CERCLA wastes resulting from a post-SARA decision document should not be transferred to any unit at a non-Subtitle C facility if the responsible agency has information indicating that an environmentally significant release of hazardous substance has occurred at that facility.

Pre-SARA decision document* resulting CERCLA wastes shall not be transferred to an off-site facility if there are environmental conditions at that facility which pose a significant threat to public health, welfare, or the environment, or affect the satisfactory operation of the facility.

---

* *Post-SARA decision documents are those CERCLA decision documents signed (such as RODs) or consent decrees lodged after October 17, 1986.*
Pre-SARA decision documents are those CERCLA decision documents signed or consent decrees lodged prior to October 17, 1986.

- Have received an appropriate facility compliance inspection within 6 months prior to receiving the CERCLA wastes. A RCRA Facility Assessment (RFA) or equivalent facility wide investigation should have been completed if the facility is being considered to receive wastes resulting from post-SARA decision documents. RCRA Subtitle C land disposal facilities must have received a comprehensive ground-water monitoring evaluation (CME) or operation and maintenance (O&M) inspection within the year preceding the determination of acceptability.

<u>Toxic Substances</u>

This section describes those specific aspects of toxic chemical control that are addressed by the Toxic Substances Control Act (TSCA) and its associated rules and regulations (40 CFR Parts 702 to 799).

The regulation of toxics under TSCA is subdivided into two components for Agency enforcement program management purposes.

- "Chemical control" covers enforcement aspects related to specific chemicals regulated under Section 6 of TSCA, such as polychlorinated biphenyls (PCBs), chlorofluorocarbons (CFCs) and asbestos.

- "Hazard evaluation" refers to the various recordkeeping, reporting, and marketing submittal requirements specified in Sections 5, 8, 12 and 13 of TSCA; although, some elements of what might be termed "chemical control" are also addressed in these sections. Sections 12 and 13 of TSCA, which pertain to chemical exports and imports, respectively, will not be covered in this manual due to their special nature and unique requirements.

Prior to discussing TSCA activities* at a facility, the investigator must present appropriate facility personnel with copies of the following two TSCA audit forms [Appendix I]:

- Notice of Inspection - Shows purpose, nature, and extent of TSCA audit

- TSCA Inspection Confidentiality Notice - Explains a facility's rights to claim that some or all of the information regarding toxic substance handling at the facility is to be considered as TSCA Confidential Business Information (CBI)

Before leaving the site, the following two forms must be completed, as appropriate.

- Receipt for Samples and Documents - Itemizes all documents, photos and samples received by the investigator during the audit

- Declaration of CBI** - Itemizes the information that the facility claims to be TSCA CBI

Inspection considerations related to the chemical control and hazard evaluation compliance are given in the following two subsections.

Chemical Control

Although the controlled substances most frequently encountered during multi-media investigations are polychlorinated biphenyls (PCBs), the investigator should determine if other regulated toxic substances are present at the facility. Currently these include metal working fluids (Part 747), fully halogenated chlorofluoroalkanes (40 CFR 762) and asbestos (40 CFR 763);

---

* *All personnel handling material claimed as Confidential Business Information under TSCA must be cleared for access to that material in accordance with Agency procedures. An annual update is required.*

** *These forms are generally completed during the closing conference. During the opening conference, facility personnel should be made aware that the latter form is used to itemize TSCA CBI material.*

additional toxic substances may be regulated in the future. Because the probability of finding PCBs and PCB items at a facility is greater than finding other TSCA-regulated substances, the following discussion is directed toward an evaluation of compliance with proper PCB and PCB item handling procedures. Should other TSCA-regulated substances be present, the investigator should consult the regulations for appropriate requirements.

Management of PCBs/PCB items is regulated under 40 CFR 761. In general, these regulations address recordkeeping, marking and labeling, audits, storage and disposal. The investigator is encouraged to use TSCA audit checklists, such as the ones provided in Appendix J.

Facilities which store and/or dispose of PCBs and PCB items often have EPA-issued Letters of Approval which contain facility operating and recordkeeping requirements in addition to those specified in 40 CFR 761. The investigator must obtain a copy of these approvals and any subsequent notifications to evaluate facility compliance. The inspector should review Part 761.30 to identify uses of PCB transformers which are prohibited beginning October 1, 1990, but with effective dates extending to October 1, 1993. The inspector should also review the requirements found in Part 761.30 which allow the installation of PCB transformers for emergency use.

In general, the compliance evaluation includes obtaining and reviewing information from Federal, State, and local regulatory agency files; interviewing facility personnel regarding material handling activity; examining facility records and inspecting material handling units.

Recordkeeping

Every facility using or otherwise handling PCBs/PCB items is required to maintain specific records. Records regarding use, storage, transport, and disposal must be reviewed for accuracy, completeness, and compliance with applicable regulations. This includes a determination of the accuracy of the PCB inventory and annual document (40 CFR 761.180). An inventory checklist is provided in Appendix J. In general, the investigator should visually inspect all PCB items in service and in storage to verify completeness/accuracy of the records. Also, current records should be compared with past records to ensure that all items have been adequately accounted for (40 CFR 761, Subpart J).

Marking/Labeling

Observe PCB and PCB suspect units in service and in storage and determine if items are properly marked/labeled. (40 CFR 761, Subpart C).

Audits (Items in Use or in Storage for Reuse)

Review records to determine if items in use or stored for reuse have been inspected, as required. Determine whether all audit and maintenance records are being maintained, as required. Review these records to determine if problems identified during the internal audit are being addressed properly. PCB items should be inspected to verify that they are not leaking [40 CFR 761.30(a)(1)].

Servicing and Use of Various PCB Items

Determine whether the facility is servicing PCB items or using PCBs for any of the following uses: Heat transfer agent, hydraulic fluid, research purposes, in capacitors or in any other special authorized use category listed in 40 CFR 761.30. If PCBs are used in these services, determine if their use complies with the special requirements for each use category (40 CFR 761.30).

Storage for Disposal

Identify all areas where PCBs/PCB items are stored for disposal. Determine the adequacy of these storage facilities, including proper marking, walls, roof, continuous floor with containment (ensure that containment is adequate), and location (above/below 100-year floodplain). Visually inspect all items in storage to determine if they are being stored properly (i.e., non-leaking, marked/labeled and dated with storage date). Review storage area records (including the required PCB annual document) for accuracy and adequacy. Determine whether or not the storage area is being properly inspected and that remedial action is being taken, as required (40 CFR 761.65).

If PCBs/PCB items are stored outside of the designated storage facilities (i.e., temporary storage), determine whether (1) items are leaking, (2) liquids stored in containers have greater than 500 ppm PCBs [liquids with PCB concentrations greater than 500 ppm cannot be stored in temporary areas (except for transformers)], and (3) items are properly marked and labeled and show dates removed from service and placed into storage (determine length of time items have been in temporary storage). If liquids with PCBs have been or are being stored in temporary storage, evaluate the required Spill Prevention Control and Countermeasure (SPCC) plan, as described in 40 CFR 112, for adequacy and accuracy. If the facility stores, in any permanent or temporary storage areas, liquid PCBs in any containers larger than those described in 40 CFR 761.65(c)(6), the facility SPCC plan must also be reviewed/evaluated.

As of October 1, 1985, installation of PCB transformers (which have been placed into storage for reuse or have been removed from another location) in or near commercial buildings, is prohibited.

Disposal

Incineration - If the facility incinerates PCBs/PCB items, determine if the facility has applied for and received the required EPA approval. Determine if the facility meets required monitoring, control, and recordkeeping requirements of the approval and of 40 CFR 761. Observe monitoring and control equipment and review the required records (including the PCB annual document) for adequacy and accuracy and to ensure that the incinerator meets the specified feed rate, combustion criteria, and combustion efficiency. Evaluate the required annual document for completeness and accuracy (40 CFR 761.70).

Landfilling - If the facility landfills PCBs/PCB items, determine if the facility has applied for and received the required EPA and State approvals. Determine if the facility meets the specified siting, liner, and geological conditions. Determine if the landfill is in the 100-year floodplain. If so, inspect for proper water diversion structures. Evaluate general landfill operating conditions to determine if waste is being handled properly (as stated in the EPA Approval Letter and/or 40 CFR 761). This includes, but is not limited to, evaluation of (1) incompatibles being landfilled with the PCBs/PCB items, (2) required facility maintenance records (including concentration of liquids disposed of and three-dimensional burial coordinates of waste), (3) adequacy of site security, (4) solidification of liquids prior to disposal, and (5) proper preparation of transformers and other PCB items (drained/triple-rinsed, etc.) prior to disposal. Evaluate the required PCB annual document for adequacy and accuracy (40 CFR 761.75).

Determine if the facility is monitoring surface water, ground water and leachates, as required by 40 CFR 761.75(b)(6). This includes identifying, locating, and evaluating operation of ground water monitoring wells, and reviewing ground water sampling and analysis procedures and sample analysis results (for adequacy of monitoring frequency and proper chemical constituents). Determine, by audit and records review, if the facility has an operating leachate collection system. Review laboratory data on leachate characterization to determine if leachate is being adequately monitored and disposed of properly (40 CFR 761.75).

Hazard Evaluation

Establishing compliance with the various hazard evaluation aspects of TSCA is best accomplished through review and evaluation of the recordkeeping, reporting and submittal data required by the various regulatory components of Sections 5 and 8. In general, Section 5 addresses "new chemicals" (i.e., those not in commercial production when TSCA was passed in 1977) and Section 8 generally provides for control of "existing chemicals" (i.e., those chemicals that were in commercial production during 1977).

Much of the information to be obtained and reviewed under these two sections of TSCA will likely be, or have been, declared as TSCA Confidential Business Information (CBI) by company officials and, thus, requires special control procedures.

The glossary [Appendix K, Table K-1] and 40 CFR Parts 703 to 723 should be consulted for an explanation of TSCA terms and definitions. The following list summarizes the different compliance objectives of the key TSCA Section 5 and 8 components. Specific checklists for the important areas to review, evaluate, and document for each pertinent section are given in Appendix K, Table K-2.

1. <u>Premanufacture Notification (PMN)</u>

   a. Verify that commercial manufacture or import did not begin prior to the 90-day review date and not more than 30 days before the Notice of Commencement (NOC) date. Verify that no NOC has been submitted if commercial manufacture or import has not begun.

   b. Verify the accuracy and documentation of the contents of the PMN itself.

   c. Verify that all commercially manufactured or imported chemicals are either on the TSCA 8(b) inventory, covered by an exemption, or not subject to TSCA.

2. <u>Research and Development (R&D) Exemption</u>

   a. Verify that the recordkeeping and notification requirements are being met for all R&D chemicals.

   b. Verify that "Prudent Laboratory Practices" and hazardous data searches are adequately documented.

3. <u>Test Marketing Exemption (TME)</u>

   a. Verify that the conditions spelled out in the TME application are being met, particularly with respect to dates of production, quantity manufactured or imported, number of customers and use(s).

b. Verify that the TME recordkeeping requirements are being met.

4. <u>Low Volume Exemption (LVE) and Polymer Exemption (PE)</u>

a. Verify that specific contents of the exemption application are being met, and that all test data have been submitted.

b. For an LVE, verify that the 1,000-Kg limit per 12-month period has not been exceeded. For a PE, assure that the chemical structure and monomer composition(s) are accurate.

c. Verify that recordkeeping requirements for both LVEs and PEs are being met.

5. <u>5(e)/5(f) Order, Rule, or Injunction</u>

a. Verify that all conditions of the order, rule, or injunction are being followed, including use of protective equipment, glove testing, training, and recordkeeping.

b. If testing trigger is specified, verify production volume and status of testing activity.

6. <u>Significant New Use Rule (SNUR)</u>

a. Verify that no commercial production has occurred prior to the 90-day review date.

b. Verify that SNUR notices have been submitted for all applicable manufactured, imported, or processed chemicals.

c. Verify technical accuracy of SNUR submittal and completeness of required recordkeeping.

7. Bona Fide Submittals

Determine the commercial production (or import) status and R&D history of those bona fide chemicals not found on the confidential 8(b) inventory. Verify findings against applicable PMN, TME or other exemption.

8. Section 8(a) Level A PAIR and CAIR Report

a. Determine if Preliminary Assessment Information Rule (PAIR) and Comprehensive Assessment Information Rule (CAIR) reports have been submitted for all 8(a) Level A listed chemicals manufactured or imported by the facility.

b. Verify the accuracy of submitted PAIR information, particularly the reported figures for total production volume and worker exposure levels.

c. Verify the accuracy of submitted CAIR information and if the report meets the date specified in the regulation.

9. Section 8(b) Inventory Update Rule (INUR)

a. Verify the accuracy of the information submitted in response to the INUR.

b. Determine that required information was submitted by the prescribed deadline for all chemicals subject to INUR.

10. Section 8(c) Recordkeeping

a. Determine if the facility has a Section 8(c) file and that allegations of significant health and environmental harm on record are properly filed and recorded.

b. Determine that all applicable allegations have been recorded and filed.

c. Determine if the facility has a written Section 8(c) policy and if the policy includes outreach to the employees.

11. Section 8(d) Reporting

Determine if copies (or lists) of all unpublished health effects studies have been submitted by manufacturers, importers, and processors for any Section 8(d) listed chemical.

12. Section 8(e) Reporting

a. Verify that all Section 8(e) substantial risk reports to the Agency were accurate and submitted within the required time frames.

b. Verify that all substantial risk incidents and/or test results have been reported to EPA.

c. Determine that the company has an adequate written policy addressing Section 8(e), and that it relieves employees of individual liability.

Pesticides

Pesticides are regulated by the Federal Insecticide, Fungicide, and Rodenticide Act (FIFRA).

The following list is for use in conjunction with the checklist in Appendix L and specific storage/use/disposal requirements found on pesticide labels. FIFRA requires a written notice of inspection and written receipt for samples and documents collected. Additional information is available in the EPA Pesticides Inspection Manual which has been revised and is being reprinted in 1989.

- Determine types and registration status of all pesticides produced, sold, stored, and used at the facility, particularly if any are restricted or experimental use pesticides

- Determine use(s) of each pesticide

- Determine certification status of facility/handlers

    - Verify who certifies facility/pesticide handlers (EPA, State, DOD)

    - Determine if commercial or private application

    - If restricted-use pesticides are used, check if pesticide applicators are authorized to use these pesticides

    - Check expiration dates on licenses/certificates

- Review applicable records

    - Check previous audit records and complaints

    - Check application records

    - Check restricted-use pesticides records (must be kept at least 2 years). Document suspected violations accordingly

    - Check inventory records

    - Check training records

    - Check equipment repair records

- Inspect storage, mixing/loading and container disposal areas

    - Check bulk storage areas for compliance with Federal/State rules

    - Check location, ventilation, segregation, shelter, and housekeeping of pesticide storage/handling areas. Check security, fire protection, and warning signs, as may be required by State regulations

    - Check mixing equipment/procedures for reducing handlers' exposures to pesticides

- Check for safety equipment/procedures/use
- Check container cleanup and disposal procedures

• Pesticide waste disposal

- Check to see that pesticides are disposed of in accordance with applicable label and RCRA requirements

• Determine measures taken to ensure worker safety

- Check pesticide use records for re-entry time limit notation
- Check pesticide use records for record of informing farmer or warning workers and/or posting fields
- Provide farmer and/or applicator copy of current worker protection standards

• Observe actual pesticide application

- Observe mixing/loading and check calculations for proper use dilution.
- Observe when spray is turned on/off with respect to ends of field.
- Watch for drift or pesticide mist dispersal pattern.
- Note direction of spraying pattern and trimming techniques.
- Record wind speed and direction, air temperature, and relative humidity.
- Observe application with respect to field workers, houses, cars, power lines, and other obstacles.
- Determine if applicator and assisting personnel are wearing safety gear required by the label.

Water Supply

Public drinking water supply systems (i.e., serve at least 25 people) are regulated by the Safe Drinking Water Act (SDWA), as amended October 31, 1988.

The water supply checklist in Appendix M should be reviewed for those items of information necessary to determine monitoring requirements for water supply systems and whether or not the system can be reasonably expected to routinely provide safe potable water. Many facilities purchase their potable water supply from a nearby municipality. If no further treatment is provided (e.g., chlorination by the facility), the facility may not be directly covered by the SDWA. Nevertheless, the facility does have a responsibility to assure that their actions do not result in contamination of the municipal water supply (e.g., through cross-connection). The audit team should be alert to these possibilities.

There are five classes of injection wells defined in the Underground Injection Control program (40 CFR Part 146.5). Generally, they can be defined as:

Class I	Industrial, Municipal or Hazardous waste disposal beneath the lowermost underground source of drinking water (USDW)
Class II	Oil and gas related wells used for produced fluid disposal, enhanced recovery
Class III	Mineral extraction wells
Class IV	Hazardous or radioactive waste disposal above or into a USDW
Class V	All other wells

The UIC program for Class I wells is also regulated under 40 CFR Parts 124, 144, 146, and 148, as amended. The new part 148 is effective

July 26, 1988. All other amendments are effective August 25, 1988. These amendments include:

- Hazardous Waste Disposal Injection Restrictions
- Amendments to Technical Requirements for Class I Hazardous Waste Injection Wells
- Additional Monitoring Requirements applicable to all Class I wells

The UIC Checklists in Appendix N should be used when inspecting a facility operating injection wells. The SDWA requires a written notice of inspection.

Community Right-to-Know Requirements

The Emergency Planning and Community Right-to-Know Act (EPCRTKA) of 1986 is a free-standing law contained within the Superfund Amendments and Reauthorization Act (SARA) of 1986. EPCRTKA is also commonly known as SARA Title III. EPCRTKA requires dissemination of information to State and community groups and health professionals on chemicals handled at regulated facilities.

An EPCRTKA audit verifies that the facility owner/operator has notified State and local agencies of regulated activities; has submitted information to specific State and local agencies; and has prepared and submitted all other required reports. The inspector should review the checklist shown in Appendix O.

Emergency Planning (Sections 301 through 303)

EPA promulgated regulations which identify extremely hazardous substances and the levels to be regulated under EPCRTKA. The inspector should determine whether the facility is subject to EPCRTKA regulation. If the facility does meet the requirements, the inspector should verify whether the facility owner/operator:

- Notified the State emergency response agency and the local emergency planning committee that the facility is regulated under EPCRTKA

- Designated a facility emergency coordinator to assist the local emergency planning committee in the planning process

- Notified the local emergency planning committee of the emergency coordinator's identity

Emergency Notification (Section 304)

The owner/operator of a facility subject to EPCRTKA must immediately report releases of hazardous substances. Substances subject to this requirement are the extremely hazardous substances listed in 40 CFR Part 355 and substances subject to the emergency notification requirements under CERCLA Section 103(a) or (c). The inspector should verify whether an immediate notification was made to the:

- State emergency response commission

- Local emergency planning committee

Community Right-to-Know Requirements (Sections 311 through 312)

Manufacturing facilities subject to the Occupational Safety and Health Act (OSHA) Hazardous Communication Regulation (29 CFR Part 1910) are required to prepare Material Safety Data Sheets (MSDS) for each hazardous chemical handled at the facility. Manufacturing facilities covered are contained within Standard Industrial Classification (SIC) Codes 20 through 39. OSHA revised its Hazardous Communication Regulation, effective September 23, 1987, to require that MSDSs be prepared by non-manufacturing facilities. The inspector should verify that the facility owner/operator has sent to the State emergency response commission, the local emergency planning committee and the local fire department the following:

- MSDS or a list of chemicals covered by MSDS found at the facility

- An annual inventory of hazardous chemicals found at the facility

Toxic Chemical Release Reporting (Section 313)

Covered facilities (40 CFR Part 372.22) that manufacture, import, process, or use certain chemicals must annually report releases to the environment. The inspector should determine whether the facility owner/ operator is required to submit a report (Form R). All of the following conditions must apply at the facility in order to meet the reporting requirements:

- The facility has ten (10) or more full-time employees

- An operation(s) identified in SIC Codes 20 through 39 is present

- The amount of chemical(s) handled exceeds the applicable threshold quantity

Laboratory and Data Quality Audits

The purpose of laboratory evaluations and data quality assessment is to determine if all analytical and monitoring requirements have been met and to characterize data usability.

Two approaches are used: Performance and systems audits. Performance audits are independent checks made to evaluate the quality of data produced by the total measurement system. This type of audit assesses the results and usually does not examine the intermediate steps to achieve these results. One example is the performance evaluation check sample which is used to validate calibration accuracy but usually not the overall effectiveness of the methodology. Another example is an audit of a particular measurement device using a reference device with known operational characteristics.

A systems audit typically involves an inspection of the components comprising the total measurement system. The Agency has certain expectations of the process used to sample, analyze, and report results. The systems audit is designed to objectively examine each important part of that process to determine deviations from required or recommended practice. The systems audit is more qualitative than the performance audit. A systems audit assesses such items as equipment, personnel, physical aspects, analytical and quality control procedures, quality assurance procedures, and other laboratory or measurement procedures. From a regulatory perspective, this type of audit may find noncompliance with equipment or procedural requirements, or even fraud.

Typically, a systems audit combined with performance audits will be conducted in order to extract the maximum amount of information.

General

A detailed list of items should be requested from the company and contract laboratory. This list should include:

- Standard Operating Procedures (SOPs)
- Quality Assurance Plan
- Personnel resumes
- Instrument maintenance and calibration records
- Monitoring data to be looked at

If performance evaluation samples are to be analyzed, these should be forwarded to the company at the earliest possible time. If preliminary data is available, it should be carefully examined for problems and if problems are found, a more careful examination of these areas can be made onsite.

During the on-site visit, every component of sample handling, sample analysis and data reduction should be examined. The auditor starts with the laboratory supervisor and QA officer to verify that the information supplied on personnel training, quality assurance/quality control, and SOPs is correct. For each parameter determined, the individual or individuals who actually make that determination are interviewed. The analyst is asked to detail exactly what happens to each sample and demonstrate the use of equipment including instrument calibration. Checklists are prepared as an aid to the inspector. Examples are shown in Appendix P. Bench data (initially recorded numbers, strip charts, etc.) is selected. Final results are calculated from the bench data by the inspector and compared with the results reported to the agency. On-site personnel will be asked to explain any discrepancies at this time. Other documents necessary to the case or as potential evidence are copied.

The final assessment and data quality determination is normally performed following the on-site audit. Critical data are re-examined for trends and anomolies. Where necessary, data is computerized and analyzed using statistical software packages. Techniques such as mass balance, solubility product determination, oxidation-reduction state consistency are used, where applicable, to indicate data problems. A propagation of error treatment may be used to establish data quality. Performance audit results are evaluated against reference data base statistics.

<u>NPDES (Water)</u>

- Determine that the exact date, time, and person who takes each sample are recorded
- Determine that the exact date, time, person, and method used for each type of determination are recorded
- Inspect permit carefully to ensure that the permittee adheres to specified conditions
- Ensure that methods used are in conformance with 40 CFR 136 unless alternate approval has been obtained

<u>RCRA Waste Handling</u>

- Determine which parts of the regulations are applicable to the site
- Determine which waste analysis plans (WAPs) were in effect during the time of records and evaluation
- Determine that the WAPs meet the specifications of the regulation.

- Determine that each type of analysis specified in the WAPs is performed in accordance with the methodology specified and under the circumstances required

- Determine that the methodology specified is adequate

RCRA Ground Water

- Determine that the sampling and analysis plan (SAP) is adequate

- Determine that the laboratory follows the methodology specified in the SAP

- Determine that this methodology is adequate

- Calculate detection limits to ensure that they are adequate for ground-water protection

Computerized Information Systems

NEIC has developed various computerized information systems to assist NEIC inspectors in their search of background information on selected facilities, and also to support data needs of users outside of NEIC, especially other EPA offices. Three listings are given below for information systems accessed by, and used by NEIC.

A. EPA Internal Systems Accessible By NEIC

Aerometric Information Retrieval System (AIRS)
Chemicals in Commerce Information System (CICIS)
Compliance Data System (CDS)
Comprehensive Environmental Response, Compensation and Liability Information System (CERCLIS)
Consent Decree Tracking System
Docket System
Emergency Response Notification System (ERNS)
Enforcement Document Retrieval System (EDRS)
Facility Index System (FINDS)
Hazardous Waste Data Management System (HWDMS)

NPDES Industrial Permit Ranking System
Permit Compliance System (PCS)
Potentially Responsible Parties System
Records of Decision System (RODS)
Site Enforcement Tracking System (SETS)
STORET
Superfund Financial Assessment System (SFFAS)
TECHLAW Evidence Audit System
Toxic Release Inventory System (TRIS)

B. Public Information Systems Accessible By NEIC

Bibliographic Retrieval Service (BRS)
Chemical Information System (CIS)
Data Times
DIALOG Information Services, Inc.
Dun and Bradstreet
Groundwater On-Line (GWOL)
Justice Retrieval and Inquiry System (JURIS)
NEWSNET
NEXIS/LEXIS
National Library of Medicine (NLM)
VU/TEXT
WESTLAW

C. Restricted Access Information Systems

Criminal Docket
Criminal Investigative Index System (CII)
National Crime Information Center (NCIC)
National Law Enforcement Teletype System (NLETS)

This Manual does not afford the opportunity to define each of these information systems. Six example systems are briefly described as follows together with NEIC application of these systems.

System	Description	Application
Compliance Data System (CDS)	A national system containing compliance information including compliance status, agency actions (e.g., inspections), etc. for major sources of the five primary air pollutants.	NEIC can acquire the Significant Violators list and compliance event data for individual sources, whole facilities, sources within a certain geographical area and sources of a specific industrial classification.
Comprehensive Environmental Response, Compensation, and Liability Information System (CERCLIS)	A national system containing names and locations of uncontrolled hazardous waste sites in the U.S., summary response event status information, alias names and site characteristic data. Recent modifications include provisions for tracking enforcement activities, and technical and chemical information at CERCLA sites.	NEIC can generate site inventory listings for geographical area, the National Priorities List, and technical event status reports for any uncontrolled hazardous waste site and cleanup expenditure reports.
Consent Decree Tracking System	A national system containing a computerized inventory of consent decrees to which EPA is a party, and computerized summaries of the contents of decrees by facility. NEIC maintains a hardcopy library of all consent decrees within the system.	NEIC can produce hard copies of all decrees in the inventory, and produce computer reports of the inventory, the entire contents of decrees, the milestones to be met in specific decrees or for decrees within a Region and the contents of all decrees for a specific issue (e.g., groundwater monitoring).

System	Description	Application
Permit Compliance System (PCS)	A national computerized management information system containing an inventory of NPDES permits, milestone forecasts, inspection events, effluent measurement data, effluent and compliance violations and enforcement actions.	NEIC can acquire limit/ measurement data for individual discharges or whole facilities, facilities within a geographic area, sources of a specific industrial classification and the Quarterly Non-Compliance Report (QNCR) by Region or State. Information on effluent and compliance schedule violations and enforcement actions/ tracking can be obtained.
Records of Decision System (RODS)	A full-text national database of over 2,000 Superfund Records of Decision	NEIC can retrieve a specific ROD by searching on-site name or ID number or can identify all RODS having selected media, contaminants or remedies.
WESTLAW	The WESTLAW system contains legal information, including the full text of cases from the Supreme Court, U.S. Court of Appeals, U.S. District Courts, and State Courts. It contains Shepards' Citations, regulatory information from the Code of Federal Regulations, Federal Register, U.S. Code and the expert witness information from Forensic Services Directory.	NEIC uses WESTLAW to identify precedent cases, to locate all cases decided by a certain judge or all cases decided by a certain attorney and to locate possible expert witnesses.

CLOSING CONFERENCE

A post-audit or wrap-up conference should be held with the facility. This should be limited to specific findings of the audit (e.g., factual observations and measurements). The audit team's main function is to observe and evaluate compliance. Any official notices of noncompliance are provided by the Regional or State office upon final review of the report and other pertinent findings. Therefore, statements on compliance status, legal aspects, or enforcement consequences of noncompliance should not be discussed with the facility or its operating personnel. It is unacceptable to recommend a particular consulting firm, if asked, but it is proper to advise that professional societies be contacted.

During the closing conference, there can be a discussion of the audit team's preliminary findings. This discussion may include observed deviations from prescribed or recommended procedures. Facility officials should be informed of any leaks, spills, or other problems that require immediate attention; however, no instructions or orders that repairs be undertaken should be issued. At this meeting, the investigators may request additional data, questions may be asked and answered, requested permit changes and process modifications are noted and necessary receipts are given. The investigators should make a final review of checklists and field notes before the conclusion of the visit. Field notes, taken by the investigators at the time of the field investigation, may not be turned over to the company officials under any circumstances.

For TSCA, FIFRA, RCRA, and CERCLA activities, written receipts are given for samples and documents taken. A Declaration of Confidential Business Information (TSCA CBI) shall include a list of items declared confidential by an authorized facility official, and procedures should be explained if the company desires to make any subsequent declaration.

THE AUDIT REPORT AND FOLLOWUP

The audit report organizes and coordinates all evidence gathered during the audit in a usable manner. It is the compilation of factual information and professional judgment resulting from the compliance audit. Information in the report must be accurate, relevant, complete, objective, and clear. The report serves to record the procedures used in gathering the data and gives factual observations and evaluations from the audit. It is the basis for any follow-up activities/enforcement that might occur.

Many different formats are possible for the audit report. A typical report can be structured in two main sections; the Executive Summary and the Technical Report. The Executive Summary establishes the objectives of the audit and presents succinct conclusions which are supported by relevant findings; recommendations are made if appropriate. Topics in the summary may include:

- Overall environmental compliance
- Adequacy of pollution control and treatment systems
- Adequacy of operation and maintenance practices
- Multi-media waste abatement needs
- Follow-up action

The Technical Report comprehensively describes the inspection by discussing such topics as facility history, investigation methods, sampling programs, and specific problem areas. The Technical Report correlates audit findings with the conclusions contained in the Executive Summary.

Where potential criminal activities are discovered during the audit, the audit team and Regional office should promptly notify the Office of Criminal Investigations in Denver or the Regional/Special-Agent-in-Charge for a determination on whether a criminal investigation should be initiated. Administrative/civil enforcement (including informal negotiations with the company) should be held in abeyance, pending a decision on the appropriateness of a criminal referral or additional field investigation.

BIBLIOGRAPHY

1. EPA Order 1000.18, *Transportation of Hazardous Materials,* February 16, 1979. Washington, D.C., Environmental Protection Agency.

2. EPA Order 1440.2, *Health and Safety Requirements for Employees Engaged in Field Activities* , July 12, 1981. Washington, D.C., Environmental Protection Agency.

3. EPA Order 1440.3, *Respiratory Protection*, July 24, 1981. Washington, D.C., Environmental Protection Agency.

4. EPA Order 1440.4, *Health and Safety Training Requirements for Mine Safety*, August 17, 1982. Washington, D.C., Environmental Protection Agency.

5. EPA Order 1440.6, *Motor Vehicle Occupant Restraint Systems*, February 2, 1984. Washington, D.C., Environmental Protection Agency.

5. EPA Order 1440.7, *Hazard Communication*, May 30, 1986. Washington, D.C., Environmental Protection Agency.

7. EPA Order 3100.1, *Uniforms, Protective Clothing and Protective Equipment*, December 8, 1972. Washington, D.C., Environmental Protection Agency.

8. EPA Order 3100.3, *Authorization of Performance of Hazardous Duty*, October 31, 1977. Washington, D.C., Environmental Protection Agency.

9. G. William Frick, October 1981. *Conducting an Environmental Audit*, Washington, D.C, Van Ness, Feldman, Sutcliffe, Curtis and Levenberg.

10. Industrial Environmental Research Laboratory, August 1979. *A Handbook of Key Federal Regulations and Criteria for Multimedia Environmental Control. Interagency Energy/Environment R&D Program Report,* Research Triangle Park, North Carolina, Environmental Protection Agency, EPA-600/7-79-175.

11. National Enforcement Investigations Center, July 1981. *A Step-by-Step Approach to Development of NPDES and RCRA Permits,* Denver, Colorado, Environmental Protection Agency, EPA-330/1-81-004.

12. National Enforcement Investigations Center, August 1979. *Enforcement Considerations for Evaluation of Uncontrolled Hazardous Waste Disposal Sites by Contractors, Draft Report,* Denver, Colorado, Environmental Protection Agency.

Bibliography (cont.)

13. National Enforcement Investigations Center, August 1979. *Performance Audit Inspections of Wastewater Sources,* Denver, Colorado, Environmental Protection Agency, EPA-300/1-79-004.

14. National Enforcement Investigations Center, March 1981. *NEIC Pesticide Sampling Guide,* EPA 330/9-81-001.

15. National Enforcement Investigations Center, (revised) May 1986. *NEIC Policies and Procedures Manual.* Denver, Colorado: Environmental Protection Agency, EPA-330/9-78-001-R.

16. National Enforcement Investigations Center, July 1981, *RCRA Inspection Manual,* Denver, Colorado, Environmental Protection Agency.

17. National Institute for Occupational Safety and Health (NIOSH), *et al.,* October 1985, *Occupational Safety and Health Guidance Manual for Hazardous Waste Site Activities.* Washington, D.C., United States Government Printing Office.

18. Office of Administration, Occupational Health and Safety Staff, *Eye Protection Program Guideline.* Washington, D.C., Environmental Protection Agency.

19. Office of Administration, Occupational Health and Safety Staff, May 1987. *Interim Health and Safety Guidelines for EPA Asbestos Inspectors* (Revised). Washington, D.C., Environmental Protection Agency.

20. Office of Administration, Occupational Health and Safety Staff, March 18, 1986. EPA 1440, *Occupational Health and Safety Manual, 1986 Edition.* Washington, D.C., Environmental Protection Agency.

21. Office of General Enforcement, February 1979. *Enforcement Workshop on Plant Inspection and Evaluation - Volume II, Inspection Procedures and Performance Evaluation,* Washington, D.C., Environmental Protection Agency.

22. Office of General Enforcement, February 1979. *Enforcement Workshop on Plant Inspection and Evaluation - Volume III, Process and Control Equipment Flow Charting Techniques,* Washington, D.C., Environmental Protection Agency.

23. Office of General Enforcement, February 1979. *Inspection Procedures for Evaluation of Electrostatic Precipitator Control System Performance,* Washington, D.C., Environmental Protection Agency, EPA-304/1-79-007.

Bibliography (cont.)

24. Office of Planning and Management, April 1973, *EPA Employee Responsibilities and Conduct,* Washington, D.C., Environmental Protection Agency.

25. Office of Water Enforcement, Enforcement Division, June 1984. *NPDES Compliance Inspection Manual,* Washington, D.C., Environmental Protection Agency.

26. Office of Solid Waste and Emergency Response, Office of Waste Programs Enforcement, September 1988, *EPA Hazardous Waste Tank Systems Inspection Manual*, Washington, D.C., Environmental Protection Agency, OSWER 9938.4.

27. Office of Water Enforcement, Enforcement Division, 1977. *NPDES Compliance Sampling Inspection Manual,* Washington, D.C., Environmental Protection Agency.

28. Oregon State Health Division, Department of Human Resources, *Small Public Water Supply Sanitary Survey Report*, 33-5 (revised January 1985).

29. PEDCO Environmental, Inc., 1980. *Standards of Performance for New Stationary Sources - A Compilation as of January 1, 1980.* Cincinnati, Ohio, Environmental Protection Agency, EPA-340/1-77-015, EPA-340/1-79-001, EPA-340/1-79-001a, EPA-340/1-80-001.

30 Pesticides and Toxic Substances Enforcement Division, January 1980. *Toxic Substances Control Act Inspection Manual, Volume One : TSCA Base Manual,* Washington, D.C., Environmental Protection Agency.

31. Pesticides and Toxic Substances Enforcement Division, March 1981, *Toxic Substances Control Act Inspection Manual, Volume Two: PCB Inspection Manual,* Washington, D.C., Environmental Protection Agency.

32 A.D. Schwope, *et al.*, March 1985, *Guidelines for the Selection of Chemical Protective Clothing, 2nd Edition.* Cambridge, MA, Arthur D. Little, Inc.

33. Technology Transfer, 1978. *Handbook, Industrial Guide for Air Pollution Control,* Environmental Protection Agency, EPA-625/6-78-004.

34. Thomas H. Truitt, *et al.*, 1971. *Environmental Audit Handbook - Basic Principles of Environmental Compliance Auditing,* Washington, D.C., Wald, Harkrader & Ross and Resource Planning Corp.

Bibliography (cont.)

35. Engineering Enterprises, Inc., February 1988: *Underground Injection Control Inspection Manual, for U.S. Environmental Protection Agency*, Washington, D.C.

36. EPA Office of Underground Storage Tanks, September 1988, *Musts for USTs: EPA/530/UST-88/008*

37. "*A Description of Automated Information Systems Accessible by NEIC*," USEPA, OECM, National Enforcement Investigation Center, Information Management Branch, Denver, Colorado, January 1989

ACRONYMS

AQCR - Air Quality Control Region

BAT - Best Available Technology

BATEA - Best Available Technology Economically Achievable

BCT - Best Conventional Pollution Control Technology

BMP - Best Management Practices

BOD - Biochemical Oxygen Demand

BPT - Best Practicable Control Technology Currently Available

Btu - British thermal units

CAA - Clean Air Act

CBI - Confidential Business Information

CEM - Continuous Emission Monitoring

CERCLA - Comprehensive Environmental Response, Compensation and Liability Act of 1980 (Superfund)

CFR - Code of Federal Regulations

COD - Chemical Oxygen Demand

CWA - Clean Water Act [aka: Federal Water Pollution Control Act (FWPCA)]

DCO - Document Control Officer

DO - Dissolved Oxygen

DOT - Department of Transportation (Federal)

EPA - Environmental Protection Agency (Federal)

EPCRTKA - Emergency Planning and Community Right-to-Know Act

ESP - Electrostatic Precipitators

FIFRA - Federal Insecticide, Fungicide and Rodenticide Act

FIP - Final Implementation Plan

F/M - Food to Microorganism Ratio

HSWA - Hazardous Solid Waste Amendments

ACRONYMS (cont.

HW-FW - Half Wave/Full Wave (electrical distribution)

INUR - Inventory Update Rule

ITC - Interagency Testing Committee

LAER - Lowest Achievable Emission Rate

MLVSS - Mixed Liquor Volatile Suspended Solids

MDSD - Material Safety Data Sheets

N/A - Not Applicable

NAA - Non-Attainment Areas

NAAQS - National Ambient Air Quality Standards

NEIC - National Enforcement Investigations Center

NESHAP - National Emission Standards for Hazardous Air Pollutants

NOC - Notice of Commencement

NPDES - National Pollutant Discharge Elimination System

NSPS - New Source Performance Standards

OECM - Office of Enforcement and Compliance Monitoring

O&M - Operation and Maintenance

ORM - Other Regulated Material

OSHA - Occupational Safety and Health Act

PAIR - Preliminary Assessment Information Rule

PCB - Polychlorinated Biphenyls

PMN - Premanufacture Notice

POTW - Publicly-Owned Treatment Works

PSD - Prevention of Significant Deterioration

QA/QC - Quality Assurance/Quality Control

RA - Regional Administrator

ACRONYMS (cont.)

RCRA - Resource Conservation and Recovery Act (enacted as amendment to the Solid Waste Disposal Act)

R&D - Research and Development

SARA - Superfund Amendments and Reauthorization Act

SDWA - Safe Drinking Water Act (enacted as amendment to the Public Health Service Act)

SIC - Standard Industrial Classification (company description)

SIP - State Implementation Plan

SNUR - Significant New Use Rule

SPCC - Spill, Prevention, Containment and Countermeasures

SPDES - State Pollutant Discharge Elimination System

SSE - Stationary Source Enforcement

TME - Test Marketing Exemption

TOC - Total Organic Carbon

T-R - Transformer-Rectifier

TSCA - Toxic Substances Control Act

TSD - Treatment, Storage and Disposal

TSDF - Treatment, Storage and Disposal Facilities (hazardous waste)

TSS - Total Suspended Solids

UIC - Underground Injection Control

U.S.C. - United States Code

USDW - Underground Source of Drinking Water

VEO - Visible Emissions Observation

WLA-TMDL - Wasteload Allocation/Total Maximum Daily Load

APPENDICES

A SUMMARY OF POLLUTION CONTROL LEGISLATION
B SAFETY PLAN
C EVIDENTIARY PROCEDURES FOR PHOTOGRAPHS/MICROFILM
D AIR POLLUTION CHECKLISTS
E WATER POLLUTION CHECKLISTS
F RCRA CHECKLISTS
G LAND DISPOSAL RESTRICTIONS CHECKLIST
H CERCLA CHECKLIST
I TSCA FORMS
J TSCA PCB CHECKLIST
K TSCA SECTIONS 5 AND 8 CHECKLIST
L PESTICIDE (FIFRA) CHECKLIST
M WATER SUPPLY CHECKLIST
N UNDERGROUND INJECTION CONTROL (UIC) CHECKLIST
0 COMMUNITY RIGHT-TO-KNOW CHECKLIST
P LABORATORY AUDIT CHECKLISTS

APPENDIX A
SUMMARY OF POLLUTION CONTROL LEGISLATION

This appendix is a synopsis of the Federal approach to environmental regulation, EPA enforcement remedies and a summary of each of the major pollution control acts: the Clean Air Act (CAA), the Clean Water Act (CWA), the Resource Conservation and Recovery Act (RCRA), the Comprehensive Environmental Response, Compensation and Liability Act (CERCLA/Superfund), the Toxic Substances Control Act (TSCA), the Federal Insecticide, Fungicide and Rodenticide Act (FIFRA), the Safe Drinking Water Act (SDWA), and the Emergency Planning and Community Right-to-Know Act (EPCRTKA). Because these laws and the regulations promulgated thereunder typically are very complex and continually are being modified, the investigator should carefully review the specific provisions which apply to the operations of the facility before conducting an inspection.

GENERAL FEDERAL APPROACH TO ENVIRONMENTAL REGULATION

National standards are established to control the handling, emission, discharge and disposal of harmful substances. Waste sources must comply with these national standards whether the programs are implemented directly by EPA or delegated to the States. In many cases, the national standards are applied to sources through permit programs which control the release of pollutants into the environment. The EPA establishes the Federal standards and requirements and approves State programs for permit issuance.

The States can set stricter standards than those required by Federal law. Some of the larger programs which have been delegated by EPA to qualifying States are the National Emissions Standards for Hazardous Air Pollutants (NESHAP), the Prevention of Significant Deterioration (PSD) permits under the CAA, the Water Quality Standards and the National Pollution Discharge Elimination System (NPDES) programs under the CWA, the Hazardous Waste Program under RCRA, and the Drinking Water and Underground Injection Control (UIC) programs under the SDWA. Conversely, TSCA is administered entirely by the Federal government.

<u>EPA ENFORCEMENT OPTIONS</u>

1. Issuance of an Administrative Compliance Order, sometimes preceded by a Notice of Violation.* A Compliance Order will specify the nature of the violation and give a reasonable time for compliance. The order, if violated, can lead to enforcement action pursuant to the civil and/or criminal process of environmental laws.

2. Issuance of an administrative complaint for civil penalties. Parties named in such complaints must be given notice and an opportunity for a hearing on the alleged violations before a penalty can be assessed by EPA.

3. Under certain statutes (e.g., SDWA) EPA may take whatever action is necessary to protect the public health, in emergency situations, without first obtaining a judicial order.

4. EPA generally may go directly to Federal court seeking injunctive relief or a civil penalty without using administrative procedures. EPA also may obtain an emergency restraining order halting activity alleged to cause "an imminent and substantial endangerment" or "imminent hazard" to the health of persons.

5. EPA may go directly to Federal court seeking criminal sanctions without using administrative procedures. Criminal penalties are available for "knowing" or for "willfull" violations.

In addition, EPA can also "blacklist" a company or party that fails to comply with the CAA or CWA by preventing it from entering into Federal contracts, loans and grants. In cases where the party had been convicted of certain criminal offenses under the CAA or CWA, Federal agencies are expressly prohibited from entering into contracts, etc., with that entity.

---

* *A concise written statement with factual basis for alleging a violation and a specific reference to each regulation, act, provision or permit term allegedly violated*

CLEAN AIR ACT

The Clean Air Act (CAA) calls for EPA to establish national ambient air standards. These standards are expressed as concentrations of designated hazardous pollutants called National Ambient Air Quality Standards (NAAQS). These standards are to be achieved by the States through State Implementation Plans (SIPs). EPA also sets the following national air emission standards: New Source Performance Standards (NSPS), National Emissions Standards for Hazardous Air Pollutants (NESHAP) and standards governing mobile sources of air pollution (including motor vehicle fuels). Moreover, special programs have been developed for prevention of significant deterioration (PSD) in clean air areas and for stringent controls in nonattainment areas (NAAs).

The SIP provides emission limitations, schedules and timetables for compliance by stationary sources, as well as transportation control plans for mobile sources. The act focuses upon "major" stationary sources or major modifications of existing sources. Major sources are defined as sources which generally emit more than 100 tons per year of a designated pollutant.

National Ambient Air Quality Standards/State Implementation Plans

EPA designates harmful pollutants and publishes criteria documents which discuss potential harmful effects of those pollutants. The Agency then sets primary and secondary ambient air standards (CAA, Section 109). Primary standards are intended to protect the health of the population, whereas, secondary standards are meant to protect the esthetic values of the environment.

Seven pollutants have been established as harmful and standards established. These pollutants include: sulfur dioxides, particulates, carbon monoxide, ozone, hydrocarbons, nitrogen oxides and lead. These standards are implemented through SIPs, (CAA, Section 110).

EPA has designated 247 Air Quality Control Regions (AQCRs). These have been rated as either "clean" or "non-attainment" for each of the criteria pollutants. SIPs must assure attainment of NAAQS by prescribed dates. SIPs must meet Federal requirements, but each State may choose its own mix of emissions for stationary and mobile sources to meet the NAAQS. Control procedures may include stationary source emission limits, transportation plans, preconstruction review of new sources, NAA and PSD permits for construction of new sources, monitoring and inspection and testing of vehicles. Other measures may include emissions charges, closing and relocation of plants, changes in operations and ways to reduce vehicular traffic including taxes, staggered work hours and mass transportation. The CAA prescribes that no SIP will be adopted without a public hearing, and sources affected by the SIP are expected to participate.

New Source Performance Standards

NSPS are established for specific pollutants in industrial categories, based upon adequately demonstrated control technology. Many States have been delegated the authority to enforce NSPS. When a State does not have the authority, EPA enforces NSPS in that state. Waivers from NSPS for up to 7 years may be obtained, the purpose of which is to encourage use of innovative technological systems (CAA, Section 111).

National Emissions Standards for Hazardous Air Pollutants

Section 112 of the CAA defines hazardous air pollutants as those for which no air quality standard is applicable but which are judged to increase mortality or serious irreversible or incapacitating illness. NESHAP standards are based on health effects with strong reliance on technological capabilities. They apply to both existing and new stationary sources. The eight substances on the NESHAP list for which there are effective regulations currently are: benzene, beryllium, asbestos, mercury, vinyl chloride, radon, arsenic, and radionuclide emissions. The NESHAP program can be delegated to any qualifying State (CAA, Section 112).

Prevention of Significant Deterioration

The purpose of PSD is to avoid significant future degradation of the nation's clean air areas. A clean air area is one where the air quality is better than the ambient primary or secondary standard. Designation is pollutant specific so that an area can be non-attainment for one pollutant but clean for another. PSD applies only to new and modified sources in clean air areas. Clean air areas are divided into three categories: Class I - only minor air quality degradation allowed, Class II - moderate degradation, and Class III - substantial degradation. In no case would PSD allow air quality to deteriorate below secondary air quality standards.

"Baseline" is the existing air quality for the area at the time the first PSD is applied for. "Increments" are the maximum amount of deterioration that can occur in a clean air area over baseline. Increments in Class I areas are smaller than for Class II and Class II increments are smaller than Class III areas. For purposes of PSD, a major emitting source is one of 26 designated categories which emits or has the potential to emit 100 tons per year of the designated air pollutant. A source that is not within the 26 designated categories is a major source if it emits more than 250 tons per year.

New sources are required to obtain permits before construction. The permit describes the level of control to be applied and what portion of the increment may be made available to that source by the State (CAA, Part C).

Non-Attainment Areas (NAA)

Non-attainment areas are those which are not in compliance with national air quality standards. New construction in an NAA is prohibited unless the SIP has been amended and approved by EPA to reflect the following conditions:

1. Total allowable emissions for the area will be less than emissions from existing sources.

2. The new source must comply with the lowest achievable emission rate (LAER).

3. All other sources within the State owned by the subject company are in compliance.

4. The SIP is being carried out for the area.

The applying source in an NAA must, therefore, obtain a greater than 1:1 reduction of the pollutant or pollutants for which the area has been designated non-attainment. The source must undergo a relatively stringent pre-construction review.

Emission offsets from existing sources may need to be obtained, especially if the new source will have emissions that would exceed the allowance for the NAA. In these situations, the source would need to obtain enforceable agreements from other sources in the NAA or from its own plants in the NAA.

Emission reductions can also be "banked" by an existing source to permit future new source growth. Banked offsets may be sold or traded to other sources.

Emission Standards for Mobile Sources/Fuel Standards

Section 202 of the CAA directs EPA to regulate air pollutants emitted by motor vehicles which "cause, or contribute to, air pollution which may reasonably be anticipated to endanger public health or welfare." In response, the Agency has set standards governing motor vehicle emissions of carbon monoxide, hydrocarbons, oxides of nitrogen and particulates. These standards have given rise to the emission control systems that first appeared in automobiles in the early 1970s. The CAA generally prohibits the removal (or rendering inoperative) of any emission control device that was installed by the vehicle manufacturer in order to meet the applicable emission standards. Most states have enacted similar laws enforcing this prohibition and/or have incorporated such prohibitions as part of SIP.

The CAA provides EPA with the authority to control or prohibit the use of fuels which pose a public health risk _or_ which "impair to a significant degree the performance of any emission control device or system." The Agency's regulations are based upon both of these rationales. (The best example of this are the regulations governing the lead content of gasoline.) Enforcement of the fuel standards is achieved through a combination of Federal and State efforts, and is based, in part, upon SIP provisions and/or State laws.

CLEAN WATER ACT (FEDERAL WATER POLLUTION CONTROL ACT)

Through the 1950s and 1960s, emphasis was on the States setting ambient water quality standards and developing plans to achieve these standards. In 1972, the Federal Water Pollution Control Act was significantly amended. These changes emphasized a new approach, combining water quality standards and effluent limitations (i.e., technology-based standards). The amendments called for compliance by all point-source discharges with the technology-based standards. A strong Federal enforcement program was created and substantial monies were made available for construction of sewage treatment plants. The Federal Water Pollution Control Act was amended in 1977 to address toxic water pollutants and in 1987 to refine and strengthen priorities under the Act as well as enhance EPA's enforcement authority. Since the 1977 amendments, the Federal Water Pollution Control Act has been commonly referred to as the Clean Water Act (CWA).

State Water Quality Standards and Water Quality Management Plans

Section 303 of the CWA authorizes the States to establish ambient water quality standards and water quality management plans. If national technology standards are not sufficient to attain desired stream water quality, the State shall set maximum daily allowable pollutant loads (including toxic pollutants) for these waters and, accordingly, determine effluent limits and compliance schedules for point sources to meet the maximum daily allowable loads.

The National Pollutant Discharge Elimination (NPDES) Program

This program was established by Section 402 of the CWA and, under it, EPA and approved States have issued more than 50,000 NPDES permits. Permits are required for all point sources from which pollutants are discharged to navigable waters. An NPDES permit is required for any direct discharge from new or existing sources. Indirect discharges through POTWs are regulated under a separate program (see discussion of pretreatment standards below). In 1979 and 1980, the permit program was revised and one of the new features was the use of Best Management Practices (BMPs) on a case-by-case basis to minimize the introduction of toxic and hazardous substances into surface waters. BMPs are industry practices used to reduce secondary pollution (e.g., raw material storage piles shall be covered and protected against rain and runoff). BMPs do not have numerical limits and, therefore, are different from effluent limits.

Section 304 of the CWA sets restrictions on the amount of pollutants discharged at industrial plant outfalls. Amounts are usually expressed as weight per unit of product (i.e., 0.5 lb/1,000 lb product manufactured). The standards are different for each industry. Effluent guidelines are applied to individual plants through the NPDES permit program.

There are three levels of technology for existing industrial sources: Best Practicable Control Technology (BPT), Best Conventional Technology (BCT) and Best Available Technology Economically Achievable (BAT). Under the 1972 Act, BPT was intended to be put in place by industry in 1977 and BAT in 1983. These timetables have been modified by subsequent amendments.

The 1987 CWA Amendments modified the compliance deadlines for the following:

- BPT limits requiring a substantially greater level of control based on a fundamentally different control technology

- BAT for priority toxic pollutants

- BAT for other toxic pollutants
- BAT for nonconventional pollutants
- BCT for conventional pollutants

For each technology the new deadline requires compliance "as expeditiously as practicable, but in no case later than 3 years after the date such limitations are promulgated. . .and in no case later than March 31, 1989."

New Source Performance Standards (NSPS) are closely related to BAT for existing sources but are not quite the same. NSPS are different for each industrial category. These standards must be achieved when the new industrial source begins to discharge. NSPS permits will be effective for a period of 10 years vs. 5 years or less for the BPT and BAT-type permits. This 10-year protection insulates against change in BCT or BAT requirements but does not hold against Section 307(a) toxic pollutant standards or against "surrogate" pollutants that are used to control hazardous or toxic pollutants.

A permit application must be made. Adequate information must be submitted including basic facility descriptions, SIC codes, regulated activities, lists of current environmental permits, descriptions of all outfalls, drawings, flows, treatment, production, compliance schedules, effluent characteristics, use of toxics, potential discharges and bio-assay toxicity tests performed.

Applicants must conduct analytical testing for pollutants for BOD, COD, TOC, TSS, ammonia, temperature and pH. The applicant, if included within any of the 34 "primary industry" categories, must sample for all toxic metals, cyanide and phenols given in EPA Application Form 2C and for specified organic toxic pollutant fractions.

The applicant must list hazardous substances believed to be present at the industrial plant. Testing is not required but analytical results must be provided, if available.

NPDES Permit

The NPDES permit, issued by EPA or the State, enforces Federal effluent limitations promulgated for individual industrial categories; NSPS; toxic effluent standards; State water quality standards under Section 303 of the CWA, if any are applicable and hazardous substances otherwise regulated under Section 311 of the CWA that may be incorporated under the NPDES permit instead. Permit elements include the amount of pollutants to be discharged expressed in terms of average monthly and maximum daily loads; compliance schedules, if applicable standards cannot be met now and monitoring, testing and reporting requirements.

Routine Non-compliance Reports - The Discharge Monitoring Form

The Discharge Monitoring Report (DMR) gives a summary of the discharger's records on a monthly or quarterly basis for flow measurement, sample collection and laboratory analyses. Noncompliance reports must be submitted quarterly on the cause of noncomplying discharges, period of noncompliance, expected return to compliance and plans to minimize or eliminate recurrence of incident.

Emergency Reporting

- Health: The EPA shall be notified within 24 hours of noncompliance involving discharge of toxic pollutants, threat to drinking water or injury to human health.

- Bypass: Noncompliance due to intentional diversion of waste shall be reported promptly to the permitting agency and may be permissable if essential to prevent loss of life or serious property damage.

- Upset: Temporary noncompliance due to factors beyond the reasonable control of the permittee shall be promptly reported to the agency.

The 1987 CWA Amendments establish a schedule for the regulation of municipal and industrial stormwater discharges under NPDES permits. Initially, (before October 1, 1992), only major dischargers and those who are significant contributors of pollutants will be required to obtain permits.

Pretreatment Standards for Indirect Discharges to Publicly-Owned Treatment Works

Coverage

New and existing industrial users who discharge to POTWs are subject to general and categorial pretreatment standards. The categorical standards are primarily directed to control of toxic pollutants in specific industries.

Requirements

- General Pretreatment Standards

  Prohibit fire or explosion hazards, corrosivity, solid or viscous obstructions, "slug" discharges, and heat sufficient to inhibit biological activity at POTWs.

- Categorical Standards

  - Standards to be expressed as concentration limits or mass weight per unit of production.

  - Source must be in compliance 3 years after promulgation of standards.

  - Variances can be obtained for fundamentally different factors or if industrial pollutants are consistently being removed by POTW.

- Reports

  Users must provide appropriate agency (EPA, State or POTWs having approved pretreatment programs) with basic information, SIC code, average and maximum daily discharge, characteristics or pollutants, applicable standards and certification whether standards are being met and, if not, what pretreatment is necessary and a compliance schedule.

- Monitoring, Sampling and Analysis

  Users shall submit sampling data for each regulated pollutant in discharge.

- Progress Reports

  Reports and information shall be submitted at 6-month intervals.

Non-Point Source Pollution Control

Section 208 of the CWA provides for control of non-point source pollution and directs States to establish planning bodies to formulate area-wide pollution control plans. NPDES permits cannot be issued where the permit may conflict with an approved Section 208 plan.

The 1987 CWA Amendments require States or EPA to develop nonpoint source management programs under Section 319.

Dredge or Fill Discharge Permit Program

Section 404 of the CWA regulates the discharge of dredged or fill material into waters of the United States. Dredged material is excavated or dredged from a water body. Fill material is that material used to replace water with dry land. The Section 404 permit program is administered by the U.S. Army Corps of Engineers. EPA provides guidelines for the issuance of permits by the Corps of Engineers. States may assume responsibility for portions of the program.

Discharge of Oil and Hazardous Substances

Section 311 of the CWA prohibits discharges of oil or hazardous substances in quantities that may be harmful to waters of the United States. The appropriate Federal agency must be immediately notified of any spill of a "reportable quantity." Section 311 provides for cleanup of spills and requires plans for preparation of Spill Prevention, Control and Countermeasures (SPCC) plans.

Over 300 substances have been defined as hazardous under Section 311 and each of these substances has a "reportable quantity" (40 CFR, Parts 116 and 117, 1980).

A person or corporation who properly notifies the Agency of the discharge of a reportable quantity of oil or hazardous substance is immune from criminal prosecution but is liable for civil penalties. Additionally, those who cause the spill are liable for the costs of cleanup and removal. If the Federal government must clean up the spill, the discharger of the spill is liable for cleanup costs. There are maximum liability limits depending upon the type of facility and spill. These limits do not apply if the discharge resulted from willfull negligence or willfull misconduct of the owner.

Certain discharges of oil and hazardous material that flow from a point source may be excluded from Section 311 liability if, during preparation of the NPDES permit covering that facility, conditions are added to the permit to avoid the occurrence of a spill.

RESOURCE CONSERVATION AND RECOVERY ACT OF 1976 (RCRA)*

RCRA was signed on October 21, 1976 and subsequently amended in 1980 and 1984. The 1984 amendments to RCRA brought about dramatic

* *43 U.S.C. §§6901 et seq. and Solid Waste Disposal Act amendments of 1980, P.L. 96-482, 94 Stat. 2334.*

changes in the coverage required by the Act. The first in a series of regulations restricting the land disposal of hazardous wastes have been promulgated. Regulations also have been proposed which will include expanded coverage in such areas as waste oil, underground tanks, etc. The Act primarily deals with current and future waste handling activities; however, one section of the act (Section 7003), addresses problems which may have arisen prior to 1976. The 7003 provision allows EPA to take action against persons conducting past and current activities that may present "an imminent or substantial endangerment to health or to the environment." The 1984 amendments also provide for corrective actions against contamination resulting from past releases of hazardous waste even without an imminent hazard. A review of the Act and the implementing regulations by the inspector is imperative before conducting an inspection, due to these changes.

Solid wastes, if land disposed, are regulated through State programs under Subtitle D of RCRA. Hazardous solid wastes are subject to regulation in their generation, transport, treatment, storage and disposal under Subtitle C of RCRA. Subtitle C of the statute authorizes a comprehensive Federal program to regulate hazardous wastes from generation to ultimate disposal. A waste is hazardous under Subtitle C if it is listed by EPA as hazardous, if it exhibits hazardous characteristics (corrosivity, reactivity, ignitability and extraction procedure toxicity) and if not delisted or excluded from regulation. There are special management provisions for hazardous wastes created by small quantity generators and hazardous wastes that are intended to be reused or recycled.

Solid waste includes garbage, refuse and sludge, other solid, liquid, semi-solid or contained gaseous material which is discarded, has served its intended purpose or is a mining or manufacturing byproduct. Most industrial and commercial byproducts can qualify as a solid waste. Exclusions from solid waste include domestic sewage, irrigation return flows, materials defined by the Atomic Energy Act, *in situ* mining waste and NPDES point sources.

Solid wastes excluded from regulation as hazardous solid wastes are household waste; crop or animal waste; mining overburden and wastes from processing and benefication of ores and minerals; flyash, bottom ash waste, slag waste and flue gas emission control waste and drilling fluids from energy development. A waste can be "delisted" from the hazardous waste listing or excluded for other reasons. Some materials intended to be reused or recycled are not fully regulated as solid/hazardous wastes, while others, depending upon the type of waste generated and the recycling process used, are fully regulated.

Statutory Restrictions/Prohibitions

- November 8, 1984 - The placement of any bulk liquid hazardous waste in salt domes, salt bed formations, underground mines or caves is prohibited until the facility receives a permit.

- May 8, 1985 - The landfilling of bulk or noncontainerized liquid hazardous waste or free liquids contained in hazardous waste is prohibited.

- November 8, 1985 - The placement of any nonhazardous waste liquid in a landfill operating under interim status or a permit, is prohibited unless the only reasonable alternative is a landfill or unlined surface impoundment which will not endanger groundwater drinking sources. See Section 3004(b)(3) for full graphics.

- November 8, 1986 - The land disposal of solvents (codes F001 through F005) and dioxins (codes F020 through F023) is prohibited unless human health and the environment will not be endangered. (Wastes generated by Superfund and RCRA enforcement actions are not affected until November 8, 1988.) See final rule, 51 Federal Register 40572 (November 7, 1986), to be codified at 40 CFR Part 268, with conforming amendments at 40 CFR Parts 260, 261, 262, 264, 265, 270 and 271.

- July 8, 1987 - Land disposal of wastes listed in Section 3004(d)(2) (the "California list") is prohibited unless human health or the environment is not endangered (wastes generated by Superfund and RCRA enforcement actions not affected until November 8, 1988.) See proposed rule, 57 Federal Register 4471 (December 11, 1986).

- May 8, 1985 - New units, lateral expansions and replacement of existing units at interim status waste piles are to have single liners and leachate collection systems.

  New units, lateral expansions and replacement of existing units at interim status landfills and surface impoundments are to have double liners and leachate collection systems.

- August 8, 1988 - Deep well injection of certain wastes is prohibited unless deemed safe by EPA. See Section 3004(d)(2) and (e)(2) for list of wastes.

List of Hazardous Wastes

Hazardous waste streams from specific major industry groups and some generic sources (40 CFR, Part 261, Subpart D, §261.31 and 261.32) and well over 200 toxic commercial chemical wastes (i.e., discarded commercial chemical products and chemical intermediates) are included on the list of hazardous waste (40 CFR §261.33). If a commercial chemical substance is on the list, its off-spec species is also considered hazardous when discarded, as are spill residues. Some of the listed wastes are acutely toxic and are more closely regulated than other hazardous wastes. See e.g., 40 CFR §§261.33(e), 261.5(e) and 261.7(b)(3).

Special Management Provisions

- Small Quantity Generators

  Small quantity generators are those that generate less than 1,000 kg per month of hazardous waste. There are two classes of small quantity generators:

1. Generators of between 100 and 1,000 kg per month that are subject to most of the requirements of 40 CFR Part 262 which apply to fully regulated generators, except that they are allowed to accumulate up to 6,000 kg of hazardous waste and to store waste for up to 180 to 270 days.

2. Generators of less than 100 kg per month that are exempt from regulation under 40 CFR Part 262 so long as they do not accumulate greater than 1,000 kg of hazardous waste, properly identify their wastes and comply with the less stringent waste treatment, storage and/or disposal requirements of 40 CFR §261.5.

Note that the classification of the generator is a function of the total wastes generated, not each waste stream. In addition, for acutely toxic wastes, if more than 1 kg per month of waste or 100 kg per month of spill residues are generated, all quantities of that waste are fully regulated.

- <u>Recycling or Reuse</u>

The type of waste generated and/or the recycling process employed will determine whether recycled/reused materials are a solid/hazardous waste. Some of these materials are not considered solid wastes, some are solid wastes but not hazardous wastes, while others are hazardous but are not subject to full regulation, and still other of these materials are both solid and hazardous wastes that are fully regulated. The circumstances surrounding the apparent recycling/reuse of waste materials should be thoroughly documented during and inspection.

Requirements for Generators*

- Identification - Hazardous wastes must be identified by list, testing or experience and assigned waste identification numbers.

- Notification - No later than 90 days after a hazardous waste is identified or listed in 40 CFR, Part 261, a notification is to be filed with EPA or an authorized State. An EPA identification number must be received.

- Manifest System - Implement the manifest system and follow procedures for tracking and reporting shipments. Beginning September 1, 1985, a waste minimization statement is to be signed by the generator [see RCRA Section 3002(b)].

- Packing - Implement packaging, labeling, marking and placarding requirements prescribed by DOT regulations (40 CFR, Parts 172, 173, 178 and 179).

- Annual Report - Submittal required March 1 using EPA Form 8700-13.

- Exception Reports - When generator does not receive signed copy of manifest from designated TSDF within 45 days, the generator sends Exception Report to EPA including copy of manifest and letter describing efforts made to locate waste and findings.

- Accumulation - When waste is accumulated for less than 90 days, generator shall comply with special requirements including contingency plan, prevention plan and staff training (40 CFR, Part 265, Subparts C, D, J and 265.16).

---

* *40 CFR Part 262*

- Permit for Storage More Than 90 Days - If hazardous wastes are retained onsite more than 90 days, generator is subject to all requirements applicable to TSDFs and must obtain a RCRA permit.

Requirements for Transporters*

- Notification - No later than 90 days after a hazardous waste is identified or listed in 40 CFR, Part 261, a notification is to be filed with EPA or an authorized State. Receive EPA identification number.

- Manifest System - The transporter must fully implement the manifest system. The transporter signs and dates manifest, returns one copy of generator, assures that manifest accompanies waste, obtains date and signature of TSDF or next receiver and retains one copy of the manifest for himself.

- Delivery to TSDF - The waste is delivered only to designated TSDF or alternate.

- Record Retention - Transporter retains copies of manifest signed by generator, himself and accepting TSDF or receiver and keeps these records for a minimum of 3 years.

- Discharges - If discharges occur, notice shall be given to National Response Center. Appropriate immediate action shall be taken to protect health and the environment and a written report shall be made to the DOT.

---

* *40 CFR Part 263*

Requirements for Treatment, Storage or Disposal Facilities (TSDFs)*

- Notification - No later than 90 days after a hazardous waste is identified or listed in 40 CFR, Part 261, a notification is to be filed with EPA or an authorized State.

- Interim Status - These facilities include TSDFs; onsite hazardous waste disposal; onsite storage for more than 90 days; in transit storage for greater than 10 days and the storage of hazardous sludges, listed wastes, or mixtures containing listed wastes intended for reuse. Interim status is achieved by:

  - Notification (see above)

  - Being in existence on November 19, 1980 or on the date of statutory or regulatory changes which require the facility to have a permit

  - Filing a Part A by the date specified in the regulation covering the facility (40 CFR, Parts 261, 264 or 265)

- Interim Status Facility Standards - The following standards and requirements shall be met.

  - General information (Subpart B)
  - Waste analysis plan
  - Security
  - Inspection plan
  - Personnel training
  - Handling requirements
  - Preparedness and prevention
  - Contingency planning and emergency procedures (Subparts C and D)
  - Records and reports

---

* *40 CFR Parts 264 and 265*

- Manifest system
- Operating logs
- Annual and other reports (Subpart E)
- Groundwater Monitoring (Subpart F)
- Closure and post-closure plans (Subpart G)
- Financial requirements (Subpart H)
- Containers, tanks, surface impoundments, piles (Subparts I, J, K, L)
- Land treatment, landfills, incinerators, thermal treatment, chemical, physical and biological treatment (Subparts M, N, O, P, Q)
- Underground injection (Subpart R)

• <u>Permit</u> - In order to obtain a permit:

  - Facilities with interim status must file a Part B RCRA permit application when directed to do so by EPA or an authorized State and final facility standards must be met or the facility must be on an approved schedule to meet those standards.

The EPA-authorized States are to issue permits or deny the application by November 8, 1988 for land disposal facilities; by November 8, 1989 for incinerators; and by November 8, 1992 for other facilities. The following is a statutory schedule for termination of interim status.

Facility	Interim Status Terminates	Unless Part B Submitted
Land Disposal	November 1985	November 1985
Incinerators	November 1989	November 1986
Other facilities	November 1992	November 1988

- New facilities and facilities which do not qualify for interim status are to receive a RCRA permit before construction can begin or a hazardous waste can be handled.

- Used/Recycled Oil - Used oil burned for energy recovery is regulated under 50 CFR Part 266. Although a number of parallel off-spec due to flashpoint, metal or halogen content. Additional regulations governing used/recycled oil are being developed.

  Underground Storage Tanks - The 1984 amendments also will cause certain underground storage tanks to be regulated. By May 8, 1986, all owners of underground tanks are to notify the designated State or local agency of the existence of the tank and specify the following:

  - Age
  - Size
  - Type
  - Location
  - Uses

  For tanks taken out of operation after January 1, 1974, the owner is to also notify the designated State or local agency of the existence of the tank and specify the following:

  - Date the tank was taken out of operation
  - Age at that time
  - Size
  - Type
  - Location
  - Type and quantity of substance left in the tank

  Rules comprehensively regulating these tanks were proposed April 17, 1987, 52 Federal Register 12662.

COMPREHENSIVE ENVIRONMENTAL RESPONSE, COMPENSATION AND LIABILITY ACT (SUPERFUND)

The Superfund Act was enacted December 11, 1980. The Federal government is authorized to clean up toxic or hazardous contaminants at closed and abandoned hazardous waste dumps and the government is permitted to recover cost of this cleanup and associated damages by suing the responsible parties involved. Cleanup monies will come out of a "superfund" created by taxes on chemicals and hazardous wastes.

The act provides that, when there is a release of hazardous substance, either real or threatened, the parties who operated the vessel or facility which created the release are liable for the containment, removal, remedial action, response and injury damages to natural resources under Section 107(a). The act also establishes limitations on liability.

If claims are presented to the liable parties but are not satisfied, the act then allows claims to be reimbursed from the Superfund.

Regulatory provisions under Sections 102 and 103 of the act require that release of hazardous substances into the environment be reported unless the release is in accordance with an established permit. Spills of any "reportable quantity", established pursuant to regulations promulgated under the Act, must be reported.

All owners or operators of any facility handling and disposing of hazardous substances or that has handled hazardous substances in the past (including previous owners and operators) were required to inform the EPA Administrator by June 1981 of their facility activities unless they have a RCRA permit or have been accorded "interim status". Failure of notification is a crime and, if the party knowingly fails to provide these data, they are not entitled to the prescribed limits and defenses of liability.

On October 17, 1986, the Superfund Act was amended under the Superfund Amendments and Reauthorization Act (SARA). Those amendments provide mandatory schedules for the completion of various phases of remedial response activities, establish detailed cleanup standards and generally strengthen existing authority to effect the cleanup of superfund sites.

[An integral part of SARA, but not an amendment to the Superfund Act, is the Emergency Planning and Community Right-to-Know Act of 1986. It addresses the handling of extremely hazardous chemicals and requires: (1) Emergency planning, (2) emergency notification, (3) community right-to-know reporting and (4) an emissions inventory.]

TOXIC SUBSTANCES CONTROL ACT (TSCA)

TSCA regulates existing and new chemical substances. TSCA applies primarily to manufacturers, distributors, processors and importers of chemicals. TSCA can be divided into five parts as follows:

Inventory and Pre-manufacture Notification

EPA has published an inventory of existing chemicals. A substance that is not on this list is considered "new" and requires Pre-manufacture Notification (PMN) to EPA at least 90 days before the chemical can be manufactured, shipped or sold (TSCA, Section 5). If EPA does not make a declaration within 90 days to restrict the product, then full marketing can begin and the chemical is added to the inventory. In addition, a manufacturer may obtain a test marketing exemption and distribute the chemical before the 90-day period has expired. Conversely, EPA, in response, may reject PMN for insufficient data, negotiate for suitable data, prohibit manufacture or distribution until risk data are available or pending development of a Section 6 rule, completely ban the product from the market or review the product data for an additional 90 days.

Testing

Under TSCA, Section 4, EPA can require product testing of any substance which "may present an unreasonable risk of injury to health or to the environment." Some testing standards are proposed, but no test requirements for specific chemicals are yet in effect.

Reporting and Recordkeeping

TSCA, Section 8(a) deals with general reporting. The "first tier" rule (PAIR) now in effect is a short form seeking production and exposure data on over 2,300 existing chemicals. A "second tier" rule is expected to obtain more detailed data on a relatively small group of chemicals that may become priority candidates for regulation.

Section 8(c) calls for records of significant adverse effects of toxic substances on human health and the environment. It requires that records of alleged adverse reaction be kept for a minimum of 5 years.

Section 8(d) allows EPA to require that manufacturers, processors and distributors of certain listed chemicals (designated under 40 CFR 716.13) submit to the EPA lists of health and safety studies conducted by, known to or ascertainable by them. Studies include individual files, medical records, daily monitoring reports, etc.

Section 8(e) requires action upon discovery of certain data. Any person who manufacturers, processes or distributes a chemical substance or mixture, or who obtains data which reasonably supports the conclusion that their chemical presents a substantial risk of injury to health or to the environment, is required to notify EPA immediately. Personal liability can only be limited if the company has a response plan in effect.

Regulation Under Section 6

EPA can impose a Section 6 rule if there is reason to believe that the manufacture, processing, distribution or use or disposal of a chemical substance or mixture causes, or may cause, an unreasonable risk of injury to health or to the environment. Regulatory action can range from labeling requirements to complete prohibition of the product. Section 6 rules are currently in effect for several chemicals including PCBs. A Section 6 rule requires informal rulemaking, a hearing, and a cost-benefit analysis.

Imminent Hazard

This is defined as a chemical substance or mixture causing an imminent and unreasonable risk of serious or widespread injury to health or the environment. When such a condition prevails, EPA is authorized by TSCA, Section 7, to bring action in U.S. District Court. Remedies include seizure of the chemical or other relief including notice of risk to the affected population or recall, replacement or repurchase of the substance.

FEDERAL INSECTICIDE, FUNGICIDE AND RODENTICIDE ACT (FIFRA)

A pesticide is defined as any substance intended to prevent, destroy, repel or mitigate pests. FIFRA requires registration of all pesticides, restricts use of certain pesticides, authorizes experimental use permits and recommends standards for pesticide applicators and the disposal and transportation of pesticides.

Pesticides are registered for 5 years and classified for either general or restricted usage. Restricted means that they are to be applied either by or under the direct supervision of a certified applicator. Pesticides must be labeled and specify ingredients, uses, warnings, registration number and any special use restrictions. Regulations also specify tolerance levels for certain pesticide chemicals in or on agricultural commodities. These limits apply to 310 different compounds and residue tolerances range from 0 to 100 ppm. A few pesticides are also regulated as toxic pollutants under Section 307(a) of the CWA and by Primary Drinking Water Standards under the SDWA.

SAFE DRINKING WATER ACT

The SDWA of 1974 was established to provide safe drinking water to the public. Both primary and secondary drinking water standards have been set by EPA regulations which apply to water after treatment by public drinking water systems. National Interim Primary Drinking Water Regulations were adopted in 1975 to protect public health (40 CFR, Part 141). Regulations covering radionuclides were added in 1976. Regulations for trihalomethanes were promulgated in 1979. Secondary regulations were established in 1979 as guidelines to States to protect the non-health-related-qualities of drinking water. The 1986 amendments to the SDWA: (1) establish a mandatory schedule, requiring the promulgation of primary drinking water regulations for 83 contaminants, (2) prohibit the use of lead in public water systems, (3) provide civil and criminal penalties for persons who tamper with public water systems and (4) require closer scrutiny of State programs, including the direct enforcement of drinking water standards, if necessary.

The SDWA also provides for protection of underground sources of drinking water. Final regulations have been issued whereby States are to establish Underground Injection Control (UIC) waste disposal programs to ensure that contaminants in water supplies do not exceed National Drinking Water Standards and to prevent endangerment of any underground source of drinking water. Injection wells are divided into five classes for regulatory handling. Construction and disposal standards are established for the permitting of Class I to III wells. Class I and IV wells are subject to RCRA requirements. Class IV wells are those used by generators of hazardous or radioactive wastes to dispose of hazardous wastes into formations within one-quarter mile of an underground source of drinking water. New Class IV wells are prohibited and existing Class IV wells must be phased out within 6 months after approval or promulgation of a UIC program in the state. There are numerous State regulatory requirements affecting groundwater which should be consulted by multi-media compliance inspectors. In addition, the 1986 amendments to SDWA strengthen EPA's enforcement authority for UIC programs.

APPENDIX B
SAFETY PLAN

The OSHA Hazardous Waste Site Worker Standards (29 CFR 1910.120), the EPA Safety Manual, Chapter 9, and other EPA protocols require certain safety planning efforts prior to field activities. The following format is aligned with these requirements. Extensive training and certifications, and further planning in the form of a more extensive Site Safety and Health Plan, may be required in addition to the following plan.

NEIC
PRELIMINARY SITE PLAN
FOR
HAZARDOUS SUBSTANCES RESPONSES AND FIELD INVESTIGATIONS

PROJECT: ____________________________ NEIC Reporting Code: ______________

Project Coordinator: __________________________ Date: ______________________

Branch Chief: _________________________________ Date: _____________________

On Scene Coordinator or
Supervisor: ________________________________ Date: _____________________

Health and Safety Manager
Approval: _________________________________ Date: _____________________

DESCRIPTION OF ACTIVITY

If any of the following information is unavailable, mark "UA"; if covered in project plan, mark "PP."

Site Name: ____

Location and approximate size: ____

Description of the response activity and/or the job tasks to be performed:
____
____
____

Duration of the Planned Employee Activity: __________________________
____

Proposed Date of Beginning the Investigation: _______________________

Site Topography: ____

Site Accessibility by Air and Roads: ______________________________

HAZARDOUS SUBSTANCES AND HEALTH HAZARDS INVOLVED OR SUSPECTED AT THE SITE

Fill in any information that is known or suspected

Areas of Concern	Chemical and Physical Properties	Identity of Substance and Precautions
Explosivity	______	______ ______ ______
Radioactivity:	______	______ ______ ______
Oxygen Deficiency: (e.g., Confined Spaces)	______	______ ______ ______
Toxic Gases:	______	______ ______ ______
Skin/Eye Contact Hazards:	______	______ ______ ______
Heat Stress	______	______ ______ ______

Pathways from site for hazardous substance dispersion: ______

______

______

______

WORK PLAN INSTRUCTIONS

A. Recommended Level of Protection: A ______ B ______ C ______

Cartridge Type, if Level C: ______

Additional Safety Clothing/Equipment: ______________________
____

Monitoring Equipment to be Used: ______________________
____
____
____
____
____

CONTRACTOR PERSONNEL:

Number and Skills: ______________________________
____
____

CONTRACTOR SAFETY CLOTHING/EQUIPMENT REQUIRED: __________
____
____
____

Have contractors received OSHA required training and certification?
(29 CFR 1910.120) Yes ______ Not Required ________

(If "yes", copy of training certificate(s) must be obtained from contractor)

B. Field Investigation and Decontamination Procedures:

Decontamination Procedures (contaminated protective clothing, instruments, equipment, etc.): ______________________________
____
____
____
____
____
____
____
____
____
____
____
____
____

Disposal Procedures (contaminated equipment, supplies, disposal items, wash-water, etc.): ____

IV. EMERGENCY CONTACTS

Hospital Phone No.: ______________________

Hospital Location: ______________________

EMT/Ambulance Phone No.: ______________________

Police Phone No.: ______________________

Fire Assistance Phone No.: ______________________

NEIC Health and Safety Manager: Ken Fischer - (303)236-5111
FTS 776-5111

Radiation Assistance:
Wayne Boliss, Director
Office of Radiation Programs
Las Vegas Facility (ORP-LVF)
(702)798-2476
FTS 545-2476

APPENDIX C

EVIDENTIARY PROCEDURES FOR PHOTOGRAPHS/MICROFILM

PHOTOGRAPHS

When movies, slides or photographs are taken which visually show the effluent or emission source and/or any monitoring locations, they are numbered to correspond to logbook entries. The name of the photographer, date, time, site location and site description are entered sequentially in the logbook as photos are taken. A series entry may be used for rapid sequence photographs. The photographer is not required to record the aperture settings and shutter speeds for photographs taken within the normal automatic exposure range. Special lenses, films, filters or other image enhancement techniques must be noted in the logbook. Chain-of-custody procedures depend upon the subject matter, type of film and the processing it requires. Film used for aerial photography, confidential information or criminal investigations require chain-of-custody procedures. Adequate logbook notations and receipts may be used to account for routine film processing. Once developed, the slides or photographic prints shall be serially numbered corresponding to the logbook descriptions and labeled.

MICROFILM

Microfilm is often used to copy documents that are or may later become TSCA Confidential Business Information (CBI). This microfilm must be handled in accordance with the TSCA CBI procedures (see Appendix I for additional information and forms). Table C-1 is the NEIC procedure for processing microfilm containing TSCA CBI documents.

Table C-1

NEIC PROCEDURE FOR MICROFILM
PROCESSING OF TSCA CBI DOCUMENTS

1. Kodak Infocapture AHU 1454 microfilm shall be used for filming all TSCA CBI documents.

2. Obtain packaging materials and instructions from the NEIC Document Control Officer or Assistant, including:

- Preprinted shipping labels
- Chain-of-custody records
- Custody seals
- Double envelopes
- Green TSCA cover sheets
- TSCA loan receipt

3. Prepare each roll of microfilm for shipment to the processor.

- Enclose the film in double-wrapped packages
- Place a green TSCA cover sheet in the inner package
- Place a TSCA loan receipt in the inner package
- Complete a Chain-of-Custody Record, place the white copy in the inner package and keep the pink copy for the field files
- Seal inner package with a custody seal and sign and date it
- Mark the inner package:

"TO BE OPENED BY ADDRESSEE ONLY
TSCA CONFIDENTIAL BUSINESS INFORMATION"

4. Ship the film via Federal Express to the Springfield, Virginia Federal Express office and instruct that it is to be held for pickup. USE SIGNATURE SECURITY SERVICE ONLY.

   This practice requires the courier to sign, the station personnel to sign and the delivery courier to sign.

   Instruct the Springfield Federal Express office to hold the shipment for pickup and to notify:

   Mr. Vern Webb
   U.S. EPA/EPIC
   Vint Hill Farms Station
   Warrenton, Virginia 22186
   (730) 557-3110

5. Telephone Mr. Webb and inform him of the date shipped, the number of rolls of film, the air bill number and your phone number.

6. Telephone the NEIC Document Control Officer or Assistant and inform them.

7. Telephone Mr. Webb the following day and verify film quality to determine if repeat microfilming is necessary.

8. The pink copy of the Federal Express form, with the shipment cost and project number indicated, must be turned in to the Assistant Director, Planning and Management. If you are in the field for an extended period of time (3 weeks or more), the pink copies must be mailed to NEIC.

APPENDIX D
AIR POLLUTION CHECKLISTS

NEW SOURCE PERFORMANCE STANDARDS (NSPS)*

Sources Covered

NSPS includes new and modified industrial stationary source categories for which construction was started after the standard was proposed. The categories are listed in Table D-1.

Requirements

- Notification to Agency

  Agency notified before construction ___Yes ___No
  before startup ___Yes ___No
  before testing ___Yes ___No

- Emissions Testing

  Performance tests of emission control equipment
  conducted using prescribed reference methods ___Yes ___No
  within 180 days of startup ___Yes ___No
  written results sent to Agency ___Yes ___No

- Monitoring

  Continuous emission monitoring (CEM) to be conducted for 10 categories [Table D-2]

  CEM recordkeeping kept in permanent form suitable for inspection ___Yes ___No

  - Records of continuous monitoring system
    maintained, including actual data ___Yes ___No
    performance specification test reports ___Yes ___No
    calibration checks ___Yes ___No
    adjustments and maintenance ___Yes ___No

  Control equipment operating parameters (flow rates, pressure drops, currents, etc.) ___Yes ___No

- Reports/Records

  Excess reports filed ___Yes ___No

  Date and time when control equipment was repaired, adjusted or inoperative ___Yes ___No

  Notification given to State/local agency ___Yes ___No

---

* *40 CFR, Part 60*

Appendix D (cont.)

Date and time when CEM was inoperative, nature of repairs _____Yes _____No

Notification given to State/local agency. _____Yes _____No

Table D-1

SOURCES SUBPART (40 CFR Part 60)
EFFECTIVE DATE OF STANDARD AND POLLUTANTS SUBJECT TO NSPS

Source	Subpart	Effective Date	Pollutant
Fossil-fuel-fired steam generators constructed after August 17, 1971	D	August 17, 1971	Particulate matter, sulfur dioxide nitrogen oxides
Fossil-fuel-fired steam generator constructed after September 18, 1978	Da	September 18, 1978	Particulate matter, sulfur dioxide nitrogen dioxide
Industrial-Commercial-Institutional steam generating units constructed after June 19, 1984	Db	June 19, 1984	Particulate matter, sulfur dioxide nitrogen oxides
Municipal incinerators	E	August 17, 1971	Particulate matter
Portland cement plants	F	August 17, 1971	Particulate matter
Nitric acid plants	G	August 17, 1971	Nitrogen oxides
Sulfuric acid plants	H	August 17, 1971	Sulfur dioxide, acid mist (sulfuric acid)
Asphalt concrete plants	I	June 11, 1973	Particulate matter
Petroleum refineries	J	June 11, 1973	Particulate matter, carbon monoxide,sulfur dioxide
Storage vessels for petroleum liquids	K	June 11, 1973	VOC
	Ka	May 18, 1978	VOC
Volatile organic liquid storage vessels	Kb	July 23, 1984	VOC
Secondary lead smelters	L	June 11, 1973	Particulate matter
Secondary brass and bronze ingot production plants	M	June 11, 1973	Particulate matter
Iron and steel plants (basic oxygen furnace)	N	June 11, 1973	Particulate matter
Iron and steel plants (secondary emissions from oxygen furnaces)	Na	January 20, 1983	Particulate matter
Sewage treatment plants (incinerators)	O	June 11, 1973	Particulate matter
Primary copper smelters	P	October 16, 1974	Particulate matter, sulfur dioxide
Primary zinc smelters	Q	October 16, 1974	Particulate matter, sulfur dioxide
Primary lead smelters	R	October 16, 1974	Particulate matter, sulfur dioxide
Primary aluminum reduction plants	S	October 23, 1974	Fluorides
Phosphate fertilizer industry (listed as five separate categories)	TUV WX	October 22, 1974	Fluorides
Coal preparation plants	Y	October 24, 1974	Particulate matter
Ferro-alloy production facilities	Z	October 21, 1974	Particulate matter, carbon monoxide
Steel plants (electric arc furnaces)	AA	October 21, 1974	Particulate matter
Steel plants, electric arc furnaces and argon-oxygen decarburization vessels	AAa	August 17, 1983	Particulate matter
Kraft pulp mills	BB	September 24, 1976	Particulate matter, TRS
Glass plants	CC	June 15, 1979	Particulate matter
Grain elevators	DD	August 3, 1978	Particulate matter
Metal furniture surface coating	EE	November 28, 1980	VOC
Stationary gas turbines	GG	September 24, 1976	Nitrogen oxides, sulfur dioxide
Lime plants	HH	May 3, 1977	Particulate matter
Lead acid battery plants	KK	January 14, 1980	Lead
Metallic mineral processing plants	LL	August 24, 1982	Particulate matter
Auto and light-duty truck, surface coating operation	MM	October 5, 1979	VOC
Phosphate rock plants	NN	September 21, 1979	Particulate matter
Ammonium sulfate plants	PP	February 4, 1980	Particulate matter
Graphic arts industry	QQ	October 28, 1980	VOC
Pressure sensitive tape manufacturing	RR	December 30, 1980	VOC
Appliance surface coating	SS	December 24, 1980	VOC
Metal coil surface coating	TT	January 5, 1981	VOC
Asphalt roofing plants	UU	November 18, 1980; May 26, 1981	Particulate matter
Synthetic organic chemicals	VV	January 5, 1981	Performance standards
Beverage can surface coating	WW	November 26, 1980	VOC
Bulk gasoline terminal	XX	December 17, 1980	VOC

Table D-1 (cont.)

SOURCES SUBPART (40 CFR Part 60)
EFFECTIVE DATE OF STANDARD AND POLLUTANTS SUBJECT TO NSPS

Source	Subpart	Effective Date	Pollutant
New residual wood heaters	AAA	July 1, 1988	Particulate matter
Rubber tire manufacturing industry	BBB	January 20, 1983	VOC
Vinyl/urethane coating	FFF	January 18, 1983	VOC
Petroleum refineries	GGG	January 4, 1983	Performance standards
Synthetic fiber plants	HHH	November 23, 1982	VOC
Petroleum dry cleaners	JJJ	September 21, 1984	VOC
Onshore natural gas processing plants	KKK	June 24, 1985	VOC
Onshore natural gas processing plants	LLL	October 1985	SO_2
Nonmetallic mineral processing plants	OOO	August 1, 1985	Particulate matter
Wool fiberglass insulation manufacturing plants	PPP	February 25, 1985	Particulate matter
Magnetic tape coating	SSS	January 22, 1986	VOC
Industrial surface coating, plastic parts for business machines	TTT	January 8, 1986	VOC

Table D-2
NSPS SOURCES REQUIRING CEM

Source	Subpart	Effective Date	Monitor
Fossil-fuel-fired steam generator	D	08/17/71	opacity, SO_2, NO_x, O_2 or CO_2
Fossil-fuel-fired electric utilities	Da	09/18/78	opacity, SO_2, NO_x, O_2 or CO_2
Nitric acid plants	G	08/17/71	NO_x
Sulfuric acid plants	H	08/17/71	SO_2
Petroleum refineries (FBCCU)	J	06/11/73	opacity, CO, SO_2, H_2S
Claus sulfur recovery unit	J	10/04/76	opacity, CO, SO_2, H_2S
Primary copper smelters	P	10/16/74	opacity, SO_2
Primary zinc smelters	Q	10/16/74	opacity, SO_2
Primary lead smelters	R	10/16/74	opacity, SO_2
Ferroalloy production facilities	Z	10/21/74	opacity
Electric arc furnaces	AA	10/21/74	opacity
Kraft pulp mills	BB	09/24/76	opacity, TRS
Lime manufacturing plants	HH	05/03/77	opacity
Phosphate rock plants	NN	09/21/79	opacity
Flexible vinyl and urethane coating and printing	FFF	01/18/83	VOC
Onshore natural gas processing plants	LLL	10/01/85	SO_2/T/TRS

NATIONAL EMISSIONS STANDARDS FOR HAZARDOUS AIR POLLUTANTS (NESHAP)*

Sources Covered

NESHAP includes new and existing stationary sources that emit or have the potential to emit any one of six hazardous air pollutants. The pollutants and sources covered are listed in Table D-3.

Existing sources must comply within 90 days but can obtain waivers for up to 2 years for installation of controls. New sources or modified sources coming online after the publication of standards must achieve immediate compliance.

Requirements

- Compliance Status

  Submit to Agency within 90 days of publication of standard adequate information on design, method of operation, weight/month of hazardous material and control devices ____Yes ____No

- Agency Notification

  Proper notice before startup and before emissions testing ____Yes ____No

- Emissions Testing

  Emission testing conducted using prescribed reference methods ____Yes ____No

  Written results sent to Agency ____Yes ____No

- Monitoring and Reporting

  Required monitoring being performed ____Yes ____No

  Reporting to Agency ____Yes ____No

---

* *40 CFR, Part 61, 1980*

Table D-3

SOURCES SUBJECT TO TITLE 40 CFR PART 61 NATIONAL EMISSIONS STANDARDS FOR HAZARDOUS AIR POLLUTANTS

Pollutant	Subpart	Source
Radon-222	B	Underground uranium mines
Beryllium	C	Extraction plants Ceramic plants Foundries Incinerators Machine shops
Beryllium	D	Rocket motor firing
Mercury	E	Ore processing plants Chlor-alkali plants Sludge incinerators Sludge drying plants
Vinyl chloride	F	Ethylene dichloride plants Vinyl chloride plants Polyvinyl chloride plants
Radionuclides	H	DOE facilities
Radionuclides	I	Facilities licensed by the Nuclear Regulatory Commission and Federal facilities not covered by Subpart H
Benzene (leaks)	J	Equipment in benzene service (plants designed to produce more than 1,000 megagrams of benzene per year)
Radionuclides	K	Elemental phosphorus plants
Asbestos	M	Asbestos mills Manufacturing Demolition and renovation Spraying Fabrication Waste disposal
Inorganic arsenic	N	Glass manufacturing plants
Inorganic arsenic	0	Primary copper smelters

Table D-3 (cont.)

SOURCES SUBJECT TO TITLE 40 CFR PART 61
NATIONAL EMISSIONS STANDARDS FOR HAZARDOUS AIR POLLUTANTS

Pollutant	Subpart	Source
Inorganic arsenic	P	Arsenic trioxide and metallic arsenic production facilities
Volatile hazardous air pollutants (VHAP)*	V	Equipment leaks (fugitive emission sources)
Radon-222	W	Licensed uranium mill tailings

* *Volatile hazardous air pollutant (VHAP) means a substance regulated under this part for which a standard for equipment leaks has been proposed and promulgated. As of February 1, 1989, benzene and vinyl chloride are VHAPs.*

Table D-4

EXAMPLE OF INSPECTION CHECKLIST*

I. GENERAL INFORMATION

A. Plant Location (mail address)____________________

B. Chief Corporate Officer (name/phone)____________________

C. Plant Manager (name/phone)____________________

D. Environmental Contact (name/phone)____________________

E. Sources Inspected____________ Production Status__________

____________________ __________

____________________ __________

____________________ __________

F. Reasons for Inspection (check appropriate items)

Routine Inspection__________ Compliance Progress__________

Complaint Investigation__________ Permit Review/Renewal__________

Stack Testing Observed__________ Tax Certification__________

Special Studies__________ Emergency Episode__________

Other__________ Equipment Malfunction__________

G. Plant Representative Contacted (name and title)____________________

____

H. Inspection Procedures and Conditions

Prior Notice (check one) Yes____ No____

Time/Date__________ Duration Onsite__________

Type Inspection (check one) Counterflow__________ Followup__________

Other__________

Weather__________ Wind Direction__________

II. PRE-INSPECTION INTERVIEW

A. Production Status: Normal__________ Abnormal__________

B. Control Equipment: Normal__________ Abnormal__________

C. Permit/Compliance Schedule Changes Needed: Yes____ No____

D. Comments____________________

____

____

---

* *Revised from Enforcement Workshop on Plant Inspection and Evaluation, Volume II, Draft, EPA, OE, SSE, February 1979*

Table D-4 (cont.)

III. INSPECTION RESULTS

A. Preliminary Conclusions

All sources in compliance with:

Mass Emission Regulations	Yes___	No___	N/A___
Visible Emission Regulations	Yes___	No___	N/A___
Fuel Quality Regulations	Yes___	No___	N/A___
Continuous Monitoring Regulations	Yes___	No___	N/A___
Sampling/Testing Requirements	Yes___	No___	N/A___
Recordkeeping Requirements	Yes___	No___	N/A___
Special Orders	Yes___	No___	N/A___
O&M Practices	Good____	Average____	Poor____
Housekeeping	Good____	Average____	Poor____

B. Specific Conclusions

Compliance questionable due to:

Changes in raw materials and/or fuels ____________________

Production rate increases ____________________

Operational changes in process ____________________

Deterioration of process equipment ____________________

Table D-4 (cont.)

Operational Problems in Control Equipment (check appropriate items below)

Electrostatic Precipitators	Fabric Filters	Wet Scrubbers
Resistivity________	Tears/pinholes_____	Low Liquor Flow ______
TR Sets__________	Blinding__________	Gas Flow Rate Low____
Insulators _________	Bleeding_________	Bed Plugging________
Discharge Wires___	Cleaning System__	Nozzle Erosion_______
High Velocity______	Hopper Overflow__	Demisters___________
Gas Distribution___	Corrosion_________	Throat Adjustment_____
Rappers__________	Tray Collapse_____	
Solids Handling___	Corrosion_________	
Plate Warpage_____		
Mass Overload____		
Other____________		

C. Samples Taken (Describe)____

____

____

D. Comments/Recommended Action_________________________________

____

____

Inspector ___________________ Date_________

Table D-5

EXAMPLE OF ASBESTOS EMISSION INSPECTION CHECKLIST

I. GENERAL INFORMATION

A. Facility Location (mail address)________________

B. Chief Corporate Officer (name/phone)________________

C. Facility Manager (name/phone)________________

D. Environmental Contact (name/phone)________________

E. Sources Inspected________________ Production Status________

________________ ________

________________ ________

________________ ________

F. Reasons for Inspection (check appropriate items)

Routine Inspection________	Compliance Progress________
Complaint Investigation________	Permit Review/Renewal________
Stack Testing Observed________	Tax Certification________
Special Studies ________	Emergency Episode________
Other ________	Equipment Malfunction________

G. Plant Representative Contacted (name and title)________________

____

H. Inspection Procedures and Conditions

Prior Notice (check one) Yes____ No____

Time/Date________________ Duration Onsite________________

Type Inspection (check one) Counterflow________ Followup________

Other________________

Weather________________ Wind Directiion________________

II. ASBESTOS MILL

Does the facility discharge to the outside air? ____Yes ____No

Are controls in place prior to discharge that meet air cleaning requirements? ____Yes ____No

(If yes, complete air cleaning standards XII.)

Table D-5 (cont.)

III. ROADWAYS

Is roadway surfaced with asbestos tailings or asbestos-contained waste material? ____Yes ____No

(Surfacing of temporary roadway in area of asbestos ore deposits is allowed.)

IV. MANUFACTURING [see 61.144(a) for applicability]

Are visible emissions possible to the outside air? ____Yes ____No

Are controls in place prior to discharge? ____Yes ____No

(If yes, complete air cleaning standards XII.)

V. DEMOLITION AND RENOVATION

A. If the facility is to be demolished, is the amount of friable asbestos at least 80 linear meters (260 linear feet) on pipes or at least 15 square meters (160 square feet) on other components? ____Yes ____No

(If no, go to B below.)

1. Was a written notice provided to the Administrator? ____Yes ____No

2. Was the notice postmarked or delivered at least 10 days before demolition/renovation began? ____Yes ____No

3. Did the notice include:

a. Name and address of owner or operator? ____Yes ____No

b. A description of the facility to be demolished or renovated including size, age and prior use? ____Yes ____No

c. The estimated amount of friable asbestos? ____Yes ____No

d. The location of the facility to be demolished/renovated? ____Yes ____No

Table D-5 (cont.)

e. A demolition/renovation schedule? ____Yes ____No

f. The methods of demolition/ renovation to be used? ____Yes ____No

g. Procedures to be followed to comply with National Emission Standards for Asbestos, 40 CFR 61, Subpart M? ____Yes ____No

h. The name and location of the asbestos disposal site? ____Yes ____No

4. Was friable asbestos material removed prior to wrecking or dismantling? ____Yes ____No

If no, was material encased in concrete or similar material? ____Yes ____No

Was material adequately wetted? ____Yes ____No

5. When asbestos covered or coated, were facility components removed? ____Yes ____No

a. Were they adequately wetted? ____Yes ____No

b. Were they carefully lowered to ground level? ____Yes ____No

6. If asbestos was stripped from facility components, were they adequately wetted? ____Yes ____No

If equipment would be damaged by wetting during renovation

a. Was Administrator supplied with sufficient information to determine that wetting would cause unavoidable damage? ____Yes ____No

b. Was a local exhaust ventilation and collection system used? ____Yes ____No

i. Are visible emissions possible to the outside air? ____Yes ____No

Table D-5 (cont.)

ii. Was the system operated according to air cleaning requirements? ____Yes ____No

(If a system was used, complete air cleaning standards XII and continue.)

7. After components were removed as units or sections,

a. Were they adequately wetted during stripping? ____Yes ____No

b. Was a local exhaust ventilation and collection system used? ____Yes ____No

(1) Are visible emissions possible to the outside air? ____Yes ____No

(2) Was the system operated to air cleaning requirements? ____Yes ____No

(If a system was used complete air cleaning standards XIII and continue.)

8. When friable material was stripped or removed,

a. Had it been adequately wetted until collected for disposal? ____Yes ____No

b. Had it been lowered, not dropped to the ground or lower floor? ____Yes ____No

c. Had it been transported via dust-tight shutes or containers if more than 50 feet above the ground level? ____Yes ____No

Table D-5 (cont.)

9. Was the temperature at the point of wetting below 0 °C (32 °F)? ____Yes ____No

(If yes, no other wetting requirements apply and components are to be removed as units or in sections to the maximum extent possible.)

B. If the facility is to be demolished,

Is the amount of friable asbestos less than 80 linear meters (260 linear feet) or pipes and less than 15 square meters (160 square feet) on other components? ____Yes ____No

(If no, go to C below.)

1. Was a written notice provided to the Administrator? ____Yes ____No

2. Was the notice postmarked or delivered at least 20 days before demolition/renovation began? ____Yes ____No

3. Did the notice include:

a. Name and address of owner or operator? ____Yes ____No

b. A description of the facility to be demolished or renovated including size, age and prior use? ____Yes ____No

c. The estimated amount of friable asbestos? ____Yes ____No

d. The location of the facility to be demolished/renovated? ____Yes ____No

e. A demolition/renovation schedule ____Yes ____No

C. Has the demolition been ordered by State or local government due to structurally unsound conditions or danger of imminent collapse? ____Yes ____No

If no, go to D below.

Table D-5 (cont.)

1. Was a written notice provided to the Administrator? ____Yes ____No

2. Was the notice postmarked or delivered as early as possible before the demolition began? ____Yes ____No

3. Did the notice include

   a. Name and address of owner or operator ____Yes ____No

   b. A description of the facility to be demolished or renovated including size, age and prior use ____Yes ____No

   c. The estimated amount of friable asbestos ____Yes ____No

   d. The location of the facility to be demolished/renovated ____Yes ____No

   e. A demolition/renovation schedule ____Yes ____No

   f. The methods of demolition/ renovation to be used ____Yes ____No

   g. Procedures to be followed to comply with national Emission Standard for Asbestos, 40 CFR 61, Subpart M ____Yes ____No

   h. The name and location of the asbestos disposal site ____Yes ____No

4. After components were removed as units or sections,

   a. Were they adequately wetted during stripping? ____Yes ____No

   b. Was a local exhaust ventilation and collection system used? ____Yes ____No

      (1) Are visible emissions possible to the outside air? ____Yes ____No

Table D-5 (cont.)

(2) Was the system operated according to air cleaning requirements? ____Yes ____No

(If a system was used, complete air cleaning standards XIII and continue.)

5. When friable material was stopped or removed,

a. Had it been adequately wetted until collected for disposal? ____Yes ____No

b. Had it been lowered, not dropped, to the ground or lower floor? ____Yes ____No

c. Had it been transported via dust-tight shutes or containers if more than 50 feet above the ground level? ____Yes ____No

6. Was the temperature at the point of wetting below 0 °C (32 °F)? ____Yes ____No

(If yes, no other wetting requirements apply and components are to be removed as units or in sections to the maximum extent possible.)

D. If the facility is to be renovated, is the amount of friable asbestos to be stripped at least 80 linear meters (260 linear feet) on pipes or at least 15 square meters (160 square feet) on other components? ____Yes ____No

1. Was a written notice provided to the Administrator? ____Yes ____No

2. Was the notice postmarked or delivered at least 10 days before demolition/renovation began? ____Yes ____No

3. Did the notice include

a. Name and address of owner or operator? ____Yes ____No

Table D-5 (cont.)

b.	A description of the facility to be demolished or renovated including size, age and prior use?	____Yes ____No
c.	The estimated amount of friable asbestos?	____Yes ____No
d.	The location of the facility to be demolished/renovated?	____Yes ____No
e.	A demolition/renovation schedule?	____Yes ____No
f.	The methods of demolition/ renovation to be used?	____Yes ____No
g.	Procedures to be followed to comply with National Emission Standards for Asbestos, 40 CFR 61, Subpart M?	____Yes ____No
h.	The name and location of the asbestos disposal site?	____Yes ____No

4. Was friable asbestos material removed prior to wrecking or dismantling? ____Yes ____No

   If no, was material encased in concrete or similar material and was material adequately wetted? ____Yes ____No

5. When asbestos covered or coated were facility components removed?

   a. Were they adequately wetted? ____Yes ____No

   b. Were they carefully lowered to ground level? ____Yes ____No

6. If asbestos was stripped from facility components, were they adequately wetted? ____Yes ____No

   If equipment would be damaged by wetting during renovation,

Table D-5 (cont.)

a. Was Administrator supplied with sufficient information to determine that wetting would cause unavoidable damage? ____Yes ____No

b. Was a local exhaust ventilation and collection system used? ____Yes ____No

(1) Are visible emissions possible to the outside air? ____Yes ____No

(2) Was the system operated according to air cleaning requirements? ____Yes ____No

(If a system was used, complete air cleaning standard XIII and continue.)

7. After components were removed as units or sections,

a. Were they adequately wetted during stripping? ____Yes ____No

b. Was a local exhaust ventilation and collection system used? ____Yes ____No

(If a system was used complete air cleaning standards XIII and continue.)

8. When friable material was stripped or removed,

a. Had it been adequately wetted until collected for disposal? ____Yes ____No

b. Had it been lowered, not dropped, to the ground or lower floor? ____Yes ____No

c. Had it been transported via dust-tight shutes or containers if more than 50 feet above the ground level? ____Yes ____No

Table D-5 (cont.)

9. Was the temperature at the point of wetting below 0 °C (32 °F)? ____Yes ____No

   (If yes, no other wetting requirements apply and components are to be removed as units or in sections to the maximum extent possible.)

VI. SPRAYING

If sprayed on asbestos material is encapsulated and the material is not friable after drying, go to 3.

A. Does material that is sprayed contain: 1% or less asbestos on a dry weight basis? ____Yes ____No

B. If greater than 1%,

1. Was the Administrator notified at least 20 days prior to the spraying? ____Yes ____No

2. Did the notice include:

   a. Name and address of owner or operator? ____Yes ____No

   b. Location of spraying operation? ____Yes ____No

   c. Procedures to be followed to comply with National Emission Standards for Asbestos, 40 CFR 61, Subpart M? ____Yes ____No

3. Are visible emissions possible to the outside air? ____Yes ____No

   Were emissions cleaned before discharge? ____Yes ____No

   (If yes, complete air cleaning standards XIII and continue.)

VII. FABRICATION (See 61.149 for applicability)

Are visible emissions to the outside air possible? ____Yes ____No

Table D-5 (cont.)

Were emissions cleaned before discharge? ____Yes ____No

(If yes, complete air cleaning standards XIII and continue.)

VIII. INSULATING MATERIALS

Was insulating material containing asbestos that was molded and friable or wet applied and friable after drying, installed or re-installed after April 5, 1984? ____Yes ____No

IX. WASTE DISPOSAL FOR ASBESTOS MILLS

A. Was asbestos-containing waste material disposed at an acceptable site? ____Yes ____No

(See Active Waste Disposal Site requirements XIV.)

B. Are visible emissions possible to the outside air? ____Yes ____No

Were emissions cleaned before discharge? ____Yes ____No

(If yes, complete air cleaning standards XIII and continue.)

C. Identify the disposal method for wastes from control devices.

____

____

1. Was the waste mixed with a wetting agent prior to disposal? ____Yes ____No

a. Was the agent recommended by the manufacturer for this use? ____Yes ____No

b. Was all asbestos containing material adequately mixed with the wetting agent? ____Yes ____No

c. Are visible emissions possible to the outside air? ____Yes ____No

Were emissions cleaned before discharge? ____Yes ____No

(If yes, complete air cleaning standards XIII and continue.)

Table D-5 (cont.)

d. Was wetting suspended when the ambient temperature at the waste disposal site dropped below -9.5 °C (15 °F)? ____Yes ____No

(1) Are hourly temperature records kept during suspension of wetting operations? ____Yes ____No

(2) Are records kept for at least 2 years? ____Yes ____No

2. Was waste mixed with water to form a slurry? ____Yes ____No

a. Are visible emissions possible to the outside air? ____Yes ____No

Were emissions cleaned before discharge? ____Yes ____No

(If yes, complete air cleaning standards and continue XIII.) ____Yes ____No

b. Was all wet asbestos-containing material in leak-tight containers? ____Yes ____No

c. Were the containers labeled with appropriate warnings? ____Yes ____No

[See 61.152(b)(1)(iv) or OSHA 29 CFR 1910.1001(g)(2)(ii) for labeling requirements.]

3. Is waste processed into nonfriable pellets or other shapes? ____Yes ____No

a. Are visible emissions possible from the operation to the outside air? ____Yes ____No

b. Were emissions cleaned before discharge? ____Yes ____No

(If yes, complete air cleaning standards XIII and continue.)

Table D-5 (cont.)

4. If an alternate method is used, was it approved by the Administrator? ____Yes ____No

X. STANDARD FOR WASTE DISPOSAL FOR MANUFACTURING, DEMOLITION, RENOVATION, SPRAYING AND FABRICATING OPERATIONS

A. Are wastes disposed at acceptable sites? ____Yes ____No

(See Active Waste Disposal Site XIV requirements.)

B. Are visible emissions possible to the outside air during collection, processing, incineration, packaging, transporting of deposition of waste? ____Yes ____No

1. Was the waste mixed with a wetting agent prior to disposal? ____Yes ____No

a. Was the agent recommended by the manufacturer for this use? ____Yes ____No

b. Was all asbestos containing material adequately mixed with the wetting agent? ____Yes ____No

c. Are visible emissions possible to the outside air? ____Yes ____No

Were emissions cleaned before discharge?

(If yes, complete air cleaning standards XIII and continue.)

d. Was wetting suspended when the ambient temperature at the waste disposal site dropped below -9.5 °C (15 °F)? ____Yes ____No

(1) Are hourly temperature records kept during suspension of wetting operations? ____Yes ____No

(2) Are records kept for at least 2 years? ____Yes ____No

Table D-5 (cont.)

2. Was waste mixed with water to form a slurry? ____Yes ____No

   a. Are visible emissions possible to the outside air? ____Yes ____No

   (If yes, complete air cleaning standards XIII and continue.)

   b. Was all wet asbestos-containing material in leak-tight containers? ____Yes ____No

   c. Were the containers labeled with appropriate warnings? ____Yes ____No

   [See 61.152(b)(1)(iv) or OSHA 29 CFR 1910.1001(g)(2)(ii) for labeling requirements.]

3. Is waste processed into nonfriable pellets or other shapes? ____Yes ____No

   a. Are visible emissions possible from the operation to the outside air? ____Yes ____No

   b. Were emissions cleaned before discharge? ____Yes ____No

   (If yes, complete air cleaning standards XIII and continue.)

4. If an alternate method is used, was it approved by the Administrator? ____Yes ____No

XI. STANDARDS FOR INACTIVE WASTE DISPOSAL SITES FOR ASBESTOS MILLS AND MANUFACTURING AND FABRICATING OPERATIONS

A. Are visible emissions possible from the site? ____Yes ____No

Is the site covered with at least 15 centimeters (6 inches) of clean compacted material? ____Yes ____No

Is a vegetation cover present? ____Yes ____No

Is the site covered with at least 60 centimeters (2 feet) of clean compacted material? ____Yes ____No

Table D-5 (cont.)

Is a dust suppression agent applied that has been recommended by the manufacturer and approved by the Administrator? ____Yes ____No

B. Is there a barrier restricting access to the site? ____Yes ____No

C. Are warning signs placed at 100-meter (330-foot) or less intervals around the site? ____Yes ____No

1. Are they easily read? ____Yes ____No

2. Do they meet the size requirements 61.153(b)(1)(ii)? ____Yes ____No

3. Do they meet the legend requirements of 61.153(b)(1)(iii)? ____Yes ____No

D. Has the Administrator approved an alternate access control method? ____Yes ____No

XII. AIR CLEANING STANDARDS

A. Are fabric filter collection devices used? ____Yes ____No

If no, go to D.

1. Is the filter pressure drop no more than .995 kilopascal (4 inches water gauge)? ____Yes ____No

2. Does the air flow permeability meet the requirements of 61.154(a)(1)(ii)? ____Yes ____No

3. Does the fabric meet the requirements of 61.154(a)(1)(iii)? ____Yes ____No

4. If a synthetic fabric is used, is the fill yarn spun? ____Yes ____No

B. Is all equipment properly installed, used, operated and maintained? ____Yes ____No

C. Are bypasses only used during suspect or emergency conditions? ____Yes ____No

D. Has the Administrator authorized wet collectors if fabric creates a fire or explosion hazard? ____Yes ____No

Table D-5 (cont.)

E. Has the Administrator authorized the use of any other alternate cleaning equipment? ____Yes ____No

XIII. REPORTING REQUIREMENTS

Has the facility submitted the following information to the Administrator by July 4, 1984 (90 days after April 5, 1984?) ____Yes ____No

A. For all sources:

1. Description of the emission control equipment for each process? ____Yes ____No

2. The pressure drop across the fabric filter, if used? ____Yes ____No

3. The airflow permeability of a woven fabric filter and of synthetic, if the fill yarn is spun? ____Yes ____No

B. For sources subject to 61.151 and 152:

1. Description of each process that generates asbestos-containing waste? ____Yes ____No

2. The average weight of material disposed in kg. per day? ____Yes ____No

3. The emission control methods used? ____Yes ____No

4. The type of disposal method or site and the name, location and operator of the site? ____Yes ____No

C. For sources subject to 61.153:

1. Description of the site? ____Yes ____No

2. Methods used to comply with the standards? ____Yes ____No

XIV. ACTIVE WASTE DISPOSAL SITE STANDARDS

A. Are visible emissions possible from the site? ____Yes ____No

Table D-5 (cont.)

Is at least 15 centimeters (6 inches) of compacted cover placed on the waste at the end of each day or 24-hour period? ____Yes ____No

Is dust suppressant used that has been approved by the Administrator? ____Yes ____No

If an alternate method is used, has it been approved by the Administrator? ____Yes ____No

B. Is there a barrier restricting access to the site? ____Yes ____No

C. Are warning signs placed at 100-meter (330-foot) or less intervals around the site? ____Yes ____No

1. Are they easily read? ____Yes ____No

2. Do they meet the size requirements of 61.153(b)(1)(ii)? ____Yes ____No

3. Do they meet the legend requirements of 61.153(b)(1)(iii)? ____Yes ____No

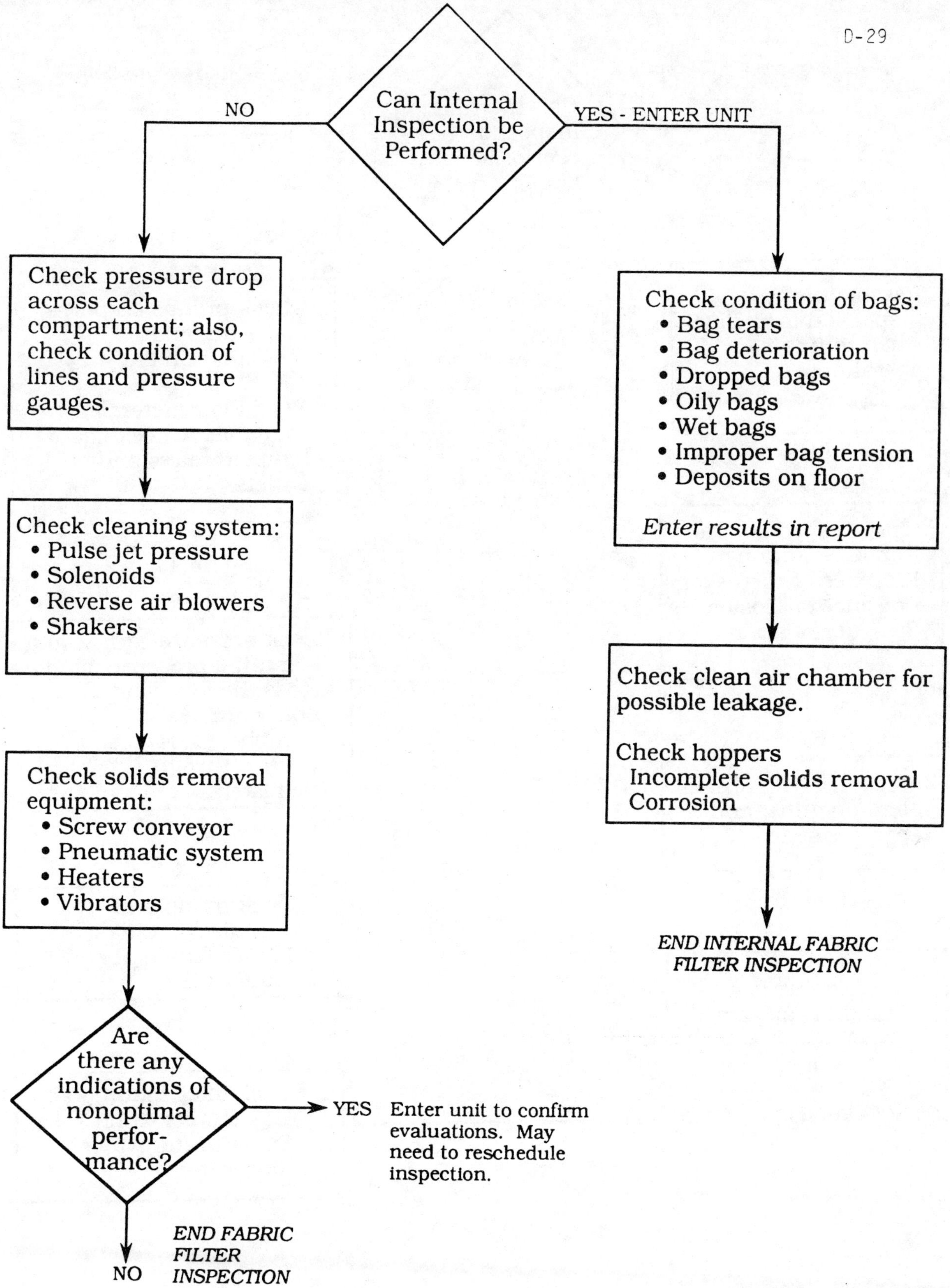

Figure D-1
Fabric Filter Inspection Flowsheet

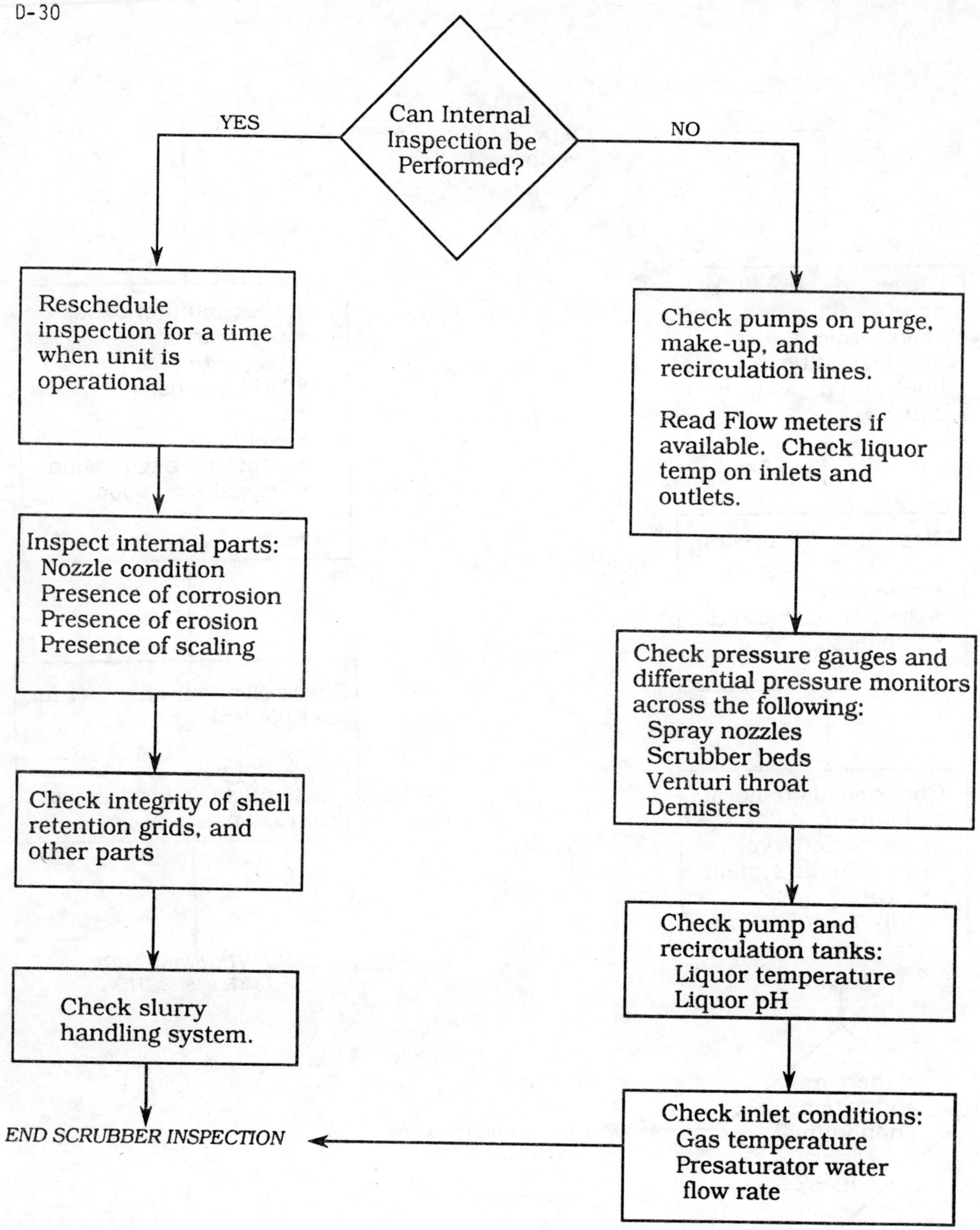

Figure D-2
Scrubber Inspection Flowsheet

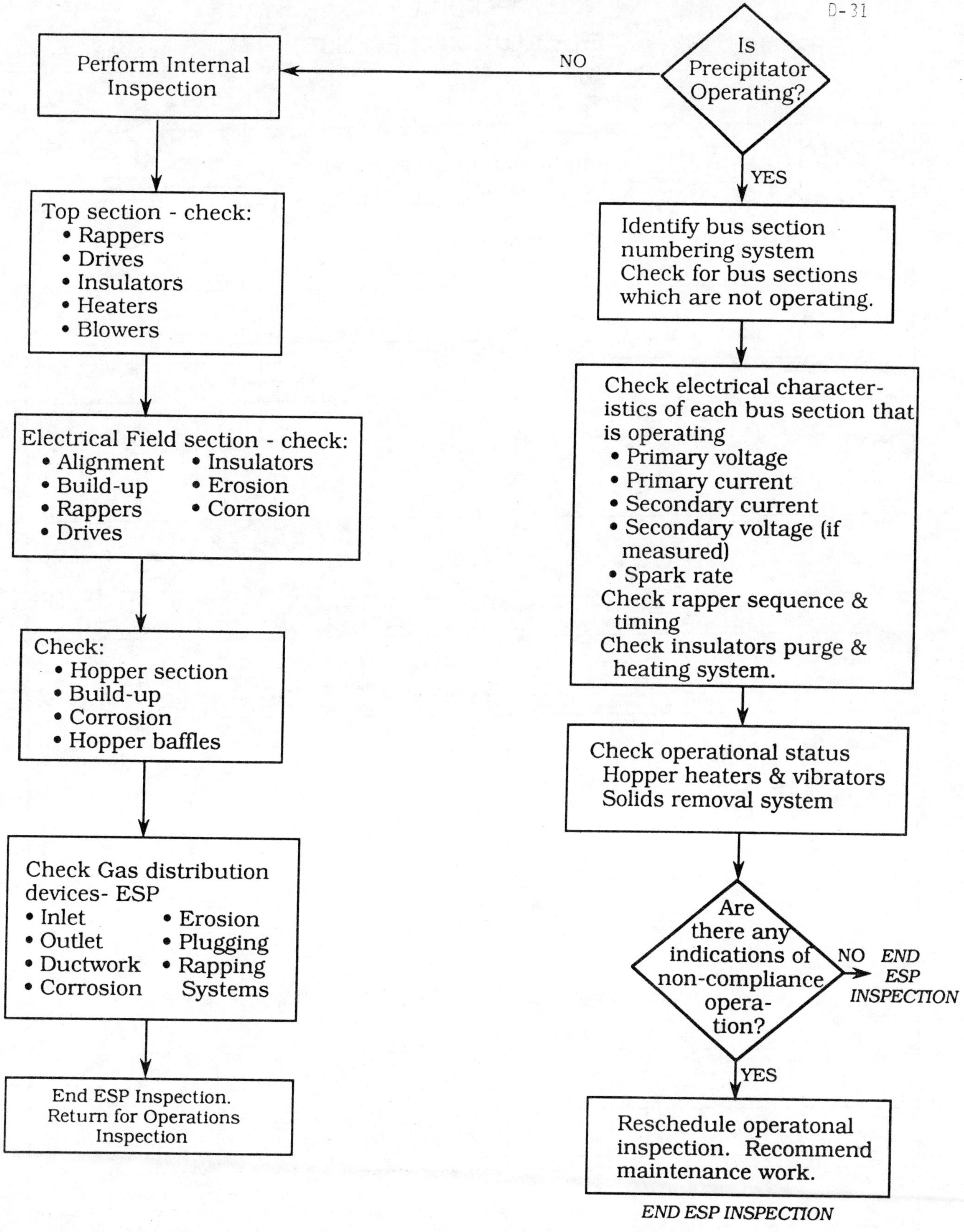

Figure D-3
Electrostatic Precipitator Inspection Flowsheet

APPENDIX E
WATER POLLUTION CHECKLISTS

United States Environmental Protection Agency
Washington, D.C. 20460

EPA

NPDES Compliance Inspection Report

Form Approved
OMB No. 2040-0003
Approval Expires 7-31-85

Section A: National Data System Coding

Transaction Code 1 ___ 2 5 ___ NPDES 3 ___ 11 yr/mo/day 12 ___ 17 Inspection Type 18 ___ Inspector 19 ___ Fac Type 20 ___

Remarks 21 ___ 66

Reserved 67 ___ 69 Facility Evaluation Rating 70 ___ BI 71 ___ QA 72 ___ Reserved 73 ___ 74 75 ___ 80

Section B: Facility Data

Name and Location of Facility Inspected

Entry Time ☐ AM ☐ PM

Permit Effective Date

Exit Time/Date

Permit Expiration Date

Name(s) of On-Site Representative(s)

Title(s)

Phone No(s)

Name, Address of Responsible Official

Title

Phone No.

Contacted ☐ Yes ☐ No

Section C: Areas Evaluated During Inspection

(S = Satisfactory, M = Marginal, U = Unsatisfactory, N = Not Evaluated)

	Permit		Flow Measurement		Pretreatment		Operations & Maintenance
	Records/Reports		Laboratory		Compliance Schedules		Sludge Disposal
	Facility Site Review		Effluent/Receiving Waters		Self-Monitoring Program		Other:

Section D: Summary of Findings/Comments *(Attach additional sheets if necessary)*

Name(s) and Signature(s) of Inspector(s)	Agency/Office/Telephone	Date
Signature of Reviewer	Agency/Office	Date

Regulatory Office Use Only

Action Taken	Date	Compliance Status ☐ Noncompliance ☐ Compliance

EPA Form 3560-3 (Rev. 3-85) Previous editions are obsolete.

INSTRUCTIONS

Section A: National Data System Coding *(i.e., PCS)*

Column 1: Transaction Code: Use N, C, or D for New, Change, or Delete. All inspections will be *new* unless there is an error in the data entered.

Columns 3-11: NPDES Permit No. Enter the facility's NPDES permit number. *(Use the Remarks columns to record the State permit number, if necessary.)*

Columns 12-17: Inspection Date. Insert the date entry was made into the facility. Use the year/month/day format (e.g., 82/06/30 = June 30, 1982).

Column 18: Inspection Type. Use one of the codes listed below to describe the type of inspection:

A — Performance Audit
B — Biomonitoring
C — Compliance Evaluation
D — Diagnostic
E — Corps of Engrs Inspection
L — Enforcement Case Support
P — Pretreatment
R — Reconnaissance Inspection
S — Compliance Sampling
X — Toxic Sampling

Column 19: Inspector Code. Use one of the codes listed below to describe the *lead agency* in the inspection.

C — Contractor or Other Inspectors *(Specify in Remarks columns)*
E — Corps of Engineers
J — Joint EPA/State Inspectors—EPA lead
N — NEIC Inspectors
R — EPA Regional Inspector
S — State Inspector
T — Joint State/EPA Inspectors—State lead

Column 20: Facility Type. Use one of the codes below to describe the facility.

1 — Municipal. Publicly Owned Treatment Works (POTWs) with 1972 Standard Industrial Code (SIC) 4952.
2 — Industrial. Other than municipal, agricultural, and Federal facilities.
3 — Agricultural. Facilities classified with 1972 SIC 0111 to 0971.
4 — Federal. Facilities identified as Federal by the EPA Regional Office.

Columns 21-66: Remarks. These columns are reserved for remarks at the discretion of the Region.

Column 70: Facility Evaluation Rating. Use information gathered during the inspection (regardless of inspection type) to evaluate the quality of the facility self-monitoring program. Grade the program using a scale of 1 to 5 with a score of 5 being used for very reliable self-monitoring programs, 3 being satisfactory, and 1 being used for very unreliable programs.

Column 71: Biomonitoring Information. Enter D for static testing. Enter F for flow through testing. Enter N for no biomonitoring.

Column 72: Quality Assurance Data Inspection. Enter Q if the inspection was conducted as followup on quality assurance sample results. Enter N otherwise.

Columns 73-80: These columns are reserved for regionally defined information.

Section B: Facility Data

This section is self-explanatory.

Section C: Areas Evaluated During Inspection

Indicate findings (S, M, U, or N) in the appropriate box. Use Section D and additional sheets as necessary. Support the findings, as necessary, in a brief narrative report. Use the headings given on the report form (e.g., Permit, Records/Reports) when discussing the areas evaluated during the inspection. The heading marked "Other" may include activities such as SPCC, BMP's, and multimedia concerns.

Section D: Summary of Findings/Comments

Briefly summarize the inspection findings. This summary should abstract the pertinent inspection findings, not replace the narrative report. Reference a list of attachments, such as completed checklists taken from the NPDES Compliance Inspection Manuals and pretreatment guidance documents, including effluent data when sampling has been done. Use extra sheets as necessary.

Appendix E (cont.)

SPILL PREVENTION, CONTROL AND COUNTERMEASURE PLAN (SPCC) CHECKLIST

1. Does this facility have:

   a. More than 1,320 gallons of above-ground oil storage capacity or a single container with a capacity of more than 660 gallons? Yes____ No____

   b. More than 42,000 gallons of underground oil storage capacity?

2. Does this facility have a Spill Prevention Control and Countermeasure (SPCC) plan? Yes____ No____

   a. Has the SPCC plan been certified by a registered professional engineer? Yes____ No____

   b. Date the SPCC plan was last certified: ____________________

   c. Original date SPCC plan was prepared: ____________________

3. Are there other State or local requirements for hazardous materials spill prevention and control plan? Yes____ No____

   a. Is this hazardous materials SPCC plan available? Yes____ No____

4. Have any reportable spills of petroleum products or hazardous materials occurred at this facility within the last review period? Yes____ No____

   List: ____

   ____

   ____

   ____

   ____

   a. Were these spills reported to the proper authorities? Yes____ No____

   b. Were these spills cleaned up properly? Yes____ No____

   c. Were measures taken to prevent future spills? Yes____ No____

Appendix E (cont.)

d. Is there evidence of these reported spills or other spills at the facility? Yes____ No____

5. Does the SPCC plan include:

a. Notification procedures? Yes____ No____

b. Inspection procedures? Yes____ No____

c. A facility drawing which includes storage tanks and containment areas? Yes____ No____

d. Oil spill prevention designee? Yes____ No____

6. Does the facility have:

a. Secondary containment or diversionary structures at oil storage areas? Yes____ No____

b. Spill cleanup materials available or information on where these materials are available? Yes____ No____

c. Security? Yes____ No____

COMMENTS:

____

____

____

____

____

____

____

____

____

____

____

____

____

____

APPENDIX F

RCRA CHECKLISTS

Table F-1
RCRA COMPLIANCE INSPECTION REPORT GENERATORS CHECKLIST

Note: State laws, in many cases are more stringent than Federal law for many of the generator requirements, but particularly in the area of accumulation time. Be aware of these differences and modify this protocol as needed!

- Does the State in which the generator is located have RCRA State authorization? Yes____ No____
- Has the generator identified the differences between the State program and the Federal program? Yes____ No____

SECTION A - EPA ID NUMBER

1. Does generator have EPA ID Number? Yes____ No____
   a. If yes, EPA ID Number ________________________________
2. Are there other EPA ID Numbers used at this location? (If yes, list the other numbers and identify where they are used and for what they were issued.) Yes____ No____

SECTION B - HAZARDOUS WASTE DETERMINATION

1. Has the generator determined whether hazardous waste(s) (§261 Sub-part D) are generated at this facility? Yes____ No____
   a. Are records of the determinations kept by the generator (262.40)? Yes____ No____
   b. List hazardous waste and quantities on an attachment (Include EPA Hazardous Waste Number. Provide waste name and description.)

---

* *These checklists are to be used only as guides and references should be made to both RCRA and the regulations (40 CFR Parts 260 through 270 except for Part 268, which is covered in Appendix G) for recent changes.*

Table F-1 (cont.)

2. Are solid wastes that exhibit hazardous characteristics generated (§261 Subpart C)? Yes____ No____

   a. If yes, list wastes and quantities on an attachment. Include EPA Hazardous Waste Number. Provide waste name and description.)

   b. How are waste characteristics determined (testing, knowledge of process)?

      (1) If determined by testing, did generator use test methods in Part 261, Subpart C (or equivalent)? Yes____ No____

      (2) If equivalent test methods used, attach copy of methods.

3. Identify total quantities of hazardous waste generated per month, for the last 12 months, for both acutely hazardous waste and other hazardous waste.

(kg/mo)	Jan	Feb	Mar	Apr	May	Jun	Jul	Aug	Sep	Oct	Nov	Dec
Acutely toxic												
Other hazardous waste												

4. Does the generator qualify as a Small Quantity Generator (SQG) for the entire last 12-month period (§261.5)? Yes____ No____

   (If no, list the months that the generator was a full generator.)

5. Is generator exempted or conditionally exempted from regulation because of:

   a. Small quantity generator (§261.5) Yes____ No____

   b. Produces nonhazardous waste at this time (§261.4) Yes____ No____

6. Are any nonhazardous wastes generated? Yes____ No____

Table F-1 (cont.)

a. If yes, did generator identify them as nonhazardous by testing or by knowledge of process? Yes____ No____

(1) If determined by testing, did generator use test methods in Part 261 Subpart C (or equivalent)? Yes____ No____

(2) If equivalent test methods used, attach copy of methods.

b. List wastes and quantities deemed nonhazardous or processes from which nonhazardous wastes were produced. Use narrative explanation sheets.

SECTION C - UNIFORM HAZARDOUS WASTE MANIFEST SYSTEM

1. Has generator shipped hazardous waste offsite since November 19, 1980 (§262 Subpart B)? Yes____ No____

a. If no skip to Section D, Question #8.

b. If yes, identify the name, EPA ID Number and site address(es) of the offsite facilities. (Use back of page for additional facilities if needed.)

Name ____________________ Address ____________________

Name ____________________ Address ____________________

Name ____________________ Address ____________________

Name ____________________ Address ____________________

2. If not exempt, is the waste manifested on the Uniform Hazardous Waste Manifest (§262, Appendix) Yes____ No____

If so, do the manifests contain:

a. Name and mailing address of generator? Yes____ No____

b. The name and EPA ID Number of each transporter? Yes____ No____

Table F-1 (cont.)

c. DOT waste description, including proper shipping name, hazardous class and DOT identification number? Yes____ No____

d. Number and type of containers (if applicable)? Yes____ No____

e. Quantity of each waste transported? Yes____ No____

f. Name, EPA ID Number and site address of facility designated to receive the waste? Yes____ No____

g. The following certification: effective September 1, 1985? Yes____ No____

"I hereby declare that the contents of this consignment are fully and accurately described above by proper shipping name and are classified, packed, marked and labeled, and are in all respects in proper condition for transport by highway according to applicable international and national government regulations.

Unless I am a small quantity generator who has been exempted by statute or regulation from the duty to make a waste minimization certification under Section 3002(b) of RCRA, I also certify that I have a program in place to reduce the volume and toxicity of waste generated to the degree I have determined to be economically practicable and I have selected the method of treatment, storage or disposal currently available to me which minimizes the present and future threat to human health and the environment."

3. Does the facility designated to receive the waste have:

a. A RCRA permit? Yes____ No____

b. Interim status? Yes____ No____

c. A permit, license or registration from a state to manage municipal or industrial solid waste? Yes____ No____

Table F-1 (cont.)

4. Does the generator retain copies of the manifests? Yes____ No____

If yes, complete 6a through 6e (§262.23).

(Inspect completed manifests at random and indicate how many manifests were inspected. Obtain copies of all manifests with violations and describe violations.)
Did the generator sign and date all manifests? Yes____ No____

Who signed the manifests for the generator?

Name ____________________ Title ____________________
Name ____________________ Title ____________________

b. Did the generator obtain the handwritten signature and date of acceptance from the initial transporter? Yes____ No____

c. Does generator retain one copy of the manifest signed by the generator and transporter? Yes____ No____

d. Do return copies of manifest include facility owner/operator signature and date of acceptance? Yes____ No____

e. If the copy of the manifest from the facility was not returned within 45 days, did generator file an Exception Report (§262.42)? Yes____ No____

If yes, did it contain:

(1) A legible copy of the manifest Yes____ No____

(2) A cover letter explaining generator's efforts to locate waste and the results of those efforts? Yes____ No____

f. Has generator retained copies for 3 years? Yes____ No____

Table F-1 (cont.)

SECTION D - PRETRANSPORT REQUIREMENTS

1. Does the generator package waste? Yes____ No____

   If not, why not? (Skip the rest of Section D) ____________________

   ____

   If yes, complete the following questions.

2. Does generator package waste in accordance with DOT requirements 49 CFR 173, 178 and 179 (§262.30)? Yes____ No____

3. Inspect containers to be shipped. (Use narrative explanation sheet to describe containers and condition.)

   a. Are containers leaking, corroding or bulging? Yes____ No____

   b. Is there evidence of heat generation from incompatible wastes in containers? Yes____ No____

   c. Are containers labeled according to DOT (49 CFR 172 Subpart E)? Yes____ No____

   d. Are containers marked according to DOT requirements (49 CFR 172 Subpart D)? Yes____ No____

   e. Is each container of 110 gallons or less marked with the following words? Yes____ No____

   "HAZARDOUS WASTE - Federal Law Prohibits Improper Disposal. If found, contact the nearest police or public safety authority or the U.S. Environmental Protection Agency."
   Generator's name and address ____________________

   ____

   Manifest Document Number____________________

   ____

(Note: During accumulation times, see below, only the words "Hazardous Waste" must appear on containers of 110 gallons or less.)

Table F-1 (cont.)

4. If there are any vehicles present onsite loading or unloading hazardous waste, <u>inspect for presence of placards</u> (49 CFR 172 Subpart F). Note this instance on narrative explanation sheet.

5. Accumulation time (§262.34)

   a. Is facility a permitted storage facility? Yes____ No____

   b. Has all hazardous waste, generated in excess of the SQG limits, been shipped offsite or sent to onsite treatment, storage or disposal within 90 days. Yes____ No____

      (1) Is the waste placed in containers and managed in accordance with the container management requirements for facility owners or operators (§265 Subpart I)? Yes____ No____

      (Generators who qualify for the SQG provided they comply with the 50-foot buffer requirement for ignitable waste.)

      (2) Is the date upon which each period of accumulation began clearly marked on each container? Yes____ No____

      (3) What system does the generator use to determine when the SQG rate is exceeded? Explain ____________

      ____

      ____

      ____

      (4) Are the words "Hazardous Waste" clearly marked on each container of 110 gallons or less and visible for inspection? Yes____ No____

Table F-1 (cont.)

(5) For quantities in excess of the respective SQG rates, is the generator complying with the facility standards for Preparedness and Prevention (Part 265 Subpart C) and Contingency Plan/Emergency Procedures (Part 265 Subpart D)? Yes____ No____

(6) For hazardous waste generated below the respective SQG rates, is the generator complying with the modified requirements for SQGs (§261.5) Yes____ No____

(7) Do the facility hazardous waste management personnel have the requisite training documented in their personnel file (§265.16) Yes____ No____

c. Have hazardous wastes, generated at a rate between 100 kg/mo and 1,000 kg/mo, been accumulated less than 180 days, or 270 days if the facility is over 200 miles away (effective September 22, 1986)? Yes____ No____

d. Is the total amount of all hazardous waste accumulated onsite and generated below 100 kg/mo, less than 1,000 kg? Yes____ No____

e. Is the total amount of hazardous waste, accumulated onsite, generated at a rate between 100 kg/mo and 1,000 kg/mo, less than 6,000 kg? Yes____ No____

f. Does the generator inspect containers for leakage or corrosion (§265.174)? Yes____ No____

(1) If yes, how often? ______________________________
(Review inspection records.)

g. Does the generator handle ignitable or reactive waste? Yes____ No____

Table F-1 (cont.)

(1) If yes, does the generator locate ignitable or reactive wastes at least 15 meters (50 feet) inside facility's property line (§265.176)? Yes____ No____

(2) Does the generator separate and protect ignitable or reactive wastes from sources of ignition (§265.17)? Yes____ No____

Note: If generator accumulates waste onsite for more than 90 days, fill out facilities checklist, Section A-9, Personnel Training; Section B - Preparedness and Prevention; and Section C - Contingency Plan and Emergency Procedures.

9. Describe storage/accumulation area(s). Use photographs and narrative explanation sheet.

SECTION E - RECORDKEEPING AND RECORDS

1. Is generator keeping the following records (§262.40)?

(Note: The following must be kept for a minimum of 3 years.)

a. Manifests or signed copies from designated facilities? Yes____ No____

b. Biennial reports (does not apply to SQGs)? Yes____ No____

c. Exception reports (does not apply to SQGs)? Yes____ No____

d. Test results or other means of determination, as required? Yes____ No____

2. Where are facility records kept (at the facility, offsite, etc.) ________

____

3. Who is responsible for keeping the records? ____________________

____________________ Title: ____________________

Table F-1 (cont.)

F. <u>SPECIAL CONDITIONS</u>

1. Have hazardous wastes been received from or transported to a foreign source (§262.50)? Yes____ No____

If yes,

a. For imports, has generator filed a notice with the Regional Administrator? Yes____ No____

b. For exports, has generator filed a notice with the Administrator, Office of International Activities, A-106, 4 weeks before the initial shipment to each country? Yes____ No____

c. For exports, are waste manifests signed by the foreign consignee? Yes____ No____

d. If the generator transported wastes out of the country, has he received confirmation of delivery of the shipment? Yes____ No____

(1) Identify those shipments for which confirmation of delivery have not been received within 90 days of shipment by manifest number.

____

____

____

(2) Has generator filed an Exception Report for all those shipments identified in 1d(1) above? Yes____ No____

e. Has the exporter filed, with the Administrator, an export summary report for the previous year by March 1? Yes____ No____

Table F-2

RCRA COMPLIANCE INSPECTION REPORT
TRANSPORTER(S) AND VEHICLE CHECKLIST

SECTION A - GENERAL TRANSPORTER INFORMATION

1. Does transporter have EPA Identification Number? Yes____ No____

   EPA ID Number ______________________

2. Does more than one transporter or address use this identification number? How many? Yes____ No____

3. Identify the mode(s) of transportation used by transporter.
   ____ Air ____ Rail ____ Highway ____ Water ____ Other (specify)
   Specification:

4. Does transporter have all necessary permits? Yes____ No____

   State permit number: ______________________
   Federal permit number: ______________________

5. Does transporter ship hazardous waste out of the U.S.? Yes____ No____

6. Does transporter ship hazardous waste into the U.S.? Yes____ No____

   If yes, complete "Generator Checklist" for these hazardous wastes.

7. Does transporter mix hazardous wastes of different DOT shipping descriptions by placing them into a single container? Yes____ No____

   If yes, complete "Generator Checklist" for these mixtures.

SECTION B - TRANSFER FACILITIES

1. Does the transporter store manifested shipments of hazardous waste in containers meeting the requirements of §262.30 at a transfer facility? Yes____ No____

Table F-2 (cont.)

2. Is all manifested hazardous waste, temporarily stored by the transporter, shipped offsite within 10 days? Yes____ No____

   If not, complete "TSDF Checklist".

SECTION C - Manifest and Recordkeeping Requirements

1. Are all shipments of hazardous wastes accompanied by an approved manifest (EPA Form 8700-22 or EPA Form 8700-22A)? Yes____ No____

2. Does all required information appear on the manifest (49 CFR 172.205)? Yes____ No____

3. Inspect completed manifests at random and indicate number inspected. Obtain copies of all manifests with deficiencies and provide narrative explanation.

4. If transporter has shipped hazardous waste(s) out of the United States, is the date of exit and the name and address of receiving facility indicated on manifest? Yes____ No____

5. Special Conditions

   a. If transportation occurs by water (bulk shipment), does the transporter:

      (1) Ship to the designated facility? Yes____ No____

      (2) Maintain shipping papers with information contained on manifest? Yes____ No____

      (3) Obtain designated facility signature and date of receipt? Yes____ No____

      (4) Retain a copy of manifest or shipping papers? Yes____ No____

   b. If transportation occurs by rail, does the transporter:

      (1) Sign and date manifest acknowledging acceptance? Yes____ No____

Table F-2 (cont.)

(2) Return signed copy to nonrail transporter? Yes____ No____

(3) Forward at least three copies of the manifest to the next appropriate destination? Yes____ No____

(4) Retain one copy of manifest and rail shipping papers? Yes____ No____

(5) Ensure shipping papers accompany the waste(s)? Yes____ No____

(6) On delivery, obtain name, date and signature of designated facility or transporter? Yes____ No____

6. Does transporter retain copies of manifests and shipping papers for the required 3-year period? Yes____ No____

SECTION D - MANIFEST COMPLIANCE

1. Does the transporter ship all waste to either the designated facility listed on the manifest or the alternate facility (when applicable) or the next designated transporter? Yes____ No____

2. Does the transporter assure delivery to the designated facility outside the U.S.? Yes____ No____

3. What procedures does the transporter follow when delivery of hazardous wastes to designated facility is prevented? (Use narrative explanation sheets.)

SECTION E - PRETRANSPORT REVIEW

1. Does the transporter check to assure that the generator has compiled with the following requirements?

   a. Has the generator packaged wastes in accordance with DOT requirements (49 CFR 173)? Yes____ No____

   b. Has the generator packaged wastes in repacks? Yes____ No____

F-14

Table F-2 (cont.)

c. Has the generator labeled wastes in accordance with DOT requirements (49 CFR 172, Subpart E)? Yes____ No____

d. Has the generator marked wastes in accordance with DOT requirements (49 CFR 172, Subpart D)? Yes____ No____

e. Has generator marked each container of 110 gallons or less used in such transportation with the following words and information displayed in accordance with the requirements of 49 CFR 172.304? Yes____ No____

HAZARDOUS WASTE - Federal Law Prohibits Improper Disposal. If found, contact the nearest police or public safety authority or the U.S. Environmental Protection Agency.

Generator's Name and Address: ______________________________

____

Manifest Document Number: ______________________________

f. Did generator placard or offer the initial transporter the appropriate placards according to DOT (49 CFR 172, Subpart F)? Yes____ No____

SECTION F - EMERGENCY ACTION

1. Has transporter ever been involved in a discharge of hazardous wastes? Yes____ No____

a. If yes, was the National Response Center (800-424-8802 or 202-426-2675), U.S. Coast Guard, the State and the principal office of transporter notified? Yes____ No____

b. Was a written report submitted to DOT within 10 days following the discharge Yes____ No____

Attach copy of report (if available).

Table F-2 (cont.)

2. Has the transporter obtained an Emergency Identification Number from EPA for the cleanup operation? Yes____ No____

   a. If yes, identify the number(s): ______________________

SECTION G - TRANSPORT VEHICLE INSPECTION

1. Company/name/designation of vehicle: ______________________
____

2. Truck driver's name: ______________________

3. What hazardous wastes are listed on manifest? List in narrative explanation.

4. Form of containerization of hazardous wastes:

______ drums, size: ______ gallons (ea), ______ amount (i.e., 30 drums)
______ portable tanks - number ____________ volume (ea) ____________
______ gondola
______ tanker-type ______________________ volume (ea) ____________

5. Narrative explanation of condition of containerization (leaking, corroded, fuming, damaged, improperly sealed, poor condition, improper lining, etc.)

6. Is truck properly placarded and marked (49 CFR, Subpart F)? Yes____ No____

7. Did generator have to repackage wastes by truck driver's request? Yes____ No____

8. Is truck driver aware of any special handling of materials? Yes____ No____

   If yes, describe.

9. Does truck driver have the National Response Center phone number accessible? Yes____ No____

Table F-2 (cont.)

COMMENTS: ____

Table F-3

RCRA COMPLIANCE INSPECTION REPORT
TREATMENT, STORAGE AND DISPOSAL FACILITIES (TSDFs)
CHECKLIST FOR INTERIM STATUS FACILITIES (PART 265)

SECTION A - GENERAL FACILITY STANDARDS

1. Does facility have EPA Identification Number (§265.11)? Yes____ No____

   If yes, EPA Identification Number: ____________________

   If no, explain: ____________________

   ____

2. Has facility received hazardous waste from a foreign source (§265.12)? Yes____ No____

   If yes, has he filed a notice with the Regional Administrator 4 weeks in advance of the initial shipment? Yes____ No____

Waste Analysis

3. Does the facility have a written waste analysis plan (§265.13)? Yes____ No____

   If yes, is a copy maintained at the facility? Yes____ No____

   If no, proceed to question 5.

4. Does the plan include:

   a. Parameters for which each waste will be analyzed? Yes____ No____

   b. Rationale for the selection of these parameters? Yes____ No____

   c. Test methods used to test for these parameters? Yes____ No____

   d. Sampling method used to obtain sample? Yes____ No____

Table F-3 (cont.)

e. Frequency with which the initial analysis will be reviewed or repeated? Yes____ No____

(1) If yes, does it include requirements to retest when the process or operation generating the waste has changed? Yes____ No____

f. (For offsite facilities) Waste analyses that generators have agreed to supply? Yes____ No____

g. (For offsite facilities) Procedures which are used to inspect and analyze each movement of hazardous waste including:

(1) Procedures to be used to determine the identity of each movement of waste? Yes____ No____

(2) Sampling method to be used to obtain representative sample of the waste to be identified? Yes____ No____

<u>Security</u>

5. Does the facility provide adequate security to minimize the possibility for the unauthorized entry of persons or livestock onto the active portions of the facility (§265.14)? Yes____ No____

If no, describe inadequacies. (Use narrative explanation sheet and include a drawing indicating any inadequacies in the facility's security system.)

If yes, is security provided through:

a. 24-hour surveillance system (e.g., television monitoring or guards)? Yes____ No____

<u>OR</u>

b. (1) Artificial or natural barrier around facility (e.g., fence or fence and cliff)? Yes____ No____

Table F-3 (cont.)

Describe type of security: ______________________

____

AND

(2) Means to control entry through entrances (e.g., attendant, television monitors, locked entrance, controlled roadway access)? Yes____ No____

Describe type of security: ______________________

____

6. Is a sign with the legend, "Danger-Unauthorized Personnel Keep Out," posted at the entrance to the active portion of the facility? Yes____ No____

Is it written in English and legible from at least 25 feet? Yes____ No____

Note: The sign must also be written in any other language predominant in the area surrounding the facility (e.g., in New Mexico and Texas areas bordering Mexico, the sign must be in Spanish).

If a sign exists with a legend other than "Danger-Unauthorized Personnel Keep Out," what does that legend say?

____

____

General Inspection Requirements

7. a. Does the owner/operator maintain a written schedule for inspecting (§265.15)? Yes____ No____

(1) Monitoring equipment, if applicable? Yes____ No____

(2) Safety and emergency equipment? Yes____ No____

(3) Security devices? Yes____ No____

(4) Operating and structural equipment, if applicable? Yes____ No____

Table F-3 (cont.)

(5) Does the schedule or plan identify the types of problems to be looked for during inspection? Yes____ No____

(a) Malfunction or deterioration (e.g., inoperative sump pump, leaking fitting, eroding dike, corroded pipes or tanks, (etc.)? Yes____ No____

(b) Operator error? Yes____ No____

(c) Discharges (e.g., leaks from valves or pipes, joint breaks, etc.)? Yes____ No____

b. Is a written schedule for these inspections maintained at the facility? Yes____ No____

(1) Are records of these inspections maintained in an inspection log (§265.15)? Yes____ No____

(2) If yes, does it include:

(a) Date and time of inspection? Yes____ No____

(b) Name of inspector? Yes____ No____

(c) Notation of observations? Yes____ No____

(d) Date and nature of repairs or remedial action? Yes____ No____

(3) Are there any malfunctions or other deficiencies noted in the inspection log that remain uncorrected? Use narrative explanation sheet. Yes____ No____

(4) Are records of the inspection log maintained at the facility for at least 3 years? (Obtain copies of incomplete or inadequate inspection records.) Yes____ No____

Table F-3 (cont.)

Personnel Training

8. Does the owner/operator maintain a personnel training program (§265.16)? Yes____ No____

   a. If yes,

      (1) Is the program directed by a person trained in hazardous waste management procedures?

      (2) Is the program designed to prepare employees to respond effectively to hazardous waste emergencies? Yes____ No____

      (3) Is a training review given annually? Yes____ No____

   b. Does the owner/operator keep the following records:

      (1) Job title and written job description of each position? Yes____ No____

      (2) Description of the type and amount of introductory and continuing training Yes____ No____

      (3) Documentation that training has been given to employees? Yes____ No____

   c. Are these records maintained at the facility? Yes____ No____

Requirements for Ignitable, Reactive or Incompatible Waste

9. Does facility handle ignitable or reactive waste (§265.17)? Yes____ No____

   a. If yes, is waste separated and confined from sources of ignition or reaction? Yes____ No____

   b. Are "No Smoking" signs posted in hazardous areas where ignitable or reactive wastes are handled? Yes____ No____

Table F-3 (cont.)

10. Observe containers (§265.17)

a. - Are containers leaking, corroding or bulging? Yes____ No____

Use narrative explanation sheet to describe containers in this condition.

b. Has the facility ever placed incompatible wastes together? Yes____ No____

If yes, what were the results? Use narrative explanation sheet. Look for signs of mixing of incompatible wastes (e.g., fire, toxic mist, heat generation, bulging containers, etc.).

SECTION B - PREPAREDNESS AND PREVENTION

1. Is there evidence of fire, explosion or contamination of the environment (§265.31)? Yes____ No____

If yes, use narrative explanation sheet to explain.

2. Is the facility equipped with (§265.32)?

a. Easily accessible internal communications or alarm system? Yes____ No____

b. Telephone or two-way radio to call emergency response personnel? Yes____ No____

c. Portable fire extinguishers, fire control equipment, spill control equipment and decontamination equipment? Yes____ No____

(1) Is this equipment tested and maintained as necessary to assure its proper operation? (Note last inspection/test date.) Yes____ No____

d. Water of adequate volume for hoses, sprinklers or water spray system? Yes____ No____

(1) Describe source of water ______________________

Table F-3 (cont.)

(2) Indicate flow rate and/or pressure and storage capacity, if applicable. ______________________

3. Is there sufficient aisle space to allow unobstructed movement of personnel and equipment (§265.35)? Yes____ No____

4. Has the owner/operator made arrangements with the local authorities to familiarize them with characteristics of the facility (§265.37)? Yes____ No____

   If no, has the owner/operator attempted to make such arrangements? Yes____ No____

5. In the case that more than one police or fire department might respond, is there a designated primary authority (§265.37)? Yes____ No____

   If yes, indicate primary authority: ______________________

   a. Is the fire department a city, volunteer or onsite fire department? ______________________

6. Does the owner/operator have phone numbers of and agreements with State emergency response teams, emergency response contractors and equipment suppliers? Yes____ No____

   Are they readily available to the emergency coordinator (§265.37)? Yes____ No____

7. Has the owner/operator arranged to familiar ize local hospitals with the properties of hazardous waste handled and typed of injuries that could result from fires, explosions or releases at the facility? Yes____ No____

   If no, has the owner/operator attempted to do this (§265.37)? Yes____ No____

8. If the State or local authorities decline to enter into the above-referenced agreements, is there documentation of this (§265.37)? Yes____ No____

Table F-3 (cont.)

SECTION C - CONTINGENCY PLAN AND EMERGENCY PROCEDURES

1. Does the facility have a contingency plan (§265.52)? Yes____ No____

   If yes, does it contain:

   (1) Actions to be taken in response to emergencies? Yes____ No____

   (2) Description of arrangements with police, fire and hospital officials? Yes____ No____

   (3) List of names, addresses, phone numbers of personnel qualified to act as emergency coordinator? Yes____ No____

   (4) List of all emergency equipment at the facility? Yes____ No____

   (5) Evacuation plan for facility personnel? Yes____ No____

2. Is a copy of the contingency plan maintained at the facility (§265.53)? Yes____ No____

3. Has a copy been supplied to local police and fire departments (§265.53)? Yes____ No____

4. Is the plan a revised SPCC plan (§265.52)? Yes____ No____

5. Is there an emergency coordinator onsite or within short driving distance of the plant at all times? Yes____ No____

   If yes, list primary emergency coordinator: ____________________

SECTION D - MANIFEST SYSTEM, RECORDKEEPING AND REPORTING

1. Has facility received hazardous waste from offsite since November 19, 1980 (§265.71)? Yes____ No____

   If no, proceed to question 5.

Table F-3 (cont.)

If yes, does the facility retain copies of all manifests? Inspect manifest at random, indicate number inspected, describe deficiencies and obtain copies of all deficient manifests.) Yes____ No____

2. Has the facility received any hazardous waste from a rail or water (bulk shipment) transporter since November 19, 1980 (§265.71)? Yes____ No____

If yes, is it accompanied by a shipping paper? Yes____ No____

(1) Has the owner/operator signed and dated the shipping paper and returned a copy to the generator? Yes____ No____

(2) Is a signed copy given to the transporter? Yes____ No____

3. Has the facility received any shipments of hazardous waste since November 19, 1980, which were inconsistent with the manifest (§265.72)?

a. If yes, has he resolved the discrepancy with the generator and transporter? Yes____ No____

b. If no, has Regional Administrator been notified? Yes____ No____

4. Has the facility received any waste (that does not come under the small generator exclusion) not accompanied by a manifest (§265.76)? Yes____ No____

If yes, has facility submitted an unmanifested waste report to the Regional Administrator? Yes____ No____

5. Does the facility have a written operating record (§265.73)? Yes____ No____

a. Is a copy maintained at the facility? Yes____ No____

b. Does the record include:

Table F-3 (cont.)

(1) Description and quantity of each hazardous waste and the methods and dates of its treatment, storage or disposal at the facility? Yes____ No____

(2) Location and quantity of each hazardous waste? Yes____ No____

(a) Is this information cross-referenced with specific manifest document numbers, if applicable? Yes____ No____

(3) Location and quantity of each hazardous waste recorded on a map or diagram of each cell or disposal area (for disposal facilities only)? Yes____ No____

(4) Record and results of waste analyses? Yes____ No____

(5) Reports of incidents involving implementation of the contingency plan (if applicable)? Yes____ No____

(6) Records and results of required inspections? Yes____ No____

(7) Monitoring, testing or analytical data where required? Yes____ No____

(8) Closure cost estimates and, for land disposal facilities, post-closure cost estimates? Yes____ No____

SECTION E - PLANS AND REPORTS

1. Have all plans and reports been visually inspected and/or been made available for inspection (§265.74)? Yes____ No____

List plans and/or reports not made available for inspection. Yes____ No____

Table F-3 (cont.)

2. Did operator provide inspector with a drawing of the facility? Yes____ No____

   If yes, identify which are hazardous waste management units on the drawing.

3. Indicate which of the following apply to wastes managed by this facility:

   ____ Groundwater Monitoring Program (Subpart F) [Table F-4]
   ____ Containers (Subpart I) [Table F-5]
   ____ Tanks (Subpart J) [Table F-6]
   ____ Surface Impoundments (Subpart K) [Table F-7]
   ____ Waste Piles (Subpart L) [Table F-8]
   ____ Land Treatment (Subpart M) [Table F-9]
   ____ Landfill (Subpart N) [Table F-10]
   ____ Incinerator (Subpart O) [Table F-11]
   ____ Thermal Treatment (Subpart P) [Table F-12]
   ____ Chemical, Physical and Biological Treatment (Subpart Q) [Table F-13]
   ____ Underground Injection (Subpart R) [Appendix M]

Table F-4
GROUNDWATER MONITORING

1. Is the facility operating under

   a. Interim status — Yes____ No____

   b. RCRA permit (or State equivalent) — Yes____ No____

2. Has the facility implemented a groundwater monitoring program under

   a. Interim status — Yes____ No____

   b. RCRA permit (or State equivalent) — Yes____ No____

3. Has a waiver demonstration been prepared? — Yes____ No____

   a. Does it describe the potential for migration of waste from the waste management unit to the uppermost aquifer? — Yes____ No____

   b. Does it describe the potential for waste to enter a water supply or surface water? — Yes____ No____

   c. Is it certified by a qualified geologist or geotechnical engineer? — Yes____ No____

4. Have required monitoring reports been submitted to EPA and/or the State? — Yes____ No____

5. Has an adequate hydrogeologic characterization investigation been conducted at the facility? — Yes____ No____

   a. Has the uppermost aquifer been adequately defined? — Yes____ No____

   b. Have flow directions been adequately defined for the uppermost aquifer? — Yes____ No____

   c. Have groundwater flow rates been determined for hydrologic units within the uppermost aquifer? — Yes____ No____

6. Has the facility developed and implemented an operation and maintenance plan for the monitoring well network and sampling equipment? — Yes____ No____

Table F-4 (cont.)

SECTION A - INTERIM STATUS PROGRAMS

1. Did the facility initially implement a detection monitoring program (40 CFR 265.92) or an assessment monitoring program (40 CFR 265.93)? Yes____ No____

2. If a detection monitoring program was implemented,

   a. Was a sampling and analysis plan prepared? Yes____ No____

   b. Was a sampling and analysis plan in effect on November 19, 1981? Yes____ No____

   c. Did the program include upgradient wells not apparently affected by the facility? Yes____ No____

   d. Did the program include at least four downgradient wells at the limit of the waste management area(s)? Yes____ No____

3. Sampling and Analysis Plan

   a. Is the sample collection adequately described? Yes____ No____

   b. Is the sample preservation adequately described? Yes____ No____

   c. Is the sample shipping adequately described? Yes____ No____

   d. Are the analytical procedures specifically identified? Yes____ No____

   e. Is the sample chain-of-custody adequate? Yes____ No____

   f. Are the quality assurance/quality control procedures identified? Yes____ No____

   g. Are parameters to be analyzed for those specified in 40 CFR 265.92(b)? Yes____ No____

Table F-4 (cont.)

h. Does the plan contain a sampling schedule? Yes____ No____

i. Does the schedule conform to regulatory requirements? Yes____ No____

4. If an assessment monitoring program was implemented,

a. Did the notification of the Regional Administrator or State Director comply with 40 CFR 265.93(d)? Yes____ No____

b. Did submittal of the plan comply with 40 CFR 265.93(d)? Yes____ No____

c. Was it certified by a qualified geologist or a geotechnical engineer? Yes____ No____

d. Was it approved by EPA or the State? Yes____ No____

e. Does it determine the rate and extent of waste migration? Yes____ No____

f. Does it determine the concentrations of waste constituents in groundwater? Yes____ No____

g. Has a groundwater quality assessment report been submitted? Yes____ No____

h. Does the facility keep records on the results of analyses and evaluations? Yes____ No____

SECTION B - RCRA PERMIT PROGRAMS

1. Which of the following programs are required by the permit? Yes____ No____

a. Detection monitoring (40 CFR 264.98) Yes____ No____

b. Compliance monitoring (40 CFR 264.99) Yes____ No____

c. Corrective action (40 CFR 264.100) Yes____ No____

2. Have sampling and analysis plans been developed for the required groundwater monitoring program(s)? Yes____ No____

Table F-4 (cont.)

a. Has the required plan(s) been approved by EPA or the State? Yes____ No____

b. Has the program been implemented? Yes____ No____

c. Are the selected monitoring parameters adequate? Yes____ No____

d. Is the point of compliance properly located? Yes____ No____

e. Is the delineation of waste management areas appropriate? Yes____ No____

f. Is leakage from non-regulated units expected to affect groundwater quality at the point of compliance? Yes____ No____

g. Have any groundwater samples been analyzed for Appendix VIII parameters (40 CFR 261)? Yes____ No____

SECTION C - MONITORING WELLS

1. Are wells

a. Adequately designed Yes____ No____

b. Properly constructed Yes____ No____

c. Appropriate materials used Yes____ No____

d. Located as indicated on map in sampling plan Yes____ No____

e. Marked with proper identifying designation Yes____ No____

f. Installed in appropriate hydrologic zones Yes____ No____

g. Secured from unauthorized entry Yes____ No____

h. Protected from damage by vehicular traffic Yes____ No____

i. Surveyed for elevation Yes____ No____

j. Marked for surveyed point Yes____ No____

Table F-4 (cont.)

2. Are the locations and numbers of wells adequate to satisfy the requirements of 40 CFR 265.91 for interim status facilities or 40 CFR 264.97 for permitted facilities? Yes____ No____

3. Are the wells being adequately maintained? Yes____ No____

4. Are the wells accessible year round? Yes____ No____

SECTION D - MONITORING PROCEDURES

1. Are adequate field procedures being used for

   a. Measuring depth to water Yes____ No____

   b. Purging the well before sampling Yes____ No____

   c. Measuring pH, conductivity and temperature Yes____ No____

   d. Other field parameters Yes____ No____

   e. Collecting samples Yes____ No____

   f. Preserving samples Yes____ No____

   g. Cleaning reused equipment between wells Yes____ No____

   h. Storing samples after collection Yes____ No____

   i. Disposal of purge water Yes____ No____

   j. Monitoring for vapors and radiation Yes____ No____

2. Is the field crew adequately trained for sampling? Yes____ No____

3. Are the records kept during sampling adequate? Yes____ No____

4. Are sampling and analysis plan procedures being followed for:

   a. Approaching the well Yes____ No____

   b. Opening the well Yes____ No____

Table F-4 (cont.)

c.	Measuring the water level	Yes____	No____
d.	Purging the well	Yes____	No____
e.	Collecting samples	Yes____	No____
f.	Preserving samples	Yes____	No____
g.	Chain-of-custody	Yes____	No____
h.	Documenting sampling	Yes____	No____
i.	Shipping samples	Yes____	No____

Table F-5

CONTAINER STORAGE CHECKLIST
(Subpart I)

1. Does the facility store hazardous waste in containers? Yes____ No____

2. Are the containers marked "Hazardous Waste" or equivalent to identify the contents? Yes____ No____

3. Are the containers in good condition (check for leaks, corrosion, bulges, etc.)? Yes____ No____

   If no, explain in narrative and document with photograph.

4. If a container is found to be leaking, does the operator transfer the hazardous waste from the leaking container? Yes____ No____

5. Is the waste compatible with the containers and/or its liner? Yes____ No____

   If no, explain in narrative.

6. Are the stored containers closed? Yes____ No____

   If no, explain in narrative.

7. Are containers holding hazardous waste opened, handled or stored in such a manner as to cause the container to rupture or leak? Yes____ No____

8. Does facility conduct weekly inspection records? Yes____ No____

   If no, explain in the narrative the frequency of inspection.

9. Does facility maintain weekly inspection records? Yes____ No____

10. Are containers holding ignitible or reactive wastes located at least 15 meters (50 feet) from the facility property line? Yes____ No____

    If no, explain in narrative and document with photograph.

11. Are incompatible wastes stored in the same containers? Yes____ No____

12. Are containers holding incompatible wastes kept apart by physical barrier or sufficient distance? Yes____ No____

Table F-5 (cont.)

If no, explain in narrative and document with photograph(s).

13. Does the facility have satellite storage at the point of hazardous waste generation §262.34(C)(1)? Yes____ No____

    Are containers in the satellite storage area clearly marked with the date accumulation began? Yes____ No____

14. Do the containers at any one generation point exceed 55 gallons of hazardous waste or 1 quart of acutely hazardous wastes? Yes____ No____

15. If yes, in the previous question:

    (a) Is the container holding the excess wastes marked with the date the material began accumulating? Yes____ No____

    (b) Has this waste been accumulating for more than 3 days? Yes____ No____

16. Are these points at or near the process generating the waste? Yes____ No____

Table F-6

TANKS CHECKLISTS
TANK SYSTEM INSPECTION GUIDANCE

NOTE: List each tank and specify compliance status. [Collective checklist(s) may be used for all similar tanks in compliance.] This checklist does not apply to covered underground tanks that cannot be entered for inspection.

Has the facility completed the form, "Notification of Underground Storage Tanks", as required by 40 CFR Part 280 (FR/vol. 53, no. 185/September 23, 1988, page 37208, 37209, and 37210) including:

I. Ownership of Tank(s)
II. Location of Tank(s)
III. Contact Person at Tank Location
IV. Type of Notification
V. Certification of Description of Tanks
VI. Description of Underground Storage Tanks (completed for each tank at facility)
VII. Certification of Compliance (completed for all new tanks at facility)

Yes____ No____

I. Small Quantity Generators - Compliance with 40CFR § 265.201 and Parts 280 and 281, as applicable

A.1 ______________________________ Tank volume (gallons)

A.2 ______________________________ Tank description (e.g., aboveground, steel, lined)

A.3 ____
Tank location (e.g., inside on cement floor, outside on asphalt pad)

B.1 Material Stored: Be as specific as possible (e.g., 20% Methylene chloride, 30% 1,1,-trichloroethane, 50% mineral spirits)

B.2 Does this tank ever contain waste other than the above? Yes___ No___
If so, list other waste:

EPA Hazardous Waste Number	Waste Description
______________________	______________________
______________________	______________________
______________________	______________________

B.3 Are hazardous wastes placed in tanks that are compatible with the waste so that the tank or inner liner may not fail prematurely? Yes____ No____

Table F-6 (cont.)

C.1 Are wastes being stored in tanks for greater than 180 days? Yes____ No____

C.2 Is the disposal site greater than 200 miles away? Yes____ No____

C.3 Are wastes being stored in tanks for greater than 270 days? Yes____ No____

C.4 SQGs, who store waste greater than 180 days (270 days if shipped over 200 miles) or who exceed the 6,000 kg limit. Has the owner/operator applied for an operating permit? Yes____ No____

C.5 Does the owner/operator inspect the tank system routinely for the following?

Discharge control equipment each operating day Yes____ No____

Data from monitoring equipment (e.g., gauges) each operating day Yes____ No____

Level of waste in tank each operating day Yes____ No____

Materials for signs of corrosion weekly Yes____ No____

Area around tank for spills or leaks weekly Yes____ No____

D. Special wastes

D.1 Is the owner/operator storing ignitable or reactive wastes so that it does not generate heat, fire, violent reactions, gases that are flammable, toxic dusts, or other means to threaten human health?

____ yes ____ no ____ NA

D.2 Does the owner/operator follow appropriate procedures for reactive or ignitable wastes? (See Special Wastes, Checklist VI)

____ yes ____ no ____ NA

E.1 Is the tank labeled "Hazardous waste"? Yes____ No____

E.2 Tank condition - Indicate presence of any of the following.

Table F-6 (cont.)

	Discolored paint or rust anywhere on tank system	Yes____	No____
	Blister, cracks, bulges, or other signs of potential failure	Yes____	No____
	Worn hoses, rips in liners	Yes____	No____
E.3	Does the area around the tank show any evidence of spills (e.g., discoloration, dead vegetation)?	Yes____	No____
E.4	Are uncovered tanks operating with a minimum of 2 feet (60 cm) freeboard or are they equipped with containment structure?	Yes____	No____
E.5	In tanks with a continuous feed system, is the system equipped with a cut-off or by-pass system?	Yes____	No____
F.	Preparedness and Prevention Plan Compliance		
F.1	Is there an emergency/response plan?	Yes____	No____
F.2	Internal communication or alarm system available?	Yes____	No____
F.3	Is telephone or other device capable of summoning emergency assistance from local police, fire or other emergency response teams available?	Yes____	No____
F.4	Are portable fire extinguishers and spill control equipment available and in operational condition?	Yes____	No____
F.5	Water available to supply water hose streams?	Yes____	No____

II. <u>Documentation of General Inspection Requirements under § 264.195, 265.195 and Parts 280 and 281, as applicable</u>

A.1	Inspection plan/procedures adequately thorough in order to identify problem areas and small leaks	Yes____	No____

A.2 Documented inspection as scheduled in permit (___________) for overfill controls

_______	_______	_______
yes	no	NA

Table F-6 (cont.)

A.2a Interim status and 90-day accumulation tank systems must have the overfill controls inspected (and documented) each operating day

________ yes   ________ no   ________ NA

A.3 Documented daily inspection of aboveground portions of tank system   Yes____ No____

A.3a Use of inspection devices

________ yes   ________ no   ________________ Provide name of device used

A.4 Documented daily inspection of monitoring and leak inspection data   Yes____ No____

A.5 Documented daily inspection of construction materials of both tank system and secondary containment, and inspection of tank location and secondary containment for signs of erosion or releases   Yes____ No____

A.6 Confirmation of proper operation of the cathodic protection system within 6 months of initial installation

________ yes   ________ no   ________________ date of inspection

A.6a Annual inspection of cathodic protection after installation

________ yes   ________ no   ________ NA

A.7 Bimonthly inspection of all sources of impressed current

________ yes   ________ no   ________ NA

A.7a Method used to inspect impressed-current system ________________

III. <u>Existing Tank Systems</u> - Compliance with § 264.191, 265.191 and Parts 280 and 281, as applicable

A.1 ________________ Tank volume (gallons)   ________________ Tank type (above-, on-, in-, below ground

Table F-6 (cont.)

B.1 Material Stored: Be as specific as possible (e.g., 20% Methylene chloride, 30% 1,1,-trichloroethane, 50% mineral spirits)

EPA Hazardous Waste Number	Waste Description
____________________	____________________
____________________	____________________
____________________	____________________
____________________	____________________

C. Secondary containment

C.1 Does this tank system have secondary containment? Yes____ No____

If yes, see Checklist IV, if no continue below

C.2 Has facility been granted a variance from secondary containment? Yes____ No____

C.3 Is a written assessment of tank system integrity on file? Yes____ No____

C.4 If assessment is provided, has it been reviewed and certified by a registered, professional engineer? Yes____ No____

C.5 ____________________ C.5a Documented Yes____ No____
Tank Age

C.6 ____________________ C.6a Documented Yes____ No____
Facility Age

C.7 ____________________
Date when secondary containment is required

D. Design Standards

D.1 The tank is constructed with: [be as specific as possible (e.g., fiberglass-reinforced plastic, mild steel, nickel based alloy)].

____

D.2 Document evaluates tank system in accordance with the most recent applicable design standards Yes____ No____

D.3 Is tank material generally compatible with waste? Yes____ No____

Table F-6 (cont.)

E. Corrosion protection measures (applicable to tank systems with metal components in contact with soil or water)

E.1 Document describes existing corrosion protection measures? Yes____ No____

E.2 Type of system employed (coatings, wraps, electrical isolation devices, sacrificial-anode, impressed-current)

____

F. <u>Non-enterable, underground tanks</u>

F.1 Method of leak testing used ______________________

F.1a Verification of annual testing Yes____ No____

F.1b Tank found to be tight Yes____ No____

F.1c Leak testing device accounts for the following changes:

Temperature Yes____ No____

High water table Yes____ No____

Tank end deflection Yes____ No____

Vapor pockets Yes____ No____

G. Other tank types

G.1 Method of leak testing used ______________________

G.1a Verification of annual testing Yes____ No____

G.1b Tank found to be tight Yes____ No____

G.2 Internal Inspections

G.2a Certification by registered, professional engineer Yes____ No____

G.2b Has the engineer checked and documented inspection of all appropriate factors? Yes____ No____

Table F-6 (cont.)

H. Tank ancillary equipment

H.1 Feed systems, safety cutoff and/or bypass systems, pressure controls are described in written assessment Yes____ No____

H.2 Has ancillary equipment been leak tested or undergone other approved integrity assessment annually? Yes____ No____

H.3 Method of leak testing used ______________________________

H.4 Have any of the leak tested tank system components been found to be leaking or unfit? Yes____ No____

If any of the tanks system components have failed the examinations or leak tests, Release Response Checklist VI should be included for this tank system.

IV. <u>New Tank Systems</u> - Compliance with § 264.192 and Parts 280 and 281, as applicable

A. New Tank Design

A.1 ____________________ Tank volume (gallons)

A.2 ____________________ Tank type (above-, on-, in-, below ground

A.3 ____________________ Tank Dimensions

A.4 ____________________ Tank shape (spherical, cylindrical, etc.)

A.5 The tank is constructed with: [be as specific as possible (e.g., fiberglass-reinforced plastic, mild steel, nickel-based alloy)]

____

B. Material Stored: Be as specific as possible (e.g., 20% Methylene chloride, 30% 1,1, trichloroethane, 50% mineral spirits)

EPA Hazardous Waste Number	Waste Description
____________________	____________________
____________________	____________________
____________________	____________________
____________________	____________________

C. Tank System Installation

Table F-6 (cont.)

C.1	Certification of inspection and supervision of installation and design by independent installation expert or qualified engineer	Yes____ No____
C.2	Did the inspection include the following:	
	Weld breaks	Yes____ No____
	Punctures	Yes____ No____
	Scrapes on protective coating	Yes____ No____
	Cracks	Yes____ No____
	Corrosion	Yes____ No____
	Other damage or inadequate construction	Yes____ No____
C.3	Has a detailed description of the installation been provided?	Yes____ No____
C.4	Has the tank passed a test for tightness prior to being covered or placed in use?	Yes____ No____
C.5	Has the ancillary equipment (e.g., piping) passed a test for tightness?	Yes____ No____
C.6	Has a detailed description of the tightness testing been provided?	Yes____ No____
D.	Secondary containment - Compliance with § 264.193	
D1	Has the facility been granted a variance? If yes, go to Section F. on this checklist	Yes____ No____
D.2	Is secondary containment for new tanks and ancillary equipment installed?	Yes____ No____
D.3	Secondary containment is: (circle one) liner, vault, double-walled component	
D.4	Secondary containment materials are	____________________
D.5	Type of leak detection equipment employed	____________________
D.6	Record of leak detection operation available	Yes____ No____
D.7	Have any leaks from the primary section into secondary containment been detected?	Yes____ No____

Table F-6 (cont.)

D.8 Was leaked waste removed from the secondary containment system within 24 hours? Yes____ No____

D.9 Was the repair to the primary system documented prior to returning tank into service? Yes____ No____

E. Exemption of secondary containment for tank systems or component §264.193(f)

E.1 Is all aboveground, straight piping that is not covered by secondary containment inspected daily? Yes____ No____

E.2 Are all welded flanges, welded joints, and welded connections inspected for leaks daily? Yes____ No____

E.3 Are all sealless or magnetic coupling pumps visually inspected for leaks daily? Yes____ No____

E.4 Are all pressurized, aboveground piping systems with automatic shutoff devices visually inspected for leaks daily? Yes____ No____

F. External Corrosion Protection for metal components or equipment §264.192

F.1 Has a corrosion potential assessment been prepared by a corrosion expert? Yes____ No____

F.2 Type of corrosion protection installed (coatings, wraps, electrical isolation devices, sacrificial-anode, impressed-current) ____________________

F.3 Has a corrosion expert supervised the installation of any field fabricated corrosion protection (e.g., cathodic-protection devices)? Yes____ No____

If any of the tank system components have failed tightness testing or have resulted in leaks that had releases outside the secondary containment, Release Response Checklist VI should be included for this tank system.

V. Tank Systems that Store or Treat Ignitable or Reactive Wastes

Compliance with § 264.198 and Parts 280 and 281, as applicable

Table F-6 (cont.)

A. Special Requirements for ignitable or reactive wastes

A.1 Has waste been treated, mixed or otherwise rendered nonreactive or not ignitable (except in emergency conditions) so that the mixture is no longer ignitable or reactive? Yes____ No____

A.2 Has complete chemical identification of waste compatability been determined prior to mixing of wastes? Yes____ No____

A.3 Is the tank protected from conditions that may cause it to ignite (e.g., use of spark proof tools) or protected from contact with materials that may cause it to react? Yes____ No____

A.4 Is the required National Fire Protection Association distance between waste management area (ignitable wastes) and public ways and adjoining properties maintained? Yes____ No____

A.5 Has an appropriate method of tank system decontamination been selected based on the type of waste residues remaining in a receiving vessel? Yes____ No____

VI. <u>Release Response</u> - Compliance with § 264.196 and Parts 280 and 281, as applicable

A.1 Notification of releases to Regional Administrator (from file review)
date: ____________________ description: ____________________
____________________ ____________________
____________________ ____________________

A.1a Did the 0/0 report to the Regional Administrator within 30 days of each release with the following information

- likely route of migration of release
- characteristics of surrounding soil
- results of sampling
- proximity to downgradient drinking water, surface water and population
- description of response actions planned or taken

____ yes ____ no ____ N/A

Table F-6 (cont.)

A.2 Did the 0/0 immediately remove the tank component from service after spill/leak?

____ yes ____ no ____ not able to verify ____ N/A

A.3 Was waste removed from leaking component of the tank system and from secondary containment?

____ yes ____ no ____ N/A

A.4 Were visible releases to the environment contained?

____ yes ____ no ____ N/A

A.5 Has secondary containment, repair, or closure of the tank system been provided?

____ yes ____ no ____ N/A

A.6 Was the repair certified by an independent, qualified, registered, professional engineer?

____ yes ____ no ____ N/A

VII. <u>Visual Tank System Inspection</u> General Operating Requirements § 264.194 and Parts 280 and 281, as applicable

A. Aboveground Portions § 264,265.194(a)

A.1 <u>Metal Tanks</u> -

Look for:	Indicate Presence
Gross leakage	____
Major corroded areas	____
Deterioration (e.g, blisters)	____
Discolored paint	____
Cracks (nozzle connections, in welded seams, under rivets)	____

Table F-6 (cont.)

Buckles and bulges ________

Defective manhead gaskets ________

Corrosion of tank tops or roofs ________

Corrosion around nozzles and valves ________

Erosion around foundation, pads and secondary containment ________

Cracks in concrete curbing and ringwalls ________

Rotting of wooden supports ________

Welds and anchor bolts between tank bottoms and ringwalls ________

Deterioration of protective coatings such as discoloration and film lifting ________

A.2 Fiberglass-Reinforced Plastic Tanks -

Look for:

Gross leakage ________

Bending, curving or flexing ________

Longitudinal cracks in horizontal tanks ________

Vertical cracks in vertical tanks ________

A.3 Concrete Tanks - Above Ground Portions

Look for:

Gross leakage ________

Cracks ________

Porous areas permeable to liquid (wet spots) ________

Deterioration of protective coatings such as discoloration and film lifting ________

B. Underground tanks § 264.192 and Parts 280 and 281, as applicable

Table F-6 (cont.)

B.1 Is the (new) tank protected from vehicular traffic (paving over tanks should extend at least 1 foot beyond perimeter in all directions)

____ yes ____ no ____ N/A

B.2 If the backfill is not covered, is it porous and homogenous?

____ yes ____ no ____ N/A

B.3 Is there water pooling or depressions in the area of the tank

____ yes ____ no ____ N/A

C. Spill and Overfill Prevention Measures § 264.194

C.1 Are spill prevention controls (e.g., check valves, dry disconnect couplings) in use? Yes____ No____

C.1a Is there any evidence of spillage from disconnect or uncoupling operations? Yes____ No____

C.2 Are overfill prevention controls (e.g., level sensing devices, high level alarms) present and operational? Yes____ No____

C.3 Is sufficient freeboard maintained in uncovered tanks to prevent overtopping due to wave or wind action or by precipitation? Yes____ No____

C.4 Is there any evidence of overtopping or major spills? Yes____ No____

D. Inspection of Ancillary Systems § 264.194 and Parts 280 and 281, as applicable

D.1 Inspect piping for the following: Indicate Presence

Pipe bends, elbows, tees, and other restrictions for leaks, external corrosion and rust spots ________

Deterioration (e.g., blisters) and discolored paint ________

Orifice plates deteriorated ________

Throttle valves w/broken stems, missing handles ________

Table F-6 (cont.)

	Wear and tear in flexible hoses	________
	Traffic passing over hoses	________
	Vibration or swaying of pipe systems while pumping	________
D.2	Inspect pumps and compressors for the following:	Indicate Presence
	Foundation cracks	________
	Excessive vibration or cavitation of pumps	________
	Leaky pump seals	________
	Missing anchor bolts	________
	Excessive dirt, burning odors, or smoke	________
	Depleted lubrication oil reservoir in compressor	________
D.3	Inspect heat exchangers and vapor control systems for:	Indicate Presence
	Rust spots or blisters	________
E.	Auxiliary systems for permitted tanks § 270.16	
	Is the following equipment the same as specified on permit and is it operational?	
E.1	Level Sensor ________________________ Identification	Yes____ No____
E.2	Alarm System ________________________ Identification	Yes____ No____
E.3	Spill proof couplings, entry points ____________ Identification	Yes____ No____
E.4	Safety Cutoff or Bypass System	Yes____ No____
E.5	Pressure controls (vents)	Yes____ No____
F.	Secondary Containment § 264.193 and Parts 280 and 281, as applicable	

Table F-6 (cont.)

F.1	Will the secondary containment (liners and vaults) contain 100% of the design capacity of the largest tank in its boundary plus a 25-year, 24-hour rainfall?	Yes____ No____
F.2	Is water collected in secondary containment system?	Yes____ No____
F.3	Does any water in secondary containment system appear discolored or otherwise contaminated or is there evidence of waste within the containment system?	Yes____ No____
F.4	Double-walled tanks: § 264.193(e)(3)	Yes____ No____
F.4a	If metal, is there appropriate corrosion protection for the outer shell?	Yes____ No____
F.4b	Does it have an operational, built-in continuous leak-detection system?	Yes____ No____
F.5	Vaults: § 264.193(e)(2)	
F.5a	Does all concrete, including sumps, have liners or coatings?	Yes____ No____
F.5b	Is a vault constructed with chemically resistant water stops at all joints?	Yes____ No____
F.5c	Is there deterioration of protective coatings such as discoloration and film lifting?	Yes____ No____
F.5d	Are there any cracks visable in the concrete?	Yes____ No____
F.6	Liners: § 264.193(e)(1)	
F.6a	Does the liner cover all the surrounding earth likely to come into contact with wastes, including berms and dikes?	Yes____ No____
F.6b	If clay liners, do liners show signs of drying and cracking?	Yes____ No____
F.6c	If polymeric liners, do liners show signs of punctures, deterioration due to sunlight, chemical spills, rips, tears, gaps, or cracks?	Yes____ No____
F.6d	If a concrete liner, is there any deterioration of its protective coating?	Yes____ No____

Table F-6 (cont.)

G.	Corrosion Control (metal tank and metal components in, on, or underground)	
G.1	Presence of trapped water near tank system (if underground tank system, is water pooling in area above tank location?)	Yes____ No____
G.2	The use of dry, crushed rock or gravel as backfill material	Yes____ No____
G.3	Existence of nearby visible metal structures	Yes____ No____
G.4	Coatings or wraps	
G.4a	Is the coverage complete?	Yes____ No____
G.4b	Has the cover or wrap dried, cracked or dissolved?	Yes____ No____
G.4c	Has the coating or wrap been damaged by spills?	Yes____ No____
G.5	Electrical isolation devices	
G.5a	Are they adequate depending upon the number of nearby, underground metal structures?	Yes____ No____
G.5b	Are the devices damaged in any way?	Yes____ No____
G.6	Sacrificial-anode system	
G.6a	How long has it been in place?	Yes____ No____
G.6b	Have the anodes decreased significantly in size?	Yes____ No____
G.6c	Is the sacrificial-anode system damaged?	Yes____ No____
G.7	Impressed-current system	
G.7a	How long has it been in place?	Yes____ No____
G.7b	Have the current requirements changed over time?	Yes____ No____
G.7c	Is the impressed-current system damaged?	Yes____ No____
G.7d	Is the impressed-current system properly maintained?	Yes____ No____

Table F-6 (cont.)

VIII. Closure, Post-closure Care - Compliance with § 264.197 and Parts 280 and 281, as applicable

A. Tank Systems with Secondary Containment - § 264.197(a) (clean closure)

A.1 Visual verification of clean closure

____ yes ____ no ____ N/A

Indicate if done

Tank system materials removed ______

Verification of proper disposal of contaminated equipment ______

Contaminated soils and residues disposed or treated properly ______

B. Tank systems that cannot be practicably decontaminated - § 264.197l(b)

B.1 Has the owner/operator demonstrated satisfactorily that all contaminated soils cannot be removed?

____ yes ____ no ____ N/A

B.2 Closure of tank site meeting § 264.310 landfill requirements

B.2a Does contaminated area have appropriate final cover? Yes____ No____

B.2b Is owner/operator maintaining cover integrity? Yes____ No____

B.2c Is 0/0 monitoring ground water according to Subpart F? Yes____ No____

C. Tank Systems without Secondary Containment - § 264.197(c)

C.1 Has 0/0 prepared a closure plan for § 264.197(a) and a contingency plan for § 264.197(b) which were submitted to EPA? Yes____ No____

C.2 If the closure plans have not been submitted, are they on file at the facility? Yes____ No____

C.3 Is or has the facility closed this tank system at the present time? Yes____ No____

If yes, evaluate closure with appropriate evaluation in A or B above.

F-53

Notification for Underground Storage Tanks

FORM APPROVED
OMB NO. 2050-0049
APPROVAL EXPIRES 6-30-88

STATE USE ONLY

I.D. Number

Date Received

GENERAL INFORMATION

Notification is required by Federal law for all underground tanks that have been used to store regulated substances since January 1, 1974, that are in the ground as of May 8, 1986, or that are brought into use after May 8, 1986. The information requested is required by Section 9002 of the Resource Conservation and Recovery Act, (RCRA), as amended.

The primary purpose of this notification program is to locate and evaluate underground tanks that store or have stored petroleum or hazardous substances. It is expected that the information you provide will be based on reasonably available records, or, in the absence of such records, your knowledge, belief, or recollection.

Who Must Notify? Section 9002 of RCRA, as amended, requires that, unless exempted, owners of underground tanks that store regulated substances must notify designated State or local agencies of the existence of their tanks. Owner means—

(a) in the case of an underground storage tank in use on November 8, 1984, or brought into use after that date, any person who owns an underground storage tank used for the storage, use, or dispensing of regulated substances, and

(b) in the case of any underground storage tank in use before November 8, 1984, but no longer in use on that date, any person who owned such tank immediately before the discontinuation of its use.

What Tanks Are Included? Underground storage tank is defined as any one or combination of tanks that (1) is used to contain an accumulation of "regulated substances," and (2) whose volume (including connected underground piping) is 10% or more beneath the ground. Some examples are underground tanks storing: 1. gasoline, used oil, or diesel fuel, and 2. industrial solvents, pesticides, herbicides or fumigants.

What Tanks Are Excluded? Tanks removed from the ground are not subject to notification. Other tanks excluded from notification are:

1. farm or residential tanks of 1,100 gallons or less capacity used for storing motor fuel for noncommercial purposes;
2. tanks used for storing heating oil for consumptive use on the premises where stored;
3. septic tanks;
4. pipeline facilities (including gathering lines) regulated under the Natural Gas Pipeline Safety Act of 1968, or the Hazardous Liquid Pipeline Safety Act of 1979, or which is an intrastate pipeline facility regulated under State laws;
5. surface impoundments, pits, ponds, or lagoons;
6. storm water or waste water collection systems;
7. flow-through process tanks;
8. liquid traps or associated gathering lines directly related to oil or gas production and gathering operations;
9. storage tanks situated in an underground area (such as a basement, cellar, mineworking, drift, shaft, or tunnel) if the storage tank is situated upon or above the surface of the floor.

What Substances Are Covered? The notification requirements apply to underground storage tanks that contain regulated substances. This includes any substance defined as hazardous in section 101 (14) of the Comprehensive Environmental Response, Compensation and Liability Act of 1980 (CERCLA), with the exception of those substances regulated as hazardous waste under Subtitle C of RCRA. It also includes petroleum, e.g., crude oil or any fraction thereof which is liquid at standard conditions of temperature and pressure (60 degrees Fahrenheit and 14.7 pounds per square inch absolute).

Where To Notify? Completed notification forms should be sent to the address given at the top of this page.

When To Notify? 1. Owners of underground storage tanks in use or that have been taken out of operation after January 1, 1974, but still in the ground, must notify by May 8, 1986. 2. Owners who bring underground storage tanks into use after May 8, 1986, must notify within 30 days of bringing the tanks into use.

Penalties: Any owner who knowingly fails to notify or submits false information shall be subject to a civil penalty not to exceed $10,000 for each tank for which notification is not given or for which false information is submitted.

INSTRUCTIONS

Please type or print in ink all items except "signature" in Section V. **This form must by completed for each location containing underground storage tanks.** If more than 5 tanks are owned at this location, photocopy the reverse side, and staple continuation sheets to this form.

Indicate number of continuation sheets attached ☐

I. OWNERSHIP OF TANK(S)

Owner Name (Corporation, Individual, Public Agency, or Other Entity)

Street Address

County

City State ZIP Code

Area Code Phone Number

Type of Owner *(Mark all that apply ☒)*

☐ Current ☐ State or Local Gov't ☐ Private or Corporate

☐ Former ☐ Federal Gov't (GSA facility I.D. no. ________) ☐ Ownership uncertain

II. LOCATION OF TANK(S)

(If same as Section 1, mark box here ☐)

Facility Name or Company Site Identifier, as applicable

Street Address or State Road, as applicable

County

City (nearest) State ZIP Code

Indicate number of tanks at this location ☐

Mark box here if tank(s) are located on land within an Indian reservation or on other Indian trust lands ☐

III. CONTACT PERSON AT TANK LOCATION

Name (If same as Section I, mark box here ☐) Job Title Area Code Phone Number

IV. TYPE OF NOTIFICATION

☐ Mark box here only if this is an amended or subsequent notification for this location.

V. CERTIFICATION (Read and sign after completing Section VI.)

I certify under penalty of law that I have personally examined and am familiar with the information submitted in this and all attached documents, and that based on my inquiry of those individuals immediately responsible for obtaining the information, I believe that the submitted information is true, accurate, and complete.

Name and official title of owner or owner's authorized representative	Signature	Date Signed

CONTINUE ON REVERSE SIDE

EPA Form 7530-1 (11-85)

F-54

Table 6-A

Owner Name (from Section I) ______________ Location (from Section II) ______________ Page No. ____ of ____ Pages

VI. DESCRIPTION OF UNDERGROUND STORAGE TANKS *(Complete for each tank at this location.)*

Tank Identification No. (e.g., ABC-123), or Arbitrarily Assigned Sequential Number (e.g., 1,2,3...)	Tank No.	Tank No.	Tank No.	Tank No.	Tank No.
1. Status of Tank *(Mark all that apply ☒)* Currently in Use	☐	☐	☐	☐	☐
Temporarily Out of Use	☐	☐	☐	☐	☐
Permanently Out of Use	☐	☐	☐	☐	☐
Brought into Use after 5/8/86	☐	☐	☐	☐	☐
2. Estimated Age (Years)					
3. Estimated Total Capacity (Gallons)					
4. Material of Construction *(Mark one ☒)* Steel	☐	☐	☐	☐	☐
Concrete	☐	☐	☐	☐	☐
Fiberglass Reinforced Plastic	☐	☐	☐	☐	☐
Unknown	☐	☐	☐	☐	☐
Other, Please Specify	____	____	____	____	____
5. Internal Protection *(Mark all that apply ☒)* Cathodic Protection	☐	☐	☐	☐	☐
Interior Lining (e.g., epoxy resins)	☐	☐	☐	☐	☐
None	☐	☐	☐	☐	☐
Unknown	☐	☐	☐	☐	☐
Other, Please Specify	____	____	____	____	____
6. External Protection *(Mark all that apply ☒)* Cathodic Protection	☐	☐	☐	☐	☐
Painted (e.g., asphaltic)	☐	☐	☐	☐	☐
Fiberglass Reinforced Plastic Coated	☐	☐	☐	☐	☐
None	☐	☐	☐	☐	☐
Unknown	☐	☐	☐	☐	☐
Other, Please Specify	____	____	____	____	____
7. Piping *(Mark all that apply ☒)* Bare Steel	☐	☐	☐	☐	☐
Galvanized Steel	☐	☐	☐	☐	☐
Fiberglass Reinforced Plastic	☐	☐	☐	☐	☐
Cathodically Protected	☐	☐	☐	☐	☐
Unknown	☐	☐	☐	☐	☐
Other, Please Specify	____	____	____	____	____
8. Substance Currently or Last Stored in Greatest Quantity by Volume *(Mark all that apply ☒)* **a. Empty**	☐	☐	☐	☐	☐
b. Petroleum					
Diesel	☐	☐	☐	☐	☐
Kerosene	☐	☐	☐	☐	☐
Gasoline (including alcohol blends)	☐	☐	☐	☐	☐
Used Oil	☐	☐	☐	☐	☐
Other, Please Specify	____	____	____	____	____
c. Hazardous Substance	☐	☐	☐	☐	☐
Please Indicate Name of Principal CERCLA Substance OR	____	____	____	____	____
Chemical Abstract Service (CAS) No.	____	____	____	____	____
Mark box ☒ if tank stores a mixture of substances	☐	☐	☐	☐	☐
d. Unknown	☐	☐	☐	☐	☐
9. Additional Information (for tanks permanently taken out of service)					
a. Estimated date last used (mo/yr)	/	/	/	/	/
b. Estimated quantity of substance remaining (gal.)	____	____	____	____	____
c. Mark box ☒ if tank was filled with inert material (e.g., sand, concrete)	☐	☐	☐	☐	☐

☆ U.S. Government Printing Office: 1986—496-735

Owner Name (from Section I) ______________ Location (from Section II) ______________ Page No. ______ of ______ Pages

VII. CERTIFICATION OF COMPLIANCE (COMPLETE FOR ALL NEW TANKS AT THIS LOCATION)

10. Installation (mark all that apply):

- ☐ The installer has been certified by the tank and piping manufacturers.
- ☐ The installer has been certified or licensed by the implementing agency.
- ☐ The installation has been inspected and certified by a registered professional engineer.
- ☐ The installation has been inspected and approved by the implementing agency.
- ☐ All work listed on the manufacturer's installation checklists has been completed.
- ☐ Another method was used as allowed by the implementing agency. Please specify:

____

11. Release Detection (mark all that apply):

- ☐ Manual tank gauging.
- ☐ Tank tightness testing with inventory controls.
- ☐ Automatic tank gauging.
- ☐ Vapor monitoring.
- ☐ Ground-water monitoring.
- ☐ Interstitial monitoring within a secondary barrier.
- ☐ Interstitial monitoring within secondary containment.
- ☐ Automatic line leak detectors.
- ☐ Line tightness testing.
- ☐ Another method allowed by the implementing agency. Please specify:

____

12. Corrosion Protection (if applicable)

- ☐ As specified for coated steel tanks with cathodic protection.
- ☐ As specified for coated steel piping with cathodic protection.
- ☐ Another method allowed by the implementing agency. Please specify:

____

13. I have financial responsibility in accordance with Subpart I. Please specify:

Method: ____

Insurer: ____

Policy Number: ____

14. OATH: I certify that the information concerning installation provided in Item 10 is true to the best of my belief and knowledge.

Installer: ______________________________ ______________________
Name Date

____
Position

____
Company

Table F-7

SURFACE IMPOUNDMENTS CHECKLIST
(Subpart K)

NOTE: List each surface impoundment and specify compliance status. Complete an individual checklist for each impoundment. [Collective checklist(s) may be used for all similar impoundments.]

1. Are there any surface impoundments which are not being used which the facility does not plan to use in the future? Yes____ No____

   If yes, has all hazardous waste and hazardous waste residue been removed from the impoundment? Yes____ No____

2. Are impoundments presently used to treat or store waste? Yes____ No____

3. Has any new unit, replacement of an existing unit or lateral expansion of an existing unit that is within the area identified in the Part A, received waste beginning 05/08/85? Yes____ No____

   a. If no, go to question 4.

   b. If yes,

      (1) Did the facility notify the Regional Administrator (RA) 60 days prior to receiving waste? Yes____ No____

      (2) Did the facility file a Part B within 6 months of receipt of such notice? Yes____ No____

   c. Does the <u>impoundment</u> have at least two liners and a leachate collection system, as required by 40 CFR 265.271? Yes____ No____

      If no, use narrative explanation to describe alternate system or, if waiver was granted, demonstration to RA (§265.221).

4. Does the impoundment have at least 2 feet (60 cm) of freeboard? Yes____ No____

   If no, what is the freeboard? ________________________________

Table F-7 (cont.)

5. Is there evidence of overtopping of the dike? Yes____ No____

   If yes, describe. ____

   ____

6. What type of dike (e.g., earthen, concrete, steel) does the impoundment have?

   a. If the dike is earthen, does it have adequate protective cover (e.g., grass, shale, rock) to minimize wind and water erosion? Use narrative explanation sheet to explain deficiencies. Yes____ No____

   b. Describe dike and its condition. ____

   ____

7. What wastes are treated or stored in the impoundment? Use narrative explanation sheets.

8. Are hazardous waste chemically treated in the impoundment? Yes____ No____

   a. If yes:

      (1) Are waste analyses and trial tests conducted on these wastes? Yes____ No____

      (2) Does the owner/operator have written documented information on similar treatment of similar wastes under similar operating conditions? Yes____ No____

   b. Is this information retained in the operating record? Yes____ No____

9. Do records indicate that freeboard level is inspected daily? Yes____ No____

10. Do records indicate the impoundment, dike and surrounding vegetation are inspected to detect leaks, deterioration or failures at least once a week? Yes____ No____

11. Does the facility maintain a record of the closure plan on site? Yes____ No____

Table F-7 (cont.)

12. Are ignitable or reactive wastes placed in the impoundment? Yes____ No____

    a. If no, proceed to question 13.

    b. If yes, are they treated, rendered or mixed before or immediately after placement in the impoundment so they no longer meet the definition of ignitable or reactive? Yes____ No____

    OR

    c. Are the wastes protected from possible ignition or reaction sources and certified as such by a qualified chemist? Use narrative explanation sheet to describe situation. Yes____ No____

    OR

    d. Is the impoundment used solely for emergencies? Yes____ No____

        (1) If yes, has treatment, storage or disposal been conducted on these wastes? Describe this situation. Yes____ No____

        ____

        ____

13. Has the facility ever placed incompatible wastes in the impoundment? Yes____ No____

    a. If yes, what were the results. Use narrative explanation sheet. Look for signs of mixing of incompatible wastes (e.g., fire, toxic mist, heat generation, bulging containers, etc.)

14. What is the impoundment lined with? ______________________________

15. Does the impoundment solely neutralize corrosive waste or waste listed in Subpart I solely because of corrosivity? Yes____ No____

Table F-8

WASTE PILES CHECKLIST
(Subpart L)

NOTE: Waste piles may also be managed as a landfill.

1. Is the pile containing hazardous waste protected from wind? Yes____ No____

2. For offsite facilities, is a representative sample of waste from each incoming shipment analyzed before the waste is added to the pile to determine the compatibility of the wastes? Yes____ No____

   a. For offsite facilities, does the analysis include a visual comparison of color and texture? Yes____ No____

3. Is the leachate or runoff from the pile considered a hazardous waste? Yes____ No____

   a. If yes, is the pile managed with the following?

      (1) An impermeable base compatible with the waste? Yes____ No____
      (2) Runon diversion? Yes____ No____
      (3) Leachate and runoff collection? Yes____ No____

   OR

   b. Is the pile protected from precipitation and runon by some other means? Describe on narrative explanation sheet. Yes____ No____

4. Are liquids or wastes containing free liquids placed in the pile? Yes____ No____

5. Are ignitable or reactive wastes placed in the pile? Yes____ No____

   a. If yes, are they treated, rendered or mixed before or immediately after placement in the pile so it no longer meets the definition of ignitable or reactive? Use narrative sheet to describe procedure. Yes____ No____

   OR

   b. Is the waste protected from sources of ignition or reaction? Yes____ No____

Table F-8 (cont.)

(1) If yes, use narrative explanation sheet to describe separation and confinement procedures.

(2) If no, use narrative explanation sheet to describe source of ignition or reaction.

6. Is there evidence of fire, explosion, gaseous emissions, leaching or other discharge from the hazardous waste pile? Use narrative explanation sheet. Yes____ No____

   a. Does the waste pile have a leachate detection, collection and removal system? Yes____ No____

   b. If no, does the inspection plan include a schedule of inspection of the devices for controlling precipitation and runon and runoff? Yes____ No____

   c. Is the waste pile periodically removed for inspection of the base? Yes____ No____

7. Have incompatible wastes ever been placed together in the waste pile? Yes____ No____

   If yes, what was the result? ____

   ____

8. Have there been other wastes previously stored at the site of the present waste pile? Yes____ No____

   a. Have hazardous wastes been piled in the same area where incompatible wastes or materials were previously piled? Yes____ No____

   b. If yes, was the area decontaminated? Use narrative explanation sheet. Yes____ No____

9. Is a closure plan available? Yes____ No____

   a. Will all waste residues, system components, subsoils, etc., be decontaminated and/or removed? Yes____ No____

   b. If the above cannot be decontaminated, will the facility be closed as a landfill? Yes____ No____

Table F-9

LAND TREATMENT CHECKLIST

(Subpart M)

<u>Note</u>: Hazardōus waste must not be placed in or on a land treatment facility unless the waste can be made less hazardous or nonhazardous by degradation, transformation, or immobilization processes occurring in or on the soil.

1. Is runon diverted away from the land treatment facility? Describe using narrative explanation sheet. Yes____ No____

2. Is runoff from the land treatment facility collected? Yes____ No____

3. Is the runoff analyzed to see if it is a hazardous waste? Yes____ No____

   a. If the runoff is considered hazardous, how is it handled? Use narrative explanation sheet. Yes____ No____

   b. If it is not a hazardous waste, is it discharged through a point source to surface waters? Yes____ No____

   If yes, list NPDES Permit No. ______________________________

4. Is wind dispersal controlled? Yes____ No____
   Describe using narrative explanation sheet.

5. What hazardous wastes are treated at the land treatment facility? Use narrative explanation sheet.

   Part 261, Subpart D Listed Wastes — Characteristic Wastes

   a. For those listed wastes, were analyses done to determine the concentrations of those constituents which caused the waste to be listed? Yes____ No____

   If yes, what are these concentrations? Use narrative explanation sheet.

   b. For those characteristic wastes designated EP toxic because of the extraction procedure, what are the concentrations of the following?

Table F-9 (cont.)

	Concentration	Waste
Arsenic		
Barium		
Cadmium		
Chromium		
Lead		
Mercury		

	Concentration	Waste
Selenium		
Silver		
Endrin		
Lindane		
Methoxychlor		
Toxaphene		
2,4 D		
2,4,5-TP Silvex		

6. Obtain a copy of the land treatment process and include it with the report.

7. Are food chain crops grown? Yes____ No____

   a. If no, go to question 9.

   b. If yes, can the owner/operator demonstrate from field testing that arsenic, lead, mercury or other toxic waste constituents:

      (1) Will not be transferred to the food portion of the crop or ingested by food chain animals. Yes____ No____

      OR

      (2) Will not occur in greater concentrations in the crops on the facility than in the same crops on untreated soils in the same region? Yes____ No____

   c. Is the following information used for making the above demonstration and is it kept at the facility?

      (1) Tests for specific wastes and application rates being used at the facility Yes____ No____

      (2) Crop characteristics Yes____ No____

      (3) Soil characteristics Yes____ No____

Table F-9 (cont.)

(4) Sample selection criteria Yes____ No____

(5) Sample size determination Yes____ No____

(6) Analytical methods used Yes____ No____

(7) Statistical procedures Yes____ No____

d. Was the Regional Administrator notified by January 19, 1981 that food chain crops had been or would be grown at the facility? Yes____ No____

e. Does the facility treat wastes that contain cadmium? Yes____ No____

(1) If no, go to question 9.

(2) If yes, list these wastes. Use narrative explanation sheet.

(3) Was the pH of the soil and waste mixture 6.5 or greater at the time of each waste application? Yes____ No____

If the pH was less than 6.5, did the waste contain cadmium concentrations of 2 mg/kg (dry weight) or less? Yes____ No____

(4) Is the annual application rate of cadmium less than 0.5 kg/ha (kilograms per hectare) for the following: tobacco, leafy vegetables, or root crops grown for human consumption? Yes____ No____

For all other food chain crops, is the annual cadmium application rate:

(i) Less than or equal to 2.0 kg/ha (through June 30, 1984) Yes____ No____

(ii) Less than or equal to 1.25 kg/ha (July 1, 1984 through December 31, 1986) Yes____ No____

Table F-9 (cont.)

(iii) Less than or equal to 0.5 kg/ha (January 1, 1987 to present) Yes____ No____

Table F-9 (cont.)

8. Does the facility have an unsaturated zone monitoring plan? Yes____ No____

   a. If no, explain circumstances on narrative explanation sheet.

   b. If yes, does the plan include:

      (1) Soil monitoring Yes____ No____

      (2) Soil pore water monitoring (water above the saturated zone) Yes____ No____

      (3) Sample depths below waste incorporation Yes____ No____

      (4) Number of samples to be taken Yes____ No____

      (5) Frequency and time of sampling Yes____ No____

      (6) Analysis of soil samples Yes____ No____

9. Does implementation of the plan yield:

   a. Background soil-pore liquid quality and chemical makeup of soil not affected by treatment zone leakage Yes____ No____

   b. The quality of soil-pore liquid and chemical makeup of soil below the treatment zone Yes____ No____

10. Have background levels of soil quality been established? Yes____ No____

11. Is monitoring occurring in the soil-pore zone immediately below the treatment zone? Yes____ No____

12. Has a sampling and analysis plan been prepared and does it include:

    a. Sample collection techniques Yes____ No____

    b. Sample preservation and shipment Yes____ No____

Table F-9 (cont.)

c. Analytical procedures Yes____ No____

d. Chain-of-custody control Yes____ No____

13. Has a statistically significant change over background been found in the soil quality? Yes____ No____

a. If yes, has the RA or State been notified? Yes____ No____

b. Have operating practices been modified? Yes____ No____

14. Is the following information (for each hazardous waste) kept at the facility?

a. Application dates Yes____ No____

b. Application rates Yes____ No____

c. Quantities Yes____ No____

d. Waste location Yes____ No____

15. Does the facility have a closure/post-closure plan? Yes____ No____

If yes, where is it kept? ____

16. Are ignitable or reactive wastes treated at the facility? (Circle appropriate waste.) Yes____ No____

a. If yes, are the wastes immediately incorporated into the soil so that they are no longer reactive or ignitable? Yes____ No____

b. Describe or attach a copy of treatment.

17. Are incompatible wastes placed in the facility? Yes____ No____

18. If so, are the incompatible wastes placed in different locations in the facility? Yes____ No____

If no, look for signs of fire, heat generation, toxic mists, etc. (Use narrative explanation sheet.)

Table F-10

LANDFILLS CHECKLIST
(Subpart N)

1. Has any new unit, replacement of an existing unit or lateral expansion of an existing unit that is within the area identified in the Part A, received waste after 05/08/85? Yes____ No____

   a. If no, proceed to question 4.

   b. If yes,

      (1) Did the facility notify the Regional Administrator 60 days prior to receiving waste? Yes____ No____

      (2) Did the facility file a Part B within 6 months of receipt of such notice? Yes____ No____

   c. Does the landfill have at least two liners and a leachate collection system? Yes____ No____

      If no, use narrative explanation sheet to describe alternate system, or, if waiver was granted, to describe demonstration to Regional Administrator (§265.301).

2. Is there a runon control system? Yes____ No____
   Describe on narrative explanation sheet.

3. Is runoff from the landfill collected? Yes____ No____

   a. Is runoff analyzed to determine if it is a hazardous waste? Yes____ No____

   b. If it is a hazardous waste, how is it managed? (Use narrative explanation sheet.)

   c. Is the collected runoff discharged through a point source to surface waters? Yes____ No____

      If yes, list NPDES permit number ______________________

4. Is the landfill managed so that wind dispersal is controlled? (Note blowing debris.) Yes____ No____

5. Is the following information maintained in the operating record? Yes____ No____

Table F-10 (cont.)

a. On a map, the exact location and dimensions, including depth of each cell with respect to permanently surveyed benchmarks? Yes____ No____

AND

b. Contents of each cell and the approximate location of each hazardous waste type within each cell? Yes____ No____

6. Are reactive or ignitable wastes placed in the landfill? Yes____ No____

   a. If yes, are they treated, rendered or mixed before or immediately after placement in the landfill so they are no longer reactive or ignitable? Yes____ No____

   b. Describe treatment, etc. or attach a copy of treatment.

7. Are incompatible wastes placed in the same landfill cell? Yes____ No____

   If yes, what are the results? Use narrative explanation sheet. (Look for signs of mixing of incompatible wastes, e.g., fire, toxic mist, heat generation, etc.)

   Describe how it is possible for incompatible wastes to be placed in the same landfill cell. (Use narrative explanation sheet.)

8. Have bulk or non-containerized, hazardous liquid wastes or wastes containing free liquids been placed in the landfill since May 8, 1985? Yes____ No____

9. Is the liquid waste treated chemically or physically so that free liquids are no longer present? (Use narrative explanation sheet.) Yes____ No____

10. Are containers holding liquid wastes placed in the landfill? Yes____ No____

    If yes,

    a. Has all free-standing liquid been removed? Yes____ No____

    OR

Table F-10 (cont.)

b. Has waste been mixed with absorbent or solidified so that free-standing liquid is no longer observed? Yes____ No____

OR

c. Is the container very small, such as an ampule? Yes____ No____

OR

d. Is the container designed to hold free liquids for use other than storage, such as a battery or capacitor? Yes____ No____

OR

e. Is the container a lab pack? Yes____ No____

11. Are empty containers placed in the landfill? Yes____ No____

a. If yes, are they reduced in volume (e.g., shredded, crushed)? Yes____ No____

12. Does the landfill or cell(s) have a cover? Yes____ No____

a. If no, go to question 13.

b. If yes, answer the following:

(1) Is there evidence of site instability (e.g., erosion, settling)? (Use narrative explanation sheet.) Yes____ No____

(2) Is there evidence of ponding of water onsite? (Use narrative explanation sheet.) Yes____ No____

(3) Is there any indication of improper or inadequate drainage? (Use narrative explanation sheet.) Yes____ No____

13. Does the facility have closure/post-closure plans? Yes____ No____

a. If yes, where are they maintained? ______________________________

b. Do the plans address the following items?

(1) Control of pollutant migration? Yes____ No____

(2) Control of surface water infiltration? Yes____ No____

(3) Prevention of erosion? Yes____ No____

Table F-11
INCINERATORS CHECKLIST
(Subpart O)

1. Is the incinerator operating at steady state conditions (temperature and air flow) before adding hazardous waste? Yes____ No____

   If no, explain in narrative.

2. Is a waste analysis performed on hazardous waste not previously incinerated at facility? Yes____ No____

3. Does it include analysis for the following?

   a. Heating value Yes____ No____
   b. Halogen content Yes____ No____
   c. Sulfur content Yes____ No____
   d. Concentration of lead Yes____ No____
   e. Concentration of mercury Yes____ No____
   f. Is the above information documented in the operating record? Yes____ No____

(NOTE: d and e are not required if the facility has written documented data that show the elements are not present.)

4. Are any of the following instruments existing on the incinerator? Does the owner/operator monitor them at least every 15 minutes when incinerating hazardous waste? Check under applicable column.

	Existing	Monitored
Waste feed	Yes____ No____	Yes____ No____
Auxiliary fuel food	Yes____ No____	Yes____ No____
Air flow	Yes____ No____	Yes____ No____
Incinerator temperature	Yes____ No____	Yes____ No____
Scrubber flow	Yes____ No____	Yes____ No____
Scrubber pH	Yes____ No____	Yes____ No____
Relevant level controls	Yes____ No____	Yes____ No____

(NOTE: Afterburner and temperature, O_2, and CO meters are examples of relevant level controls.)

   a. Does the owner/operator monitor the stack plume (emissions) at least hourly for:

      (1) Color (normal) Yes____ No____

Table F-11 (cont.)

(2) Opacity Yes____ No____

b. Does the owner/operator monitor the incinerator and associated equipment at least daily including: (circle those not in compliance)

(1) Pumps, valves, conveyors, pipes for leaks, spills and fugitive emissions. (Use narrative explanation sheet.) Yes____ No____

(2) Emergency shutdown controls Yes____ No____

(3) System alarms Yes____ No____

c. Are these inspections referenced in the inspection log? Review inspection plan, note deficiencies in narrative. Yes____ No____

5. Is a closure plan maintained for the incinerator? Yes____ No____

If yes, is it kept at the facility? Yes____ No____

6. What wastes are incinerated onsite?

EPA Hazardous Waste No.	Description	Weight or Volume Incinerated Daily

Table F-12

THERMAL TREATMENT CHECKLIST
(Subpart P)

NOTE: Applies to thermal treatment of hazardous waste in devices other than incinerators.

1. Is the process a non-continuous (batch) process? Yes____ No____

If no, is the process operating at steady State conditions (including temperature) before adding hazardous waste? Yes____ No____

2. Does the operating record document weak analysis, for all wastes burned? Yes____ No____

a. Does it include analyses for the following:

(1) Heating value Yes____ No____
(2) Halogen content Yes____ No____
(3) Sulfur content Yes____ No____
(4) Concentration of lead Yes____ No____
(5) Concentration of mercury Yes____ No____

b. Is this information documented in the operating record? Yes____ No____

(NOTE: 4 and 5 are not required if the facility has written documented data that show the elements are not present.)

3. Are the existing instruments which relate to combustion and emission control monitored at least every 15 minutes?

		Existing	Monitored
a.	Waste feed	Yes____ No____	Yes____ No____
b.	Auxiliary fuel feed	Yes____ No____	Yes____ No____
c.	Treatment process temp.	Yes____ No____	Yes____ No____
d.	Relevant process flow	Yes____ No____	Yes____ No____
e.	Relevant controls (e.g., afterburner and temperature controls, O_2 and CO meters)	Yes____ No____	Yes____ No____

Table F-12 (cont.)

4. Are stack plume (emissions) monitored at least hourly? Yes____ No____

   a. Color (normal) Yes____ No____
   b. Opacity Yes____ No____

5. Is thermal treatment process equipment monitored at least daily including: (NOTE: circle those not in compliance). Yes____ No____

   a. Pumps, valves, conveyors, pipes, etc., (for leaks, spills and fugitive emissions) Yes____ No____
   b. Emergency shutdown controls Yes____ No____
   c. System alarms Yes____ No____

6. Is a closure plan maintained at the facility? Yes____ No____

7. Is open burning or detonation of waste explosives conducted? Yes____ No____

   If yes, is the detonation performed in accordance with the following table? Yes____ No____

Pounds of Waste Explosives or Propellants	Minimum Distance From Open Burning or Detonation to the Property of Others
0-100	204m (670 ft.)
101-1,000	380m (1,250 ft.)
1,001-10,000	530m (1,730 ft.)
10,001-30,000	690m (2,260 ft.)

8. Is there evidence of open burning of hazardous wastes except for waste explosives? Yes____ No____

   Use narrative explanations sheet to describe details.

Table F-13

CHEMICAL, PHYSICAL AND BIOLOGICAL TREATMENT CHECKLIST
(Subpart Q)

NOTE: Applies to treatment in other than tanks, surface impoundments and land treatment facilities.

1. Describe treatment process (include information on wastes treated).

2. Inspect treatment process and equipment:

   Are there any leaks, corrosion or other failures evident? Yes____ No____

   If yes, describe. ____

   ____

3. Is the process a continuous feed system? Yes____ No____

   If yes, is it equipped with a means to stop waste inflow (e.g., waste feed cutoff system or bypass). Yes____ No____

4. If hazardous waste is to be treated which is substantially different from any hazardous waste previously treated at the facility or if a substantially different process than any previously used at the facility is to be used to chemically treat hazardous wastes, are the following obtained:

   a. Waste analyses and trial treatment tests (e.g., bench scale)? Yes____ No____

   OR

   b. Written, documented information on similar treatment or similar wastes? Yes____ No____

5. Does the owner/operator inspect the following, where present (indicate which items are present)?

   a. At least daily

      (1) Discharge control and safety equipment (e.g., waste feed cutoff, bypass, drainage or pressure relief systems)? Yes____ No____

      (2) Data gathered from monitoring equipment (e.g., pressure and temperature gauges)? Yes____ No____

Table F-13 (cont.)

b. At least weekly

(1) Construction materials of treatment process or equipment to detect erosion or obvious signs of leakage? Yes____ No____

(2) Construction materials of an area immediately surrounding discharge confinement structures? Yes____ No____

6. Does the facility have a closure plan? Yes____ No____

7. Where is the plan maintained? ______________________________

8. Are ignitable or reactive wastes placed in the treatment process (circle appropriate waste). Yes____No____

   If yes, is the waste treated, rendered or mixed before or immediately after being placed in the treatment process so it no longer meets the definition of ignitable or reactive? Describe or attach a copy of the treatment. Yes____ No____

9. Has the facility treated incompatible wastes? Yes____ No____

   If yes, what were the results. Use narrative explanation sheet. Look for signs of mixing of incompatible wastes (e.g., fire, toxic mist, heat generation, etc.)

10. If a waste is to be placed in treatment equipment that previously held an incompatible waste, was that equipment washed? Yes____ No____

    If yes, describe washing procedures. Use narrative explanation sheet.

    Describe how it is possible for incompatible wastes to be placed in the same treating equipment. Use narrative explanation sheet.

Table F-14

RCRA CHECKLIST FOR RECYCLABLE WASTES AND WASTES BURNED FOR ENERGY RECOVERY (40 CFR Part 266)

Name of Facility: ______________________________

Address: ______________________________

____

EPA I.D. Number ______________________________

Facility Inspection Representative: ______________________________

Title: ______________________________

Telephone Number: ______________________________

SECTION A - RECYCLABLE MATERIALS USED IN A MANNER CONSTITUTING DISPOSAL

The following questions are to assist in evaluating compliance with 40 CFR Part 266, Subpart C.

1. Is the waste applied to the land? Yes____ No____

   If no, the regulations do not apply.

   If yes, is it mixed with other substances? Yes____ No____

   If it is mixed with other substances, do they react with waste? Yes____ No____

2. If mixed, is the combined material produced for public use in a manner which constitutes disposal? Yes____ No____

   If yes, have the recyclable materials undergone a chemical reaction when producing the product such that the material is not separable from the product by physical means? Yes____ No____

If yes to both of the above, the material is not regulated.

3. If waste oil or other material is being used for dust suppression or road treatments, has it been tested for dioxin? Yes____ No____

4. Is the waste subject to Subpart D of 40 CFR Part 268 (Land Disposal Restrictions)? Yes____ No____

Table F-14 (cont.)

If yes, does it meet the applicable treatment standard? Yes____ No____

5. Are the requirements of 40 CFR Part 262 applicable to the transporter of the material? Yes____ No____

6. Are the requirements of 40 CFR Part 263 applicable to the transporter of the material? Yes____ No____

7. Is the use of the recyclable materials such that the owner/operator is subject to any requirements of 40 CFR Parts 264/265, Subparts A through N, Parts 270 and 124? Yes____ No____

SECTION B - ENERGY RECOVERY

These are questions pertaining to facilities that recycle wastes to be burned for energy recovery (Marketers and Burners) that are regulated by 40 CFR Part 266, Subparts D and E.

NOTE: Regarding generators and waste as fuel standards. Generators of used oil or hazardous waste are subject to the waste as fuel marketer standards if they sell waste fuels directly to burners for energy recovery. Generators are subject to the burner standards if they burn used oil or hazardous waste for energy recovery.

1. Does the facility receive used oils or hazardous waste for the purpose of marketing waste as fuel for energy recovery? Yes____ No____

If yes, complete the marketer checklist of Section B.1.

2. Does the facility burn its waste as fuel for energy recovery? Yes____ No____

If yes, complete the burner checklist of Section B.2.

SECTION B.1 - MARKETERS/PROCESSORS OF WASTE FUELS

Site Characterization

1. Does the facility accept waste oil? Yes____ No____

Specify types and source: ____

____

Table F-14 (cont.)

2. Does the facility blend hazardous waste with waste oil to be marketed as fuel? Yes____ No____

3. Does the facility accept hazardous waste fuel (i.e., used oil previously blended with hazardous waste)? Yes____ No____

4. Does the facility accept hazardous waste? Yes____ No____

   Specify waste and generator type: ____________________

   ____

5. Does the facility accept only used oil? Yes____ No____

6. Does the facility have Interim Status or a permit (RCRA §3005)? Yes____ No____

   Specify: ____________________

7. Does the facility generate hazardous waste? Yes____ No____

   If yes, refer to the generator checklist, also.

8. Inspect the following general operating practices:

Storage	Treatment	Disposal
____Drum	____Settling	____Landfill
____Above-ground tank(s)	____Heat addition	____Land Treatment
____Under-ground tank(s)	____In-Line Filtering	____Surface Impoundment
____Other	____Certrifugation	
____Tank sizes	____Screen Filtration	____Other
________	____Dehydration	
________	____Emulsion Breaking	
	____Blending	

Descriptions and Observations: ____________________

____

9. Specify other material recycled as fuel. ____________________

____

Table F-14 (cont.)

10. Has the facility notified the Agency of their waste fuel activity [§266.34(b), or §266.43(b)(3)]? Yes____ No____

If no, explain: ______________________________

____

11. Does the facility have manifests for all shipments of hazardous waste and blended hazardous waste fuel (received or sent) (§265.70)? Yes____ No____

Review manifests and obtain copies of deficient documents.

12. Does the facility have a copy of the required notice burners or marketers to whom waste fuel is marketed [§266.34(e) or §266.43(b)(5)]? Yes____ No____

13. Does the facility have invoice information for shipments of used oil claimed to be specification used oil fuel [§266.43(b)(6)]? Yes____ No____

14. Does the above invoice information for specification used oil fuel have a cross-reference to analysis or other information? Yes____ No____

15. Does the facility analyze for metals and halogens? Yes____ No____

Specify methods: ______________________________

____

16. Does the facility have records of analysis or other information documenting that the used oil meets the specification? Yes____ No____

17. Does the facility have the records required under §266.34(f) or §266.43(b)(6)? Yes____ No____

Comments: ______________________________

____

____

NOTE: If a facility markets hazardous waste fuel, the facility is subject to storage requirements of Parts 262, 264 or 265 and 270, Subparts A through L. Complete the TSDF checklist.

Table F-14 (cont.)

<u>SECTION B.2 - BURNERS OF USED OIL FUEL AND HAZARDOUS WASTE FUEL</u>

The following questions pertain to facilities regulated under Part 266 who burn waste fuel for energy recovery. These do not necessarily apply to incineration under Subpart O of Part 265.

1. Does the facility burn used oil fuel? Yes____ No____

   Specify: Off-specification____ Specification____

2. Does the facility burn hazardous waste fuel? Yes____ No____

   If yes, was the facility in existence before May 26, 1986?* Yes____ No____

3. Does the facility's burning unit(s) classify as industrial boiler(s) or industrial furnace(s)? Yes____ No____

   If no, does the facility have records of analysis or other information documenting that the used oil meets the required specifications [§266.44(b)]? Yes____ No____

4. Has the owner/operator notified EPA of their waste fuel activity [§266.35(b) or §266.44(b)]? Yes____ No____

5. Does the facility have records of the <u>required notices</u> sent to the fuel suppliers (marketers) for hazardous waste fuel or off-specification used oil [§266.35(d) or §266.44(c)]? Yes____ No____

6. Does the facility have Interim Status or a permit (§3005)? Yes____ No____

   Comments: ____

   ____

   ____

* *Storage requirements for hazardous waste fuel under Subparts A through L, Parts 262, 264 or 265 and 270 apply to these facilities as of May 29, 1986. Therefore, refer to the checklist for inspection of TSDF.*

Table F-14 (cont.)

SECTION C - RECYCLABLE MATERIALS USED FOR PRECIOUS METAL RECOVERY

The following questions are to assist in evaluating compliance with 40 CFR Part 266, Subpart F.

1. Is the recyclable material being kept for speculative purposes, as defined in Part 261.1(c)(8)? Yes____ No____

If yes, owner/operator is subject to all applicable provisions of 40 CFR Parts 262 through 265, 270, and 124.

2. Are any of the following metals reclaimed or expected to be reclaimed from the material: gold, silver, platinum, paladium, irridium, osmium, rhodium, ruthenium, or any combination of these? Yes____ No____

   If yes, has the person notified EPA pursuant to section 3010 of RCRA? Yes____ No____

3. Do storage records show:

   a. The volume of materials stored at the beginning of the calendar year? Yes____ No____

   b. The amount of these materials generated or received during the calendar year? Yes____ No____

   c. The amount of materials remaining at the end of the calendar year? Yes____ No____

4. If the wastes are shipped offsite for recycling, are the shipments accompanied by a hazardous waste manifest [266.70(b)(2)]? Yes____ No____

   If they are manifested as hazardous wastes, do land ban notifications accompany the shipments? Yes____ No____

   Are copies of the manifest and land ban notifications kept by the generator for at least 3 years? Yes____ No____

Table F-14 (cont.)

SECTION D - SPENT LEAD-ACID BATTERIES BEING RECLAIMED

The following questions are to assist in evaluating compliance with 40 CFR Part 266, Subpart G.

1. Does the facility reclaim lead-acid batteries? Yes____ No____

   If yes, the regulations apply.

2. Has the facility complied with the notification requirements of section 3010 of RCRA? Yes____ No____

3. Has the facility complied with applicable provisions of Part 264, as identified in 40 CFR Part 266.80(b)(2)? Yes____ No____

APPENDIX G

LAND DISPOSAL RESTRICTIONS PROGRAM CHECKLIST

Does the facility use one or more of the following methods for disposal of hazardous waste:

Landfill	___ Yes	___ No
Surface impoundment	___ Yes	___ No
Waste pile	___ Yes	___ No
Injection well*	___ Yes	___ No
Land treatment	___ Yes	___ No
Salt dome	___ Yes	___ No
Salt beds	___ Yes	___ No
Underground mines or caves	___ Yes	___ No
Concrete vaults or bunkers	___ Yes	___ No
Other land disposal including unlined ditches	___ Yes	___ No

If the answer is yes to one or more of the above, then the facility uses a method of land disposal regulated by the Land Disposal Restrictions Program. Proceed with the checklist.

Directions: Review process descriptions and determine what wastes are handled at the facility. Use Part A of the checklist, Sections I through VI to determine if the waste stream is restricted under the Land Disposal Restrictions Program, and if applicable, to determine the effective dates of the restriction. Proceed to Part B of the checklist to see general requirements applicable to all facilities. Refer to Part B Section II to determine the other applicable requirements depending on the operating status (i.e., generator, transporter, TSD), then refer to the referenced Parts of the checklist [e.g., generator (Part C), transporter (Part D), etc.].

---

* *Refer to 40 CFR Part 148 for specific dates applicable to disposal of restricted wastes in injection wells.*

PART A- Determination of Restricted Constituents

Section A-I- Solvent Wastes(268.30) (effective November 8,1986, except for disposal into injection wells, which was effective August 8,1988)

Does the facility generate any of the following F001 through F005 constituents as the result of being used in the process either in pure form or commercial grade?

F001

Tetrachloroethylene	___ Yes ___ No
Trichloroethylene	___ Yes ___ No
Methylene chloride	___ Yes ___ No
1,1,1-trichloroethane	___ Yes ___ No
Carbon tetrachloride	___ Yes ___ No

F002

Tetrachloroethylene	___ Yes ___ No
Trichloroethylene	___ Yes ___ No
Methylene chloride	___ Yes ___ No
1,1,1-trichloroethane	___ Yes ___ No
Chlorobenzene	___ Yes ___ No
Trichlorofluoromethane	___ Yes ___ No
1,1,2-trichloro-1,2,2-trifluoroethane	___ Yes ___ No
1,2-dichlorobenzene (same as ortho)	___ Yes ___ No

F003

Xylene	___ Yes ___ No
Acetone	___ Yes ___ No
Ethyl acetate	___ Yes ___ No
Ethyl benzene	___ Yes ___ No
Ethyl ether	___ Yes ___ No
Methyl isobutyl ketone	___ Yes ___ No
n-butyl alcohol	___ Yes ___ No
Cyclohexanone	___ Yes ___ No
Methanol	___ Yes ___ No

If the F003 waste stream has been mixed with a non-restricted solid or nonlisted hazardous waste, does the resultant mixture exhibit the ignitability characteristic? ___ Yes ___ No

If the answer is no, then land ban does not apply to this waste stream.

F004

Cresols and cresylic acid	___ Yes ___ No
Nitrobenzene	___ Yes ___ No

F005

Toluene	___ Yes ___ No
Methyl ethyl ketone	___ Yes ___ No
Carbon disulfide	___ Yes ___ No
Isobutanol	___ Yes ___ No
Pyridine	___ Yes ___ No

a. If any of the above constituents are used as a solvent (i.e., as a cleaning agent, wetting agent, paint remover, degreaser, or dilutant, etc.,), where the substance is not chemically altered, then the substance when spent, is restricted under the Land Disposal Restrictions Program. Solvents are restricted both above and below the treatment standards listed in Table G-1. If the substance is chemically altered during the process or it has not been used as a solvent it is not restricted under land ban.

b. If the waste is a mixture of constituents, answer this to determine whether it is a "solvent mixture" covered under Part 268.30 (a)(3).

1. If the waste stream is mixed and contains two or more of the F001 through F005 constituents determine the concentration, before use, of all the constituents in the mixture. If the waste stream is a mixture containing a total of 10% or more (by volume) of one or more of the F001, F002, F004 or F005 constituents then it is a restricted waste. For example:

Solvent mixture before use

5%	methylene chloride
2%	trichloroethylene
25%	1,1,1-trichloroethane
68%	mineral spirits
100%	

With respect to the F003 solvent wastes, if, before use, the waste stream is mixed and contains only F003 constituents, it is a restricted waste. For example:

33%	acetone
16%	methanol
51%	ethyl ether
100%	

Table G-1

TREATMENT STANDARDS* FOR F-SOLVENTS AND DIOXINS IN WASTE EXTRACT

F001-F005 Spent Solvents	Concentration (in mg/L) Wastewaters	Other Wastes
Acetone	0.05	0.59
N-butyl alcohol	5.0	5.0
Carbon disulfide	1.05	4.81
Carbon tetrachloride	0.05	0.59
Chlorobenzene	0.15	0.05
Cresols (and cresylic acid)	2.82	0.75
Cyclohexanone	0.125	0.75
1,2-dichlorobezene	0.65	0.125
Ethyl acetate	0.05	0.75
Ethyl benzene	0.05	0.053
Ethyl ether	0.05	0.75
Isobutanol	5.0	5.0
Methanol	0.25	0.75
Methylene chloride	0.20	0.96
Methyl ethyl ketone	0.05	0.75
Methyl isobutyl ketone	0.05	0.33
Nitrobenzene	0.66	0.125
Pyridine	1.12	0.33
Tetrachloroethylene	0.079	0.05
Toluene	1.12	0.33
1,1,1-Trichloroethane	1.05	0.41
1,1,2-Trichloro-1,2,2-trifluoroethane	1.05	0.96
Trichloroethylene	0.062	0.091
Trichlorofluoromethane	0.05	0.96
Xylene	0.05	0.15

F020-F023 and F026-F028 Dioxin Containing Wastes	Concentration
HxCDD-all hexachlorodibenzo-p-dioxins	< 1 ppb
HxCDF-all hexachlorodibenzofurans	< 1 ppb
PeCDD-all pentachlorodibenzo-p-dioxins	< 1 ppb
PeCDF-all pentachlorodibenzofurans	< 1 ppb
TCCD-all tetrachlorodibenzo-p-dioxins	< 1 ppb
TCDF-all tetrachlorodibenzofurans	< 1 ppb
2,4,5-trichlorophenol	< 0.05 ppm
2,4,6-trichlorophenol	< 0.05 ppm
2,3,4,6-tetrachlorophenol	< 0.10 ppm
Pentachlorophenol	< 0.01 ppm

* *Table CCWE from 268.41*

If the waste stream is a mixture containing F003 constituents and a total of 10% or more of one or more of the F001, F002, F004 and F005 listed constituents before use, it is a restricted waste. For example:

50%	xylene	(F003)
12%	TCE	(F001)
38%	mineral spirits	
100%		

If (a) or (b) above indicate that the F001 through F005 constituents are restricted, refer to Part B of this checklist for applicable requirements.

Section A-II- Dioxin Wastes (268.31) (effective date November 8,1986)

Does the facility generate wastes with the codes F020 through F023 or F026 through F028? ___ Yes ___ No

These wastes are restricted and can not be land disposed between November 1986 and November 1988 unless the disposal facility meets the requirements of 268.5(h)(2). Refer to 40 CFR Part 268.31(d) for exemptions, extensions and variances to this rule.

If the facility generates the above wastes, refer to Part B of this checklist for applicable requirements.

Section A-III-California List Wastes (268.32) (effective July 8,1987)

Does the facility generate any of the following hazardous wastes (the wastes must be RCRA hazardous wastes as defined in Part 261)?

a. Liquid wastes with a pH less than or equal to 2

b. Liquid wastes containing polychlorinated biphenyls (PCBs) at concentrations greater than or equal to 50 ppm

c. Liquid wastes that are primarily water and contain halogenated organic compounds (HOCs) in total concentration greater than or equal to 1,000 mg/L and less than 10,000 mg/L [See Table G-2]

d. Liquid wastes including free liquids associated with any solid or sludge, containing free cyanides at concentrations greater than or equal to 1,000 mg/L

e. Liquid wastes, including free liquids associated with any solid or sludge, containing the following metals (or elements) or compounds of these metals (or elements) at concentrations greater than or equal to those specified

Table G-2
List of Halogenated Organic Compounds

Appendix III to Part 268—List of Halogenated Organic Compounds Regulated Under § 268.32

In determining the concentration of HOCs in a hazardous waste for purposes of the § 268.32 land disposal prohibition. EPA has defined the HOCs that must be included in the calculation as any compounds having a carbon-halogen bond which are listed in this Appendix (see § 268.2). Appendix III to Part 268 consists of the following compounds:

Volatiles

Bromodichloromethane
Bromomethane
Carbon Tetrachloride
Chlorobenzene
2-Chloro-1.3-butadiene
Chlorodibromomethane
Chloroethane
2-Chloroethyl vinyl ether
Chloroform
Chloromethane
3-Chloropropene
1.2-Dibromo-3-chloropropane
1.2-Dibromomethane
Dibromomethane
Trans-1.4-Dichloro-2-butene
Dichlorodifluoromethane
1.1-Dichloroethane
1.2-Dichloroethane
1.1-Dichloroethylene
Trans-1.2-Dichloroethene
1.2-Dichloropropane
Trans-1.3-Dichloropropene
cis-1.3-Dichloropropene
Iodomethane
Methylene chloride
1.1.1.2-Tetrachloroethane
1.1.2.2-Tetrachloroethane
Tetrachloroethene
Tribromomethane
1.1.1-Trichloroethane
1.1.2-Trichloroethane
Trichloroethene
Trichloromonofluoromethane
1.2.3-Trichloropropane
Vinyl chloride

Semivolatiles

Bis(2-chloroethoxy)ethane
Bis(2-chloroethyl)ether
Bis(2-chloroisopropyl) ether
p-Chloroaniline
Chlorobenzilate
p-Chloro-m-cresol
2-Chloronaphthalene
2-Chlorophenol
3-Chloropropionitrile
m-Dichlorobenzene
o-Dichlorobenzene
p-Dichlorobenzene
3.3'-Dichlorobenzidine
2.4-Dichlorophenol
2.6-Dichlorophenol
Hexachlorobenzene
Hexachlorobutadiene
Hexachlorocyclopentadiene
Hexachloroethane
Hexachloroprophene
Hexachloropropene
4.4'-Methylenebis(2-chloroaniline)
Pentachlorobenzene
Pentachloroethane
Pentachloronitrobenzene
Pentachlorophenol
Pronamide
1.2.4.5-Tetrachlorobenzene
2.3.4.6-Tetrachlorophenol
1.2.4-Trichlorobenzene
2.4.5-Trichlorophenol
2.4.6-Trichlorophenol
Tris(2.3-dibromopropyl)phosphate

Organochlorine Pesticides

Aldrin
alpha-BHC
beta-BHC
delta-BHC
gamma-BHC
Chlordane
DDD
DDE
DDT
Dieldrin
Endosulfan I
Endosulfan II
Endrin
Endrin aldehyde
Heptachlor
Heptachlor epoxide
Isodrin
Kepone
Methoxyclor
Toxaphene

Phenoxyacetic Acid Herbicides

2.4-Dichlorophenoxyacetic acid
Silvex
2.4.5-T

PCBs

Aroclor 1016
Aroclor 1221
Aroclor 1232
Aroclor 1242
Aroclor 1248
Aroclor 1254
Aroclor 1260
PCBs not otherwise specified

Dioxins and Furans

Hexachlorodibenzo-p-dioxins
Hexachlorodibenzofuran
Pentachlorodibenzo-p-dioxins
Pentachlorodibenzofuran
Tetrachlorodibenzo-p-dioxins
Tetrachlorodibenzofuran
2.3.7.8-Tetrachlorodibenzo-p-dioxin

1.	Arsenic and or compounds (as As)	500 mg/L
2.	Cadmium and/or compounds (as Cd)	100 mg/L
3.	Chromium (VI) and/or compounds (as Cr VI)	500 mg/L
4.	Lead and/or compounds (as Pb)	500 mg/L
5.	Mercury and/or compounds (as Hg)	20 mg/L
6.	Nickel and/or compounds (as Ni)	134 mg/L
7.	Selenium and/or compounds (as Se)	100 mg/L
8.	Thallium and/or compounds (as T1)	130 mg/L

f. Nonliquid and liquid hazardous wastes containing HOCs in total concentrations greater than or equal to 1,000 mg/kg are prohibited from land disposal on July 8,1989 [refer to 268.32(g)(2) for exemptions)]

If any of (a) through (f) above constituents are generated at or above (or less than for pH) the concentrations specified, then the waste stream is restricted. Refer to Part B of this checklist for applicable requirements.

<u>Section A-IV- First-Third wastes (268.10 and 268.33)</u> (effective date August 8,1988)

Determine if the facility generates any of the wastes listed in 268.10 (also listed in Table G-3). If the wastes are listed both in Table F-3 and 40 CFR Part 268.33, then applicable treatment standards have been established for the waste stream.

If the waste stream is listed in Table G-3 but not listed in 268.33 (i.e., listed for wastewaters but not for nonwastewaters, or vice versa, or the waste is not listed at all), then the waste is a "soft hammer" waste.

A soft hammer waste can not be land disposed in a surface impoundment or landfill unless the unit meets minimum technology requirements outlined in 268.5(h)(2)* (double liner, leachate detection system, groundwater monitoring system, etc.), and <u>prior to disposal</u> the generator must certify to the Administrator that they have investigated the availability of treatment capacity and have determined that disposal in the landfill or surface impoundment is the only practical alternative available to the generator (RCRA Section 3004(g)(6)(a) and 268.8) [Refer to Part C of this checklist for further information about generator requirements].

Soft hammer wastes are not prohibited from other forms of land disposal until May 8,1990, when a "hard hammer" falls as stipulated in Section 3004(g)(6)(c) of RCRA. If the Administrator fails to publish treatment standards for any listed waste by May 8,1990, then the waste is prohibited from land disposal.

---

* *Before November 8,1988, the <u>facility</u> had to meet minimum technology requirements, but after November 8,1988 the disposal unit receiving the waste must meet minimum technology standards.*

Table G-3
First-Third Listed Wastes

§ 268.10

Subpart B—Schedule for Land Disposal Prohibition and Establishment of Treatment Standards

SOURCE: 51 FR 19305, May 28, 1986, unless otherwise noted.

§ 268.10 Identification of wastes to be evaluated by August 8, 1988.

EPA will take action under sections 3004(g)(5) and 3004(m), of the Resource Conservation and Recovery Act, by August 8, 1988, for the following wastes (for ease of understanding the wastes have been listed by the section of 40 CFR Part 261 under which they were listed):

§ 261.31 Wastes

F006—Wastewater treatment sludges from electroplating operations except from the following processes: (1) Sulfuric acid anodizing of aluminum; (2) tin plating on carbon steel; (3) zinc plating (segregated basis) on carbon steel; (4) aluminum or zinc-aluminum plating on carbon steel; (5) cleaning/stripping associated with tin, zinc and aluminum plating on carbon steel; and (6) chemical etching and milling of aluminum.
F007—Spent cyanide plating bath solutions from electroplating operations.
F008—Plating bath sludges from the bottom of plating baths from electroplating operations where cyanides are used in the process.
F009—Spent stripping and cleaning bath solutions from electroplating operations where cyanides are used in the process.
F019—Wastewater treatment sludges from the chemical conversion coating of aluminum.

§ 261.32 Wastes

K001—Bottom sediment sludge from the treatment of wastewaters from wood preserving processes that use creosote and/or pentachlorophenol.
K004—Wastewater treatment sludge from the production of zinc yellow pigments.
K008—Over residue from the production of chrome oxide green pigments.
K011—Bottom stream from the wastewater stripper in the production of acrylonitrile.
K013—Bottom stream from the acetonitrile column in the production of acrylonitrile.
K014—Bottoms from the acetonitrile purification column in the production of acrylonitrile.
K015—Still bottoms from the distillation of benzyl chloride.
K016—Heavy ends or distillation residues from the production of carbon tetrachloride.
K017—Heavy ends (still bottoms) from the purification column in the production of epichlorohydrin.
K018—Heavy ends from the fractionation column in ethyl chloride production.
K020—Heavy ends from the distillation of vinyl chloride in vinyl chloride monomer production.
K021—Aqueous spent antimony catalyst waste from fluoromethanes production.
K022—Distillation bottom tars from the production of phenol/acetone from cumane.
K024—Distillation bottoms from the production of phthalic anhydride from naphthalene.
K030—Column bottom or heavy ends from the combined production of trichloroethylene and perchloroethylene.
K031—By-products salts generated in the production of MSMA and cacodylic acid.
K035—Wastewater treatment sludges generated in the production of creosote.
K036—Still bottoms from toluene reclamation distillation in the production of disulfoton.
K037—Wastewater treatment sludge from the production of disulfoton.
K044—Wastewater treatment sludges from the manufacturing and processing of explosives.
K045—Spent carbon from the treatment of wastewater containing explosives.
K046—Wastewater treatment sludges from the manufacturing, formulation and loading of lead-based initiating compounds.
K047—Pink/red water from TNT operations.
K048—Dissolved air flotation (DAF) float from the petroleum refining industry.
K049—Stop oil emulsion solids from the petroleum refining industry.
K050—Heat exchange bundle cleaning sludge from the petroleum refining industry.
K051—API separator sludge from the petroleum refining industry.
K052—Tank bottoms (leaded) from the petroleum refining industry.
K060—Ammonia still lime sludge from coking operations.
K061—Emission control dust/sludge from the primary production of steel in electric furnaces.
K062—Spent pickle liquor from steel finishing operations in chlorine production.
K069—Emission control dust/sludge from secondary lead smelting.
K071—Brine purification muds from the mercury cells process in chlorine production, where separately prepurified brine is not used.
K073—Chlorinated hydrocarbon waste from the purification step of the diaphragm cell process using graphite anodes
K083—Distillation bottoms from aniline production.
K084—Wastewater treatment sludges generated during the production of veterinary pharmaceuticals from arsenic or organoarsenic compounds.
K085—Distillation of fractionation column bottoms from the production of chlorobenzenes.
K086—Solvent washes and sludges; caustic washes and sludges, or water washes and sludges from cleaning tubs and equipment used in the formulation of ink from pig-

Table G-3 Cont.

ments, driers, soaps, and stabilizers containing chromium and lead.

K087—Decanter tank tar sludge from coking operations.

K099—Untreated wastewater from the production of 2,4-D.

K101—Distillation tar residues from the distillation of aniline-based compounds in the production of veterinary pharmaceuticals from arsenic or organo-arsenic compounds.

K102—Residue from the use of activated carbon for decolorization in the production of veterinary pharmaceuticals from arsenic or organo-arsenic compounds.

K103—Process residues from aniline extraction from the production of aniline.

K104—Combined wastewater streams generated from nitrobenzene/aniline production.

K106—Waste water treatment sludge from the mercury cell process in chlorine production.

§ 261.33(e) Wastes

P001—Warfarin, when present at concentration greater than 0.3%
P004—Aldrin
P005—Allyl alcohol
P010—Arsenic acid
P011—Arsenic (V) oxide
P012—Arsenic (III) oxide
P015—Beryllium dust
P016—Bis-(chloromethyl) ether
P018—Brucine
P020—Dinoseb
P030—Soluble cyanide salts not elsewhere specified
P036—Dichlorophenylarsine
P037—Dieldrin
P039—Disulfoton
P041—Diethyl-p-nitrophenyl phosphate
P048—2,4-Dinitrophenol
P050—Endosulfan
P058—Fluoracetic acid, sodium salt
P059—Heptachlor
P063—Hydrogen cyanide
P068—Methyl Hydrazine
P069—Methyllactonitrile
P070—Aldicarb
P071—Methyl parathion
P081—Nitroglycerine
P082—N-Nitrosodimethylamine
P084—N-Nitrosomethylvinylamine
P087—Osmium tetraoxide
P089—Parathion
P092—Phenylmercuric acetate
P094—Phorate
P097—Famphur
P102—Propargyl alcohol
P105—Sodium azide
P108—Strychnine and salts
P110—Tetraethyl lead
P115—Thallium (I) sulfate
P120—Vanadium pentoxide
P122—Zinc phosphide, when present at concentrations greater than 10%
P123—Toxaphene

§ 261.33(f) Wastes

U007—Acrylamide
U009—Acrylonitrile
U010—Mitomycin C
U012—Aniline
U016—Benz(c)acridine
U018—Benz(a)anthracene
U019—Benzene
U022—Benzo(a)pyrene
U029—Methyl bromide
U031—n-Butanol
U036—Chlordane, technical
U037—Chlorobenzene
U041—n-Chloro-2,3-epoxypropane
U043—Vinyl chloride
U044—Chloroform
U046—Chloromethyl methyl ether
U050—Chrysene
U051—Creosote
U053—Crotonaldehyde
U061—DDT
U063—Dibenz o (a, h) anthracene
U064—1,2:7,8 Dibenzopyrene
U066—Dibromo-3-chloropropane 1,2-
U067—Ethylene dibromide
U074—1,4-Dichloro-2-butene
U077—Ethane, 1,2-dichloro-
U078—Dichloroethylene, 1,1-
U086—N,N Diethylhydrazine
U089—Diethylstilbestrol
U103—Dimethyl sulfate
U105—2,4-Dinitrotoluene
U108—Dioxane, 1,4-
U115—Ethylene oxide
U122—Formaldehyde
U124—Furan
U129—Lindane
U130—Hexachlorocyclopentadiene
U133—Hydrazine
U134—Hydrofluoric acid
U137—Indeno(1,2,3-cd)pyrene
U151—Mecury
U154—Methanol
U155—Methapyrilene
U157—3-Methylcholanthrene
U158—4,4-Methylene-bis-(2-chloroaniline)
U159—Methyl ethyl ketone
U171—Nitropropane, 2-
U177—N-Nitroso-N-methylurea
U180—N-Nitrosopyrrolidine
U185—Pentachloronitrobenzene
U188—Phenol
U192—Pronamide
U200—Reserpine
U209—Tetrachloroethane, 1,1,2,2-
U210—Tetrachloroethylene
U211—Carbon tetrachloride
U219—Thiourea
U220—Toluene
U221—Toluenediamine
U223—Toluene diisocyanate
U226—Methylchloroform
U227—Trichloroethane, 1,1,2-
U228—Trichloroethylene
U237—Uracil mustard
U238—Ethyl carbamate
U248—Warfarin, when present at concentrations of 0.3% or less
U249—Zinc phosphide, when present at concentrations of 10% or less

Exceptions to the general rules of applicability:

a. For wastes that are both first-third and California list wastes the following hierarchy applies

1. First-third treatment standards (268.41 and 43), when effective, supersede the California list prohibitions, because they are more specific and more stringent.

2. If the first third waste is a "soft hammer" waste and California list waste it may be subject to the California list prohibitions and the soft hammer requirements. If treatment standards are listed in 40 CFR Parts 268.42 [e.g., PCBs greater than or equal to 50 ppm and HOCs greater than or equal to 1000 ppm (as of April 1988)],the California list treatment standards apply, otherwise the soft hammer prohibitions apply. Whichever is the most stringent applies.

The effect of this distinction is that treatment residues from the California list treatment (PCBs and HOCs) can be disposed in non-minimum technology landfills and surface impoundments. For those without treatment standards in 268.41 or 268.43 the treatment residues must meet the California list prohibition levels [Section III of this Part] at a minimum <u>and</u> the soft hammer prohibition [i.e., the generator must notify that the waste is both first third and California list waste and certify that the waste meets the treatment standards for California list, but the treatment residues still have to go into a facility meeting minimum technology standards of 268.5(h)(2)].

b. Several treatment residues derived from the treatment of first-third wastes have been reclassified as third-third wastes and are not currently regulated under the "soft hammer"; refer to 268.12(b) for these wastes.

c. Some types of surface impoundments and landfills are permitted to receive soft hammer wastes as described in 268.5(h)(2) or 3004(o)(2), because they have demonstrated equivalency to minimum technology standards.

If the waste stream generated is restricted as listed in this Section, refer to Part B of this checklist for applicable requirements.

<u>Section A-V- Second-third wastes (268.11)</u> (proposed effective date June 8,1989)

Refer to 40 CFR Part 268.11 (also Table G-4) for a list of the wastes proposed to be listed in the second-third restrictions. Further requirements have not been developed to date.

Table G-4
Second-Third Listed Wastes

§ 268.11 Identification of wastes to be evaluated by June 8, 1989.

EPA will take action under sections 3004(g)(5) and 3004(m) of the Resource Conservation and Recovery Act, by June 8, 1989, for the following wastes (for ease of understanding the wastes have been listed by the section of 40 CFR Part 261 under which they were listed):

§ 261.31 Wastes

F010—Quenching bath sludge from oil baths from metal heat treating operations where cyanides are used in the process.
F011—Spent cyanide solutions from salt bath pot cleaning from metal heat treating operations.
F012—Quenching wastewater treatment sludges from metal heat operations where cyanides are used in the process.
F024—Wastes including but not limited to, distillation residues, heavy ends, tars and reactor clean-out wastes from the production of chlorinated aliphatic hydrocarbons, having carbon content from one to five, utilizing free radical catalyzed processes. [This listing does not include light ends, spent filters and filter aids, spend desiccants, wastewater, wastewater treatment sludges, spent catalysts, and wastes listed in § 261.32.].

§ 261.32 Wastes

K009—Distillation bottoms from the production of acetaldehyde from ethylene.
K010—Distillation side cuts from the productions of acetaldehyde from ethylene.
K019—Heavy ends from the distillation of ethylene dichloride in ethylene dichloride production.
K025—Distillation bottoms from the production of nitrobenzene by the nitration of benzene.
K027—Centrifuge and distillation residues from toluene diisocyanate production.
K028—Spent catalyst from the hydrochlorinator reactor in the production of 1,1,1-trichloroethane.
K029—Waste from the product steam stripper in the production of 1,1,1-trichloroethane.
K038—Wastewater from the washing and stripping of phorate production.
K039—Filter cake from the filtration of diethylphosphoro-dithioic acid in the production of phorate.
K040—Wastewater treatment sludge from the production of phorate.
K041—Wastewater treatment sludge from the production of toxaphene.
K042—Heavy ends or distillation residues from the distillation of tetrachlorobenzene in the production of 2,4,5-T.
K043—2,6-Dichlorophenol waste from the production of 2,4-D.
K095—Distillation bottoms from the production of 1,1,1-trichloroethane.
K096—Heavy ends from the heavy ends column from the production of 1,1,1-trichloroethane.
K097—Vacuum stripper discharge from the chlordane chlorinator in the production of chlordane.
K098—Untreated process wastewater from the production of toxaphene.
K105—Separated aqueous stream from the reactor product washing step in the production of chlorobenzenes.

§ 261.33(e) Wastes

P002—1-Acetyl-2-thiourea
P003—Acrolein
P007—5-(Aminoethyl)-3-isoxazolol
P008—4-Aminopyridine
P014—Thiophenol
P026—1-(o-Chlorophenyl)thiourea
P027—Propanenitrile, 3-chloro
P029—Copper cyanides
P040—O,O-Diethyl o-pyrazinyl phosphorothioate
P043—Diisopropyl fluorophosphate
P044—Dimethoate
P049—2,4-Dithiobiuret
P054—Aziridine
P057—Fluoracetamide
P060—Isodrin
P062—Hexaethyltetraphosphate
P066—Methomyl
P067—2-Methylaziridine
P072—Alpha-naphthylthiourea (ANTU)
P074—Nickel cyanide
P085—Octamethylpyrophosphoramide
P098—Potassium cyanide
P104—Silver cyanide
P106—Sodium cyanide
P107—Strontium sulfide
P111—Tetraethylpyrophosphate
P112—Tetranitromethane
P113—Thallic oxide
P114—Thallium (I) selenite

§ 261.33(f) Wastes

U002—Acetone
U003—Acetonitrile
U005—o-Acetylaminofluorene
U008—Acrylic acid
U011—Amitrole
U014—Auramine
U015—Azaserine
U020—Benzenesulfonyl chloride
U021—Benzidine
U023—Benzotrichloride
U025—Dichloroethyl ether
U026—Chlornaphazine
U028—Bis(2-ethylhexyl)phthalate
U032—Calcium chromate
U035—Chlorambucil
U047—Beta-chloronaphthalene
U049—4-Chloro-o-toluidine, hydrochloride
U057—Cyclohexanone
U058—Cyclophosphamide
U059—Daunomycin
U060—DDD
U062—Diallate
U070—o-Dichlorobenzene
U073—Dichlorobenzidene, 3,3-
U080—Methylene chloride
U083—Dichloropropane, 1,2-
U092—Dimethylamine
U093—Dimethylaminoazobenzene
U094—Dimethylbenz(a)anthracene,7,12-
U095—Dimethylbenzidine,3,3'-
U097—Dimethylcarbamoyl chloride
U098—Dimethylhydrazine, 1,1-
U099—Dimethylhydrazine, 1,2-
U101—Dimethylphenol, 2,4-
U106—Dinitrotoluene, 2,6-
U107—Di-n-octyl phthalate
U109—1,2,-Diphenylhydrazine
U110—Dipropylamine
U111—Di-N-Propylnitrosamine
U114—Ethylenebis-(dithiocarbamic acid)
U116—Ethylene thiourea
U119—Ethyl methanesulfonate
U127—Hexachlorobenzene
U128—Hexachlorobutadiene
U131—Hexachloroethane
U135—Hydrogen sulfide
U138—Methyl iodide
U140—Isobutyl alcohol
U142—Kepone
U143—Lasiocarpine
U144—Lead acetate
U146—Lead subacetate
U147—Maleic anhydride
U149—Malononitrile
U150—Melphalan
U161—Methyl isobutyl ketone
U162—Methyl methacrylate
U163—N-Methyl-N-nitro-N-nitrosoguanidine
U164—Methylthiouracil
U165—Naphthalene
U168—Napthylamine, 2-
U169—Nitrobenzene
U170—p-Nitrophenol
U172—N-Nitroso-di-n-butylamine
U173—N-Nitroso-diethanolamine
U174—N-Nitroso-diethylamine
U176—N-Nitroso-N-ethylurea
U178—N-Nitroso-N-methylurethane
U179—N-Nitrosopiperidine
U189—Phosphorus sulfide
U193—1,3-Propane sultone
U196—Pyridine
U203—Safrole
U205—Selenium disulfide
U206—Streptozotocin
U208—Terachloroethane, 1,1,1,2-
U213—Tetrahydrofuran
U214—Thallium (I) acetate
U215—Thallium (I) carbonate
U216—Thallium (I) chloride
U217—Thallium (I) nitrate
U218—Thioacetamide
U235—Tris (2,3-Dibromopropyl) phosphate
U239—Xylene
U244—Thiram

<u>Section A-VI- Third-third wastes (268.12)</u> (proposed effective date May 8,1990)

Refer to 40 CFR Part 268.12 (also Table G-5) for a list of the wastes proposed to be listed in the third-third. Further requirements have not been developed to date.

Part B- General Requirements and Operation Status

<u>Section B-I- General Requirements Applicable To All Facilities</u>

If the facility generates any restricted wastes; the treatment residues derived from the treatment of these wastes are also restricted [see 261.3(c)(2)(i)].

If the answer to any or all of questions 1 through 6 below is yes, then the waste is <u>not</u> restricted under the land disposal restrictions program, except as number 4 is applicable.

1. Has the facility been granted a case-by-case extension to the effective date pursuant to 268.5? ___ Yes ___ No

2. Has the facility been granted an exemption from a prohibition, pursuant to a petition under 268.6? ___ Yes ___ No

3. Has the facility applied for a variance from a treatment standard under 268.44? ___ Yes ___ No

4. Are the wastes contaminated soil or debris resulting from a response action taken under CERCLA Sections 104 or 106, or a corrective action required under RCRA? ___ Yes ___ No

If the answer is yes, the following effective dates for prohibitions apply:

- Solvent wastes, except soil and debris are prohibited from land disposal effective November 8,1988

- Solvent contaminated soil or debris is prohibited from land disposal effective November 8,1990. The unit receiving the waste must meet minimum technology standards in 268.5(h)(2).

- Wastes listed in 268.31 and 268.32, where the wastes are contaminated soil or debris are prohibited effective November 8,1990 as long as the disposal unit meets the minimum technology requirements of 268.5(h)(2).

5. Is the facility a small quantity generator of less than 100 kilograms of non-acute hazardous waste per month or less than one kilogram of acute hazardous waste per month as defined in 261.5? ___ Yes ___ No

6. Is the generator a farmer disposing of waste pesticides in accordance with 262.70? ___ Yes ___ No

Table G-5
Third-Third Listed Wastes

§ 268.12 Identification of wastes to be evaluated by May 8, 1990.

(a) EPA will take action under sections 3004(g)(5) and 3004(m) of the Resource Conservation and Recovery Act, by May 8, 1990, for the following wastes (for ease of understanding, the wastes have been listed by the section of 40 CFR Part 261 under which they were listed):

§ 261.32 Wastes

K002—Wastewater treatment sludge from the production of chrome yellow and orange pigments.
K003—Wastewater treatment sludge from the production of molybdate orange pigments.
K005—Wastewater treatment sludge from the production of chrome green pigments.
K006—Wastewater treatment sludge from the production of chrome oxide green pigments (anhydrous and hydrated).
K007—Wastewater treatment sludge from the production of iron blue pigments.
K023—Distillation light ends from the production of phthalic anhydride from naphthalene.
K026—Stripping still tails from the production of methyl ethyl pyridines.
K032—Wastewater treatment sludge from the production of chlordane.
K033—Wastewater and scrub water from the chlorination of cyclopentadiene in the production of chlordane.
K034—Filter solids from the hexachlorocyclopentadiene in the production of chlordane.
K093—Distillation light ends from the production of phthalic anhydride from ortho-xylene.
K094—Distillation bottoms from the production of phthalic anhydride from ortho-xylene.
K100—Waste leaching solution from acid leaching of emission control dust/sludge from secondary lead smelting.

§ 261.33(e) Wastes

P006—Aluminum phosphide
P009—Ammonium picrate
P013—Barium cyanide
P017—Bromoacetone
P021—Calcium cyanide
P022—Carbon disulfide
P023—Chloroacetaldehyde
P024—p-Chloroaniline
P028—Benzyl chloride
P031—Cyanogen
P033—Cyanogen chloride
P034—4,6-Dinitro-o-cyclohexylphenol
P038—Diethylarsine
P042—Epinephrine
P045—Thiofanox
P046—Alpha, alpha-Dimethylphenethylamine
P047—4,6-Dinitro-o-cresol and salts
P051—Endrin
P056—Fluorine
P064—Methyl isocyanate
P065—Mercury fulminate
P073—Nickel carbonyl
P075—Nicotine and salts
P076—Nitric oxide
P077—p-Nitroaniline
P078—Nitrogen dioxide
P088—Endothall
P093—N-Phenylthiourea
P095—Phosgene
P096—Phosphine
P099—Potassium silver cyanide
P101—Propanenitrile
P103—Selenourea
P109—Tetraethyldithiopyrophosphate
P116—Thiosemicarbazide
P118—Trichloromethanethiol
P119—Ammonium vanadate
P121—Zinc cyanide

§ 261.33(f) Wastes

U001—Acetaldehyde
U004—Acetophenone
U006—Acetyl chloride
U017—Benzal chloride
U024—Bis(2-chloroethoxy)methane
U027—Bis(2-chloroisopropyl)ether
U030—Benzene, 1-bromo-4-phenoxy
U033—Carbonyl fluoride
U034—Chloral
U038—Ethyl-4,4'-dichlorobenzilate
U039—4-Chloro-m-cresol
U042—Vinyl ether, 2-chloroethyl
U045—Methyl chloride
U048—o-Chlorophenol
U052—Cresols
U055—Cumene
U056—Cyclohexane
U068—Methane, dibromo
U069—Dibutyl phthalate
U071—m-Dichlorobenzene
U072—p-Dichlorobenzene
U075—Dichlorodifluoromethane
U076—Ethane, 1,1-dichloro-
U079—1,2-Dichlorethylene
U081—2,4-Dichlorophenol
U082—2,6-Dichlorophenol
U084—1,3-Dichloropropene
U085—2,2'-Bioxirane
U087—0,0,-Diethyl-S-methyl-dithiophosphate
U088—Diethyl phthalate
U090—Dihydrosafrole
U091—3,3'-Dimethoxybenzidine
U096—alpha,alpha-Dimethylbenzylhydroxyperoxide
U102—Dimethyl phthalate
U112—Ethyl acetate
U113—Ethyl acrylate
U117—Ethyl ether
U118—Ethylmethacrylate
U120—Fluoranthene
U121—Trichloromonofluoromethane
U123—Formic acid
U125—Furfural
U126—Glycidylaldehyde
U132—Hexachlorophene
U136—Cacodylic acid
U139—Iron dextran
U141—Isosafrole
U145—Lead phosphate
U148—Maleic hydrazide
U152—Methacrylonitrile
U153—Methanethiol
U156—Methyl chlorocarbonate
U160—Methyl ethyl ketone peroxide
U166—1,4-Naphthaquinone
U167—1-Naphthylamine
U181—5-Nitro-o-toluidine
U182—Paraldehyde
U183—Pentachlorobenzene
U184—Pentachloroethane
U186—1,3-Pentadiene
U187—Phenacetin
U190—Phthalic anhydride
U191—2-Picoline
U194—1-Propanamine
U197—p-Benzoquinone
U201—Resorcinol
U202—Saccharin and salts
U204—Selenious acid
U207—1,2,4,5-tetrachlorobenzene
U222—o-Toluidine hydrochloride
U225—Bromoform
U234—Sym-Trinitrobenzene
U236—Trypan blue
U240—2,4-D, salts and esters
U243—Hexachloropropene
U246—Cyanogen bromide
U247—Methoxychlor

Wastes identified as hazardous based on a characteristic alone (i.e., corrosivity, reactivity, ignitability and EP toxicity).

(b) Wastewater residues (less than 1% total organic carbon and less than 1% suspended solids) resulting from the following well-designed and well-operated treatment methods for wastes listed in § 268.10 for which EPA has not promulgated wastewater treatment standards: metals recovery, metals precipitation, cyanide destruction, carbon adsorption, chemical oxidation, steam stripping, biodegradation, and incineration or other direct thermal destruction. The treatment standards applicable to wastes prohibited under §§ 268.30–268.33 of this part still apply.

(c) Leachate derived from the treatment, storage or disposal of wastes listed in § 268.10 for which EPA has not promulgated wastewater treatment standards, and contaminated ground water that contains such wastes. The treatment standards applicable to wastes prohibited under §§ 268.30–268.33 of this Part still apply.

(d) Hazardous wastes listed in § 268.10 which are mixed hazardous/radioactive wastes. The treatment standards applicable to wastes prohibited under §§ 268.30–268.32 of this part still apply.

7. Is the facility (generator, TSD, transporter, etc) diluting a restricted waste or the residual from treatment of a restricted waste as a substitute for adequate treatment? ___ Yes ___ No

   If yes, this is prohibited, refer to 268.3.

8. Is the facility treating a restricted waste in a surface impoundment?

   ___ Yes ___ No

   If yes, refer to 268.4 to determine if the operation is exempted.

9. If the generator, treatment, storage or disposal facility is managing a waste covered by site specific variance from a treatment standard in accordance with 268.44, has the facility complied with the waste analysis requirements under 268.7?

   ___ Yes ___ No

   If no, refer to 268.44(k)

Section B-II- Operation Status

Generators- Refer to Part C for additional requirements
Transporters-Refer to Part D for additional requirements
Treatment, Storage or Disposal facilities- Refer to Part E for additional requirements

If more than one of the above apply refer to each section as noted.

Part C- Generator Requirements

If the answer to any of the following questions is "no", refer to the referenced section of the regulations to document noncompliance.

1. Has the generator tested the waste or an extract developed using the TCLP method [Appendix I of 268] or used knowledge to determine if the wastes produced are restricted [268.7(a)]?

   ___ Yes ___ No

2. Has each shipment of restricted waste, which does not comply with applicable treatment standards [268.32 or RCRA 3004(d)], been accompanied with a notification [268.7(a)(1)]?

   ___ Yes ___ No

3. Does each notification include all of the following items?

   a. EPA hazardous waste number ___ Yes ___ No

   b. Treatment standards and all applicable prohibitions in 268.32 or RCRA Section 3004(d) ___ Yes ___ No

   c. The manifest number associated with the shipment of waste ___ Yes ___ No

   d. Waste analysis data where available ___ Yes ___ No

4. If the generator has determined that he is managing a restricted waste, but the waste meets treatment standards and can be land disposed, is each shipment accompanied with both a notification (as above) and certification as required in 268.7(a)(2)?
___ Yes ___ No

5. If the waste is subject to a case-by-case extension (268.5), exemption (268.6), an extension under 268.1(c)(3), or a nation-wide variance under Subpart C, has the generator forwarded a notice with the waste to the TSD receiving the waste as required in 268.7(a)(3)? ___ Yes ___ No

6. If the generator is managing wastes subject to 268.33 (f) but not 268.3, has the generator submitted a notification with each shipment of waste [268.7(a)(4)]? ___ Yes ___ No

7. If the generator determines that the waste is restricted based solely on knowledge of the waste, is all of the supporting data used to make that determination kept onsite in the files (starting August 8, 1988) [268.7(a)(5)]? ___ Yes ___ No

8. Has the generator retained onsite a copy of all notices, certifications, determinations, waste analysis data, etc., required by Part 268, for the last 5 years (starting August 8,1988) [268.7(a)(6)]? ___ Yes ___ No

9. Has the generator prepared and submitted demonstrations and certifications required by 268.8 to the Regional Administrator and/or TSD facility as applicable? ___ Yes ___ No

10. If the generator is storing wastes for the purpose of accumulation, does the storage comply with the requirements in 262.34 (Storage < 90 days) [268.50(a)(1)]? ___ Yes ___ No

Part D Transporter Requirements

Has the transporter stored manifested shipments of restricted wastes for more than 10 days? ___ Yes ___ No

If yes, refer to 268.50(a)(3).

Part E Treatment, Storage and Disposal Facilities

<u>Section E-I General Requirements Applicable to all Treatment, Storage and Disposal Facilities</u>

If the answer to any of the following questions is "no" refer to the referenced section of the regulations to document noncompliance.

1. Before a facility treats, stores or disposes of a hazardous waste have they obtained a detailed chemical and physical analysis which contains all of the information necessary to treat, store or dispose of the waste in accordance with Part 268, as required in 264.13(a)(1) or 265.13(a)(1)? ___ Yes ___ No

2. Has the waste analysis plan been updated with the methods which will be used to meet the additional requirements for specific waste management methods specified in 268.7 [264.13(b)(6) or 265.13(b)(6)]? ___ Yes ___ No

3. Does the waste analysis plan include the procedures and schedule required in 264.13(b)(7) or 265.13(b)(7) for surface impoundments exempted from land disposal restrictions (treatment impoundments) under 268.4(a)? ___ Yes ___ No

4. Do hazardous waste treatment, storage or disposal facilities store wastes in tanks or containers for the purpose of accumulation to facilitate proper recovery, treatment or disposal?

   a. If so, is each <u>container</u> marked to identify the contents and the date each period of accumulation begins [268.50 (a)(2)(i)] ___ Yes ___ No

   b. If so, is each <u>tank</u> clearly marked with a description of the contents, the quantity of each hazardous waste received and the date each period of accumulation begins (or the required information can be in the operating record) 285.50(a)(2)(ii)? ___ Yes ___ No

5. Does the facility have copies of the notice and/or certification required by generators and treatment facilities for each restricted waste received [268.7(c) and 264.73(b)(11-16) or 265.73(b)(9-14)]? ___ Yes ___ No

6. Has the facility stored restricted wastes onsite for in excess of one year? ___ Yes ___ No

Refer to 268.50(d-f) for exemptions to storage requirements for restricted wastes.

<u>Section E-II Treatment Facility Specific Requirements</u>

If the answer to any of the following questions is "no" refer to the referenced section of the regulations to document noncompliance.

1. Has the treatment facility tested their wastes according to the frequency in the waste analysis plan required by 264.13 or 265.13 [268.7(b)]? ___ Yes ___ No

2. For wastes with treatment standards expressed as concentrations in the waste extract (268.41), has the treatment facility tested treatment residues or an extract of the residues (using the TCLP method in 268 Appendix I) to assure that the residues meet applicable treatment standards [268.7(b)(1)]? ___ Yes ___ No

3. For wastes prohibited under 268.32 or RCRA 3004(d) but without treatment standards, has the treatment facility tested the treatment residues according to generator testing requirements specified in 268.32 [268.7(b)(2)]? ___ Yes ___ No

4. For wastes with treatment standards expressed as concentrations in the waste (268.43), has the facility tested the treatment residues to assure that the residues meet applicable treatment standards [268.7(b)(3)]? ___ Yes ___ No

5. Has a notification complying with the requirements of 268.7(b)(4) been sent with each waste shipment to the land disposal facility? ___ Yes ___ No

6. Has a certification complying with the requirements of 268.7(b)(5) been sent with each shipment of waste or treatment residue of a restricted waste to the land disposal facility when the waste or treatment residue has been treated in compliance with applicable treatment standards? ___ Yes ___ No

7. If the waste or treatment residues do not comply with applicable treatment standards or prohibitions, has the treatment facility sent applicable notice and/or certification with the wastes which are to be stored or treated at a different facility as required in 268.7(b)(6 and 7)? ___ Yes ___ No

8. If the wastes are recyclable materials used in a manner constituting disposal subject to provisions of 266.20(b), has the owner/operator submitted with each shipment a notification and certification in accordance with 268.7(b)(8)? ___ Yes ___ No

9 Has the treatment, recovery or storage facility kept copies of the generator demonstrations (if applicable) and certification in the operating record [268.8(c)]? ___ Yes ___ No

10. Has the treatment or recovery facility certified that wastes have been treated in accordance with the generators demonstration [268.8)(c)(1)]? ___ Yes ___ No

11. Has the treatment, recovery, or storage facility sent a copy of the generators demonstration (if applicable) and certification under 268.8(a)(2) and certification under 268.8(c)(1) (if applicable) to the facility receiving the waste or treatment residues [268.8(c)(2)]? ___ Yes ___ No

Section E-III Disposal Facility Specific Requirements

If the answer to any of the following questions is "no" refer to the referenced section of the regulations to document noncompliance.

1. Does the facility have a record of the quantities (and date of placement) for the wastes disposed as required in 264.73(b)(10) or 265.73(b)(8)? ___ Yes ___ No

2. Has the disposal facility tested the waste or extract of the waste according to the requirements in 268.7(c) to assure that the wastes or treatment residues are in compliance with applicable treatment standards in 268 Subpart D, 268.32 or RCRA Section 3004(d)? ___ Yes ___ No

3. Has the disposal facility tested incoming restricted wastes at the frequency specified in the waste analysis plan required by 264.13 or 265.13 [268.7(c)(2)]? ___ Yes ___ No

4. Does the land disposal unit meet the requirements of 268.5(h)(2), if it is a surface impoundment or landfill? ___ Yes ___ No

5. Has the facility complied with the certification requirements for wastes specified in 268.7(c)(3) and 268.8(d)? ___ Yes ___ No

APPENDIX H

CERCLA CHECKLIST

1. Notification

   a. Has the facility notified the proper regulatory authorities concerning sites of past hazardous substance releases and former hazardous substance storage, treatment and disposal areas [CERCLA 103(a) and (c)]? Yes____ No____

   b. What sites have been listed in any notification?

   ____

   ____

   ____

   ____

2. Unreported Sites

   a. Are there indications of other sites at the facility which may be appropriate for notification (from records review, interviews, evidence of spills, aerial photographs, etc.)? Yes____ No____

   b. List any potentially contaminated sites which have not been reported.

   ____

   ____

   ____

   ____

3. CERCLA Response Actions

   a. (1) Has the preliminary assessment (40 CFR 300.64) been completed? Yes____ No____

   (2) Was the preliminary assessment adequate? Yes____ No____

Appendix H (cont.)

(3) Findings and status:

____

____

____

____

b. (1) Were immediate removals (40 CFR 300.65) conducted at any of the sites? Yes____ No____

(2) Was the removal adequate (verification data)? Yes____ No____

(3) Findings and status:

____

____

____

____

c. (1) Has there been a site evaluation phase and National Priorities List (NPL) determination to assist with any planned removals and/or remedial actions (40 CFR 300.66)? Yes____ No____

(2) Was this evaluation and determination adequate? Yes____ No____

(3) Status:

____

____

____

____

d. (1) Has a Hazardous Ranking System (HRS) score been determined for these sites [40 CFR 300.66(b)]? Yes____ No____

(2) Was this ranking adequate? Yes____ No____

Appendix H (cont.)

(3) Status:

____

____

____

____

e. (1) Was a planned removal or remedial action (40 CFR 300.67 and 68) taken? Yes____ No____

(2) Was this planned removal or remedial action successful? Yes____ No____

(3) Status:

____

____

____

____

4. Comments:

____

____

____

____

____

APPENDIX I
TSCA FORMS

CONFIDENTIALITY NOTES AND DISCUSSIONS

The TSCA Notice of Inspection [Figure I-1] and Inspection Confidentiality Notice [Figure I-2] are presented to the facility owner or agent in charge during the opening conference. These notices inform facility officials of their right to claim as confidential business information any information (documents, physical samples or other material) collected by the inspector.

Authority to Make Confidentiality Claims

The inspector must ascertain whether the facility official, to whom the notices were given, has the authority to make business confidentiality claims for the company. The facility official's signature must be obtained at the appropriate places on the notices certifying that he does or does not have such authority.

- The facility owner is assumed to always have the authority to make business confidentiality claims. In most cases, it is expected that the agent in charge will also have such authority. It is possible that the officials will want to consult with their attorneys (or superiors in the case of agents in charge) regarding this issue.

- If no one at the site has the authority to make business confidentiality claims, a copy of the TSCA Inspection Confidentiality Notice and Notice and Declaration of Confidential Business Information form [Figure I-3] are to be sent to the chief executive officer of the firm within 2 days of the inspection. He will then have 7 calendar days in which to make confidentiality claims.

- The facility official may designate a company official, in addition to the chief executive officer, who should also receive a copy of the notices and any accompanying forms.

FIGURE I-1

EPA	US ENVIRONMENTAL PROTECTION AGENCY WASHINGTON, DC 20460 TOXIC SUBSTANCES CONTROL ACT **NOTICE OF INSPECTION**	Form Approved OMB No. 2070-0007 Expires 3-31-88

1. INVESTIGATION IDENTIFICATION			2. TIME	3. FIRM NAME
DATE	INSPECTOR NO.	DAILY SEQ. NO.		

4. INSPECTOR ADDRESS	5. FIRM ADDRESS

REASON FOR INSPECTION

Under the authority of Section 11 of the Toxic Substances Control Act:

☐ For the purpose of inspecting (including taking samples, photographs, statements, and other inspection activities) an establishment, facility, or other premises in which chemical substances or mixtures or articles containing same are manufactured, processed or stored, or held before or after their distribution in commerce (including records, files, papers, processes, controls, and facilities) and any conveyance being used to transport chemical substances, mixtures, or articles containing same in connection with their distribution in commerce (including records, files, papers, processes, controls, and facilities) bearing on whether the requirements of the Act applicable to the chemical substances, mixtures, or articles within or associated with such premises or conveyance have been complied with.

☐ In addition, this inspection extends to *(Check appropriate blocks)*:

☐ A. Financial data

☐ B. Sales data

☐ C. Pricing data

☐ D. Personnel data

☐ E. Research data

The nature and extent of inspection of such data specified in A through E above is as follows:

INSPECTOR SIGNATURE		RECIPIENT SIGNATURE	
NAME		NAME	
TITLE	DATE SIGNED	TITLE	DATE SIGNED

FIGURE I-2

EPA

US ENVIRONMENTAL PROTECTION AGENCY
WASHINGTON, DC 20460

TOXIC SUBSTANCES CONTROL ACT

TSCA INSPECTION CONFIDENTIALITY NOTICE

Form Approved
OMB No. 2070-0007
Expires 3-31-88

1. INVESTIGATION IDENTIFICATION			2. FIRM NAME
DATE	INSPECTOR NO.	DAILY SEQ. NO.	
3. INSPECTOR NAME			4. FIRM ADDRESS
5. INSPECTOR ADDRESS			
			6. CHIEF EXECUTIVE OFFICER NAME
			7. TITLE

TO ASSERT A CONFIDENTIAL BUSINESS INFORMATION CLAIM

It is possible that EPA will receive public requests for release of the information obtained during inspection of the facility above. Such requests will be handled by EPA in accordance with provisions of the Freedom of Information Act (FOIA), 5 USC 552; EPA regulations issued thereunder, 40 CFR Part 2; and the Toxic Substances Control Act (TSCA), Section 14. EPA is required to make inspection data available in response to FOIA requests unless the Administrator of the Agency determines that the data contain information entitled to confidential treatment or may be withheld from release under other exceptions of FOIA.

Any or all the information collected by EPA during the inspection may be claimed confidential if it relates to trade secrets or commercial or financial matters that you consider to be confidential business information. If you assert a CBI claim, EPA will disclose the information only to the extent, and by means of the procedures set forth in the regulations (cited above) governing EPA's treatment of confidential business information. Among other things, the regulations require that EPA notify you in advance of publicly disclosing any information you have claimed as confidential business information.

A confidential business information (CBI) claim may be asserted at any time. You may assert a CBI claim prior to, during, or after the information is collected. The declaration form was developed by the Agency to assist you in asserting a CBI claim. If it is more convenient for you to assert a CBI claim on your own stationery or by marking the individual documents or samples "TSCA confidential business information," it is not necessary for you to use this form. The inspector will be glad to answer any questions you may have regarding the Agency's CBI procedures.

While you may claim any collected information or sample as confidential business information, such claims are unlikely to be upheld if they are challenged unless the information meets the following criteria:

1. Your company has taken measures to protect the confidentiality of the information, and it intends to continue to take such measures.

2. The information is not, and has not been, reasonably obtainable without your company's consent by other persons (other than governmental bodies) by use of legitimate means (other than discovery based on showing of special need in a judicial or quasi-judicial proceeding).

3. The information is not publicly available elsewhere.

4. Disclosure of the information would cause substantial harm to your company's competitive position.

At the completion of the inspection, you will be given a receipt for all documents, samples, and other materials collected. At that time, you may make claims that some or all of the information is confidential business information.

If you are not authorized by your company to assert a CBI claim, this notice will be sent by certified mail, along with the receipt for documents, samples, and other materials to the Chief Executive Officer of your firm within 2 days of this date. The Chief Executive Officer must return a statement specifying any information which should receive confidential treatment.

The statement from the Chief Executive Officer should be addressed to:

and mailed by registered, return-receipt requested mail within 7 calendar days of receipt of this Notice. Claims may be made any time after the inspection, but inspection data will not be entered into the special security system for TSCA confidential business information until an official confidentiality claim is made. The data will be handled under the agency's routine security system unless and until a claim is made.

TO BE COMPLETED BY FACILITY OFFICIAL RECEIVING THIS NOTICE:		If there is no one on the premises of the facility who is authorized to make business confidentiality claims for the firm, a copy of this Notice and other inspection materials will be sent to the company's chief executive officer. If there is another company official who should also receive this information, please designate below.
I have received and read the notice		
SIGNATURE		NAME
NAME		TITLE
TITLE	DATE SIGNED	ADDRESS

FIGURE I-3

US ENVIRONMENTAL PROTECTION AGENCY
WASHINGTON, DC 20460

TOXIC SUBSTANCES CONTROL ACT

EPA

Form Approved
OMB No. 2070-0007
Expires 5-31-89

DECLARATION OF CONFIDENTIAL BUSINESS INFORMATION

1. INVESTIGATION IDENTIFICATION			2. FIRM NAME
DATE	INSPECTOR NO.	DAILY SEQ. NO.	
3. INSPECTOR ADDRESS			4. FIRM ADDRESS

INFORMATION DESIGNATED AS CONFIDENTIAL BUSINESS INFORMATION

NO.	DESCRIPTION

ACKNOWLEDGEMENT BY CLAIMANT

The undersigned acknowledges that the information described above is designated as Confidential Business Information under Section 14(c) of the Toxic Substances Control Act. The undersigned further acknowledges that he/she is authorized to make such claims for his/her firm.

The undersigned understands that challenges to confidentiality claims may be made, and that claims are not likely to be upheld unless the information meets the following guidelines: (1) The company has taken measures to protect the confidentiality of the information and it intends to continue to take such measures; (2) The information is not, and has not been reasonably attainable without the company's consent by other persons (other than governmental bodies) by use of legitimate means (other than discovery based on a showing of special need in a judicial or quasi-judicial proceeding); (3) The information is not publicly available elsewhere; and (4) Disclosure of the information would cause substantial harm to the company's competitive position.

INSPECTOR SIGNATURE		CLAIMANT SIGNATURE	
NAME		NAME	
TITLE	DATE SIGNED	TITLE	DATE SIGNED

EPA Form 7740-2 (12-82)

INSPECTION FILE

Appendix I (cont.)

Confidentiality Discussion

Officials should be informed of the procedures and requirements that EPA must follow in handling TSCA confidential business information. The inspector should explain that these procedures were established to protect the companies subject to TSCA and cover the following points during the discussion.

- Data may be claimed confidential business information during the closing conference if a person authorized to make such claims is onsite at the facility.

- It is suggested that a company official accompany the inspector during the inspection to facilitate designation (or avoidance, if possible) of confidential business data.

- A detailed receipt for all documents, photographs, physical samples, and other materials [Figure I-4] collected during the inspection will be issued at the closing conference.

- An authorized person may make immediate declarations that some or all of the information is confidential business information. This is done by completing the Declaration of Confidential Business Information form. Each item claimed must meet all four of the criteria shown on the TSCA Inspection Confidentiality Notice.

- If no authorized person is available onsite, a copy of the notices, along with the Receipt for Samples and Documents, will be sent by certified, return-receipt-requested mail to the Chief Executive Officer of the firm and to another company official, if one has been designated.

Appendix I (cont.)

Four copies are made of the Declaration of Confidential Information form and distributed to:

- Facility owner or agent in charge
- Other company official (if designated)
- Document Control Officer
- Inspection report

FIGURE I-4

EPA	US ENVIRONMENTAL PROTECTION AGENCY WASHINGTON, DC 20460 TOXIC SUBSTANCES CONTROL ACT **RECEIPT FOR SAMPLES AND DOCUMENTS**	Form Approved. OMB No. 2070-0007 Approval expires 3-31-88

1. INVESTIGATION IDENTIFICATION			2. FIRM NAME
DATE	INSPECTOR NO.	DAILY SEQ. NO.	
3. INSPECTOR ADDRESS			4. FIRM ADDRESS

The documents and samples of chemical substances and/or mixtures described below were collected in connection with the administration and enforcement of the Toxic Substances Control Act.

RECEIPT OF THE DOCUMENT(S) AND/OR SAMPLE(S) DESCRIBED IS HEREBY ACKNOWLEDGED:

NO.	DESCRIPTION

OPTIONAL:

DUPLICATE OR SPLIT SAMPLES: REQUESTED AND PROVIDED ☐ NOT REQUESTED ☐

INSPECTOR SIGNATURE		RECIPIENT SIGNATURE	
NAME		NAME	
TITLE	DATE SIGNED	TITLE	DATE SIGNED

EPA Form 7740-1 (12-82)

INSPECTOR'S FILE

APPENDIX J
TSCA PCB CHECKLIST

PCB COMPLIANCE INSPECTION REPORT
(40 CFR PART 761)

A. FACILITY SUMMARY

Name and address of facility (include county, state and zip code)

____

____

____

________________	________________	________________
(Responsible Official)	(Title)	(Phone)
________________	________________	________________
(Facility Representative)	(Title)	(Phone)

____

Type of facility (utility, salvage yard, etc.)

B. INSPECTION/REVIEW

Inspected by:	________________ (Signature)	________________ (Agency and Date)
Reviewed by:	________________ (Signature)	________________ (Agency and Date)

COMMENTS: __________________________________

____

____

____

____

____

____

____

____

____

____

____

Appendix J (cont.)

C. INVENTORY

1. As of July 2, 1978, did facility contain in-service, stored for future use, or disposal:

   a. 50 or more large high- or low-voltage PCB capacitors? Yes___No___N/A___C/A___*

   b. One or more PCB transformers? Yes___No___N/A___C/A___

   c. 45 kgs (99.4 lbs.) or more PCB chemicals, substances or mixtures? Yes___No___N/A___C/A___

2. Disposition of PCB items at time of inspection:

Identify source of the above information (company records, manufacturer's labels, etc.)

____

____

____

* *N/A - Not applicable*
C/ A - Comments attached

Appendix J (cont.)

If any PCB items are not properly marked, describe deficiencies below. Description must include information on amount of PCBs involved.

____

____

____

____

3. If company has PCB-contaminated transformers, explain how company determined the transformers contained 50 to 500 ppm PCB.

____

____

4. Does the facility have any other PCB items (electromagnets, hydraulic systems, etc.)? Yes___No___N/A___C/A___

If yes, list number and type of item; whether it is in-service, storage or sent to disposal; and if it is properly marked.

____

____

____

5. a. Were there observations of leaks or spills or any sign of improper disposal of PCB substances or mixtures. Yes___No___N/A___C/A___

   b. If yes, document, sample and describe below. Description must include information on amount of PCBs involved.

   ____

   ____

   ____

6. a. Was there any indication that waterways in the vicinity have been contaminated by spills, leaks or improper disposal? Yes___No___N/A___C/A___

Appendix J (cont.)

b. If yes, document, sample and describe below. Description must include information on the amount of PCBs involved and the name of the waterway.

____

____

____

7. a. Were samples collected for analysis of PCB residual concentration? Yes___No___N/A___C/A___

b. If yes, describe below.

____

____

D. STORAGE AND HANDLING

1. Location:

a. Does the facility have its own storage site for PCBs? Yes___No___N/A___C/A___

b. If the storage site is not within the boundary of the facility, give the site's name and address.

____

____

2. Does storage site meet physical requirements [761.42(a) - Physical Requirements] Yes___No___N/A___C/A___

a. Provide protection from rainfall? Yes___No___N/A___C/A___

b. Meet floor requirements with 6-inch continuous curbing? Yes___No___N/A___C/A___

c. Meet containment volume requirements? Yes___No___N/A___C/A___

Appendix J (cont.)

(1) What is total containment volume of storage site?

____

(Length x Width x Height)

(2) What is the internal volume of the largest PCB article or container stored within the storage site?

____

(3) What is the total internal volume of all PCB articles and containers within the storage site?

____

Is item 1 greater than two times item 2? Yes___No___N/A___C/A___

or

25% of item 3? Yes___No___N/A___C/A___

d. (1) Is the area within the curbed area void of drains, valves, expansion joints or other openings? Yes___No___N/A___C/A___

(2) If no, document location of opening, drainage patch and ultimate disposal location in logbook and describe below.

____

____

____

e. Is storage site located above the 100-year flood water elevation level? Yes___No___N/A___C/A___

f. Are storage areas adequately marked? Yes___No___N/A___C/A___

g. Any deficiencies in permanent storage facility must be documented with photographs and described below. Description must include amount of PCBs involved.

____

____

Appendix J (cont.)

3. Containers:

a. Are all PCB items which are located within storage areas dated [761.65(c)(8)]? Yes___No___N/A___C/A___

b. Do PCB containers comply with DOT specifications except as noted in 3c and 3d below [761.65(c)(6)]? Yes___No___N/A___C/A___

c. Are any non-liquid PCBs being stored in containers larger than those specified in DOT regulations [761.65(c)(6)]? Yes___No___N/A___C/A___

(1) Do these containers provide as much protection and have the same strength as DOT containers? Yes___No___N/A___C/A___

d. Are any liquid PCBs being stored in containers larger than those specified in DOT regulations [761.42(c)(7)]? Yes___No___N/A___C/A___

(1) Do containers comply with OSHA specifications? Yes___No___N/A___C/A___

(2) Has SPCC plan been prepared and implemented? Yes___No___N/A___C/A___

4. Storage Site Operations:

a. Are all PCB items arranged so they can be located by date? [761.65(c)(8)] Yes___No___N/A___C/A___

b. Do observations indicate good housekeeping procedures? Yes___No___N/A___C/A___

Appendix J (cont.)

c. Is moveable equipment decontaminated by approved procedures? Yes___No___N/A___C/A___

d. Are PCB items stored and handled in a manner that protects them from accidental breakage or damage? Yes___No___N/A___C/A___

5. Other Storage Areas:

a. Are any of the following temporarily being stored outside the prescribed area: [761.65(c)(1)]

(1) Nonleaking PCB articles and PCB equipment? Yes___No___N/A___C/A___

Is date removed from service noted on the article or equipment? Yes___No___N/A___C/A___

Have they been there fewer than 30 days? Yes___No___N/A___C/A___

(2) Leaking PCB articles and PCB equipment placed in a non-leaking PCB container? Yes___No___N/A___C/A___

Is the date removed from service noted on the container? Yes___No___N/A___C/A___

Have they been there fewer than 30 days? Yes___No___N/A___C/A___

(3) Containers of liquid PCBs at concentrations of 50 to 500 ppm? Yes___No___N/A___C/A___

Is SPCC plan available pertaining to temporary storage area? Yes___No___N/A___C/A___

Appendix J (cont.)

Are containers marked to indicate the liquid does not exceed 500 ppm? Yes___No___N/A___C/A___

Is the date removed from service noted on the containers? Yes___No___N/A___C/A___

Have containers been there fewer than 30 days? Yes___No___N/A___C/A___

b. Are there any large high voltage capacitors or PCB contaminated transformers next to the storage site [761.65(c)(2)]? Yes___No___N/A___C/A___

Are they on pallets? Yes___No___N/A___C/A___

Is there adequate space within the storage site to contain 10% of the volume of these capacitors and transformers? Yes___No___N/A___C/A___

c. Any deficiencies in temporary storage must be documented with photographs and described below. Descriptions must include information on the amount of PCBs involved.

____

____

E. <u>DECONTAMINATION</u>

1. Does the facility drain or cleanse PCB transformers or other equipment containing PCB substances or mixtures prior to disposal or decontaminate movable equipment? Yes___No___N/A___C/A___

2. Does the facility claim to have an exemption from incineration [761.60(e)] or exemptions under 761.80? Yes___No___N/A___C/A___

Appendix J (cont.)

3. Is the drainage and solvent filling site adequate to protect against spills and leaks and consequent contamination of surrounding areas and waterways? Yes___No___N/A___C/A___

4. Do solvents to be used for removing PCBs contain less than 50 ppm PCBs [761.79]? Yes___No___N/A___C/A___

5. Was a sample of the solvent which was used for PCB removal obtained? Yes___No___N/A___C/A___

6. Was the rinse volume of the dilutant approximately equal to 10% of the container's total volume [761.79(a)]? Yes___No___N/A___C/A___

7. Are PCB transformers completely filled with solvent and allowed to stand for at least 18 hours before being drained [761.60(b)(1)]? Yes___No___N/A___C/A___

8. Are the drained PCB chemical substances or PCB solvent mixtures properly disposed of or stored? Yes___No___N/A___C/A___

9. Are solvents or materials which have been used for decontamination of PCB equipment disposed of or stored in the same manner as PCB mixtures? Yes___No___N/A___C/A___

10. If decontamination procedures were not observed during inspection, did facility representative demonstrate knowledge of proper decontamination procedures? Yes___No___N/A___C/A___

11. Does facility have written decontamination procedures? Yes___No___N/A___C/A___

Appendix J (cont.)

12. Any deficiencies in the decontamination procedures must be described below.

____

____

____

F. <u>RECORDKEEPING</u>

1. Do records indicate the date PCBs were:

   a. Removed from service? Yes___No___N/A___C/A___

   b. Placed in storage for disposal? Yes___No___N/A___C/A___

   c. Placed in transport for disposal? Yes___No___N/A___C/A___

2. Do records indicate the quantity of the above items as follows:

   a. The weights of PCBs and PCB items in PCB containers? Yes___No___N/A___C/A___

   b. The identification of contents of PCB containers? Yes___No___N/A___C/A___

   c. The number of PCB transformers? Yes___No___N/A___C/A___

   d. The weight of PCBs in PCB transformers? Yes___No___N/A___C/A___

   e. The number of PCB large, high- and low-voltage capacitors? Yes___No___N/A___C/A___

3. Do records indicate the quantities of PCBs remaining in service broken down as follows:

   a. The weight of PCBs and PCB items in PCB containers? Yes___No___N/A___C/A___

Appendix J (cont.)

b. The identification of contents of PCB containers? Yes___ No___ N/A___ C/A___

c. The number of PCB transformers? Yes___ No___ N/A___ C/A___

d. The weight of PCBs in PCB transformers? Yes___ No___ N/A___ C/A___

e. The number of PCB large, high- and low-voltage capacitors? Yes___ No___ N/A___ C/A___

4. a. Is the information requested in paragraphs 1, 2 and 3 above compiled in an annual document? (This document must be prepared by July 1 and cover the previous calendar year.) Yes___ No___ N/A___ C/A___

b. List years for which annual documents are available.

________ ________ ________ ________ ________

5. Any deficiencies in recordkeeping must be described below including information on amount of PCBs involved.

____

____

6. If owners or operators maintain more than one facility that contains PCBs in the quantities prescribed in paragraph C 1, are records and documents kept at a single location? Yes___ No___ N/A___ C/A___

If yes, list location. ______________________________

7. Do records provide information on a PCB disposal facility? Yes___ No___ N/A___ C/A___

Appendix J (cont.)

If yes, list name, location and type of facility (i.e., incinerator, boiler, landfill, etc.)

____

____

____

G. DISPOSAL

1. Are PCB articles or containers, which were stored for disposal after January 1, 1983, disposed of within 1 year? Yes____ No____

2. Were items stored for disposal before January 1, 1983? Yes____ No____

   a. Were they disposed of by January 1, 1984? Yes____ No____

3. What items are disposed and state the disposal methods?

____

____

APPENDIX K

TSCA SECTIONS 5 AND 8 CHECKLIST

Table K-1

GLOSSARY OF TERMS AND ACRONYMS:
TOXIC SUBSTANCES CONTROL ACT SECTIONS 5 AND 8

SECTION 5.	"New Chemicals"
	(Note: TSCA Chemicals do not include pesticides, drugs, cosmetics, firearms, etc., by definition)
PMS	Premanufacture Notification to EPA is required for all "new" TSCA chemicals, i.e., those not listed on the §8(b) existing chemical inventory.
SNURs	Significant New Use Rules require subsequent notification to EPA when usage/exposure changes (i.e., in addition to PMN).
NOC	Notice of Commencement to Agency is required before manufacture begins (after PMN review period has expired).
TME	Test Marketing Exemption to PMN requirement can be obtained on application to and approval by EPA - usually subject to specific restrictions.
R & D	Research and Development Exemption - automatic exemption, does not require Agency review or approval.
SECTION 5(e) Order	An administrative order prohibiting or limiting the manufacture, processing, distribution, use and/or disposal of a chemical for which a PMN is required because there is insufficient information to permit evaluation.
"*Bona fide*" Inquiry	Inquiry by manufacturer that intends to manufacture a specific chemical to determine whether that chemical is on the confidential portion of the Section 8(b) inventory. (Manufacturer must establish intent to manufacture to get reply from EPA.) If the chemical in question is not on the inventory and no PMN is filed subsequently, the manufacturer may be targeted for an inspection.
SECTION 5(f) Order/Rule	An administrative order or rule prohibiting/limiting the manufacture, etc., of a chemical for which a PMN is required because there is a reasonable basis to conclude that such activities present an unreasonable risk to health/environment.

Table K-1 (cont.)

SECTION 8	"Existing Chemicals"
PAIR	Preliminary Assessment Information Reporting Rules Promulgated under Section 8(a) Level A - require reporting to Agency of production, uses and exposure of specific chemicals or classes of chemicals.
ITC	Interagency Testing Committee - designates chemicals listed in PAIR rules as well as some of the chemicals in section 8(d) rules. ITC is established under section 4(e) of TSCA. It also recommends chemicals for inclusion in testing rules under section 4(a).
SECTION 8(a) Level A Inspection	An inspection to determine compliance with PAIR rules.
SECTION 8(b) Inventory	Inventory compiled by EPA of all chemicals manufactured/processed in U.S. that were manufactured, imported or processed in the period 1975-77. Chemicals for which PMN is submitted are added to inventory when manufacturing/processing commences (i.e., upon receipt of NOC). A major updating of the inventory will be undertaken in 1986.
SECTION 8(c) Inspection	An inspection to determine whether the manufacturer, processor, etc., has kept required records concerning allegations of previously unknown significant adverse reactions to health or environment.
SECTION 8(d) Inspection	An inspection to determine compliance with rules requiring submission of health and safety studies for chemicals or classes of chemicals designated by the Agency or the ITC.
SECTION 8(e) Inspection	An inspection to determine whether the manufacturer, processor, etc., has properly notified EPA (within 15 days of knowledge) regarding chemicals that present a substantial risk to health or environment.

Table K-2

INSPECTION NO.	______________
FACILITY/CITY	______________
INSPECTION DATE	______________

TSCA SECTIONS 5 AND 8 CHECKLIST

		Completed	#
I.	Inspection Management	________	
II.	Nature of Facility	________	
III.	§5 General Information	________	
IV.	*Bona fide* Review	________	_____
V.	Specific PMN Review	________	_____
VI.	5(e) and 5(f) Order	________	_____
VII.	TME Review	________	_____
VIII.	TSCA §5 Research & Development (R&D)	________	_____
IX.	Low Volume Exemption (LVE)	________	_____
X.	Polymer Exemption	________	_____
XI.	Significant New Use Rule (SNUR)	________	_____
XII.	TSCA §8(a) Level A and 8(d) Compliance Review	________	_____
XIII.	TSCA §8(c) and 8(e) Compliance Review	________	

INSPECTION NO. ________________
FACILITY/CITY ________________
INSPECTION DATE ________________

TSCA SECTION 5/8 CHECKLIST

I. INSPECTION MANAGEMENT (Attach additional information as necessary)

1. Name and Address of Facility: ________________________
____
____

2. Telephone No.: ______________ DUNS No.: ______________

3. Telephone Contact (Name, Title and Date):
____ ______________

4. Written Notification (Date): ________________________ [Exhibit 1]

5. Date and Time of Inspection: ______________ ______________

6. Inspection Team: ________________________ __________ (lead)
________________________ __________
________________________ __________

7. TSCA Notice of Inspection Issued to (Name, Title):
____ [Exhibit 2]

8. TSCA ICN Notice Issued to (Name, Title):
____ [Exhibit 3]

9. Other Company Inspection Participants (Names, Titles):
1. ____
2. ____
3. ____
4. ____
5. ____

10. Type of Inspection: ____Routine ____Special Request
____Followup

INSPECTION NO. ____________________
FACILITY/CITY ____________________
INSPECTION DATE ____________________

INSPECTION MANAGEMENT (cont.)

11. Scope of Inspection (List by Federal Register, CAS No. or other designation):

___ Gen. Inv.:	__________	___ 8(a) L(A):	____________________
___ Spec. PMN:	__________		____________________
	__________	___ 8(b):	____________________
	__________	___ 8(c):	____________________
___ TMEs:	__________	___ 8(d):	____________________
___ LVEs:	__________	___ 8(e):	____________________
___ PEs:	__________	___ Sect. 4:	____________________
___ 5(e)/5(f):	__________	___ Other:	____________________
___ BFs:	__________	___ Other:	____________________

12. Walk-through: Yes____ No____
Areas: ____

13. TSCA Receipt for Samples and Documents Issued to:

(Name and Title) ____ [Exhibit 4]

TSCA Declaration of CBI Issued to:

(Name and Title) ____ [Exhibit 5]

14. Followup Information Requested: Yes____ No____
Date Received: ________________

15. Remarks:

INSPECTION NO. ______________
FACILITY/CITY ______________
INSPECTION DATE ______________

II. NATURE OF THE FACILITY (Attach additional information as necessary):

1. Facility History, Organization and Corporate Relationship:

2. Scope, Size and Functions of the Facility:

3. Facility Description and Layout:

INSPECTION NO. ________________
FACILITY/CITY ________________
INSPECTION DATE ________________

III. TSCA §5 GENERAL CHEMICAL INVENTORY COMPLIANCE REVIEW

A. Interviewee(s): 1. ____________________________
2. ____________________________

B. Chemicals: __ Manufactured __ Imported __ Processed __ Other

1. Prepared list of chemicals available by CASR No. Yes____ No____
2. List verified against company business records: Yes____ No____
   What records: ____________________________
3. Records reviewed in lieu of prepared list (type and dates):
   ____
   ____
4. Chemicals reviewed on open inventory by ________________
   via ____________________________

   Date search completed: ________________
   No. unlisted chemicals: ________________ (attach list)
   Date unlisted chemicals sent to OCM: ________________
   Date reply: ____________________________
   No. chemicals unlisted in conf. inventory: ________________
   Date followup with facility: ________________ (attach copy)
   Date reply: ________ Status: ________________
   ____

5. Additional Notes and Remarks: ________________
   ____
   ____
   ____
   ____
   ____
   ____

INSPECTION NO. ____________
FACILITY/CITY ____________
INSPECTION DATE ____________

IV. TSCA §5 *BONA FIDE* REVIEW:

A. Interviewee(s): (1) ____________
(2) ____________

B. 1. EPA Accession No. ____________
2. Name of chemical: ____________
3. CAS Registry No. if known: ____________
4. Date of submission: ____________
5. Date of response by Agency: ____________
6. Was chemical found on confidential inventory? ____________
If yes, did company commercialize product? ____________
7. What records were reviewed during inspection? ____________
____
____
8. Remarks: ____________
____
____

C. 1. Was PMN filed for chemical? ____________
2. Date of submission: ____________ PMN No.: ____________
3. Was NOC submitted: ____________
4. Was PMN reviewed during this inspection? ____________
5. Remarks: ____________
____
____
____
____
____

INSPECTION NO. ______________
FACILITY/CITY ______________
INSPECTION DATE ______________

V. SPECIFIC PREMANUFACTURE NOTIFICATION (PMN) COMPLIANCE REVIEW - (One PMN per form)

A. Interviewees: (1) ______________________________
(2) ______________________________

B. General Information:

1. PMN No.: ______ 90-day Date: ______ NOC Date: _______
2. Advance copy available: Yes____ No____
   Copy at site: Yes____ No____
3. Chemical Name: ______________________________
   ____
4. Other Names: ______________________________
5. Use at site: ___ Manufacture ___ Import ___ Process
   ___ R&D ___ Other

C. Production Compliance:

1. Date of first commercial manufacture or import (circle): _____
   How verified (records reviewed and dates): ______________
   ____
   ____
2. Dates and amounts of R & D Production: (1) ______________
   Use ______________
   (2) ______________
   Use ______________
   (Attach if more than 2 R&D batches)
   How verified (records reviewed and dates): ______________
   ____
   ____
   ____
   ____

INSPECTION NO. ______________
FACILITY/CITY ______________
INSPECTION DATE ______________

V. SPECIFIC PREMANUFACTURE NOTIFICATION (PMN) COMPLIANCE REVIEW (cont.)

Mass balance and disposition of R&D material: ______________

3. PMN and R&D records complete as per 40 CFR Part 720.78:

Yes____ No____

Description of PMN records: ______________

Description of R&D records: ______________

4. Additional remarks: ______________

INSPECTION NO. ____________
FACILITY/CITY ____________
INSPECTION DATE ____________

V. SPECIFIC PREMANUFACTURE NOTIFICATION (PMN) COMPLIANCE REVIEW (cont.)

D. Technical Content

1. Chemical identity: ____________________
____

2. Monomer verifications (for polymers only): ____________
____

3. Impurities: ____________________
____

4. By-products: ____________________
____

5. Use(s): ____________________
____

6. Operation: ____________________
____

7. Exposure: ____________________
____

8. Env. Release: ____________________
____

9. Processing: ____________________
____

10. Test data: ____________________
____

11. Additional Information: ____________________
____
____
____
____
____
____

INSPECTION NO. ______________
FACILITY/CITY ______________
INSPECTION DATE ______________

VI. SPECIFIC PMN-§5(e) and 5(f) ORDER

A. Interviewee(s): (1) ______________________________
(2) ______________________________

B. Compliance Restrictive Elements:

Was PMN chemical in commercial production at time of inspection?
Yes____ No____

1. Testing Trigger

Specified Testing Production Volume Trigger ____________
Was a Trigger volume reached? Yes____ No____
If yes, when ______________________________
If yes, has prescribed testing been initiated? Yes____ No____
If yes, was commercial production stopped? Yes____ No____

Remarks: ______________________________
____

2. Gloves

Was glove testing a requirement? Yes____ No____
If yes, was imperviosity testing conducted? Yes____ No____

Was testing conducted by PMN Submitter/Contractor (circle one)?
Did testing protocol meet Agency guidelines? Yes____ No____
Were gloves demonstrated to be impervious? Yes____ No____
Was glove usage observed? Yes____ No____

Remarks: ______________________________
____

INSPECTION NO. ____________________
FACILITY/CITY ____________________
INSPECTION DATE ____________________

VI. SPECIFIC PMN-§5(e) and 5(f) ORDER (cont.)

3. Protective Devices and Hazard Communication

What were protective clothing requirements? ______________

____

Were employees observed to be wearing protective clothing as described in consent order? Yes____ No____

Were other protective measures and equipment in use by employees as described in consent order? Yes____ No____

Describe: ______________________________________

Were employees instructed and trained in the proper use of protective equipment and measures? Yes____ No____

How was this documented? ____________________________

Were affected employees notified in training sessions with respect to the hazards, dangers and concerns of the PMN chemical? Yes____ No____

Were signed attendance sheets available for review by the inspector? Yes____ No____

Had all operators received appropriate training? Yes____ No____

How verified: ______________________________________

____

4. Waste Disposal

What was specified disposal requirement? ______________

____

Was evidence of proper disposal present? Yes____ No____

How verified: ______________________________________

____

INSPECTION NO. ____________
FACILITY/CITY ____________
INSPECTION DATE ____________

VI. SPECIFIC PMN-§5(e) and 5(f) ORDER (cont.)

5. Label Requirements

What was type size specification? ____________
Actual type size on label: ____________
Remarks: ____________

6. Evidence for Customer Compliance

Was there evidence of customer compliance with Agency restrictions on use as described in manufacturer's letter to final users? Yes____ No____

Remarks: ____________

____

7. General (Cleanliness and Housekeeping)

Was the production area of PMN Chemical clean and well-maintained? Yes____ No____

Was there any evidence of spillage or environmental release? Yes____ No____

Remarks: ____________

____

INSPECTION NO. ____________________
FACILITY/CITY ____________________
INSPECTION DATE ____________________

VII. TSCA §5 TEST MARKETING EXEMPTION

A. Interviewees: (1) ____
(2) ____

B. General

1. TME No.: __________ Date of Receipt: ________________

2. Chemical: ______________________________________
CASR No.: ______________________________________
Verification of Chemical Structure: ________________
____

C. Restrictions

1. Period of Approved Use: __________ to ________________
Verified via: ______________________________
____
____

2. Production Volume Allowed: _________ Actual ___________
Verified via: ______________________________
____
____

3. Number of Customers: Allowed: ________ Actual ________
Verified via: ______________________________
____
____

INSPECTION NO. ____________

FACILITY/CITY ____________

INSPECTION DATE ____________

VII. TSCA §5 TEST MARKETING EXEMPTION (cont.)

4. Use: Allowed: ____________ Actual ____________

Verified via: ____________

5. Worker/Consumer Exposure: Actual: ____________

Allowed: ____________

Verified via: ____________

6. Additional Remarks: ____________

INSPECTION NO. ____________________
FACILITY/CITY ____________________
INSPECTION DATE ____________________

VIII. TSCA §5 RESEARCH & DEVELOPMENT (R&D)

A. Interviewees: (1) ______________________________

(2) ______________________________

B. Background

1. Does facility conduct TSCA defined R&D activities? Yes____ No____

2. If not, where is basic R&D conducted for company?

____

____

3. Does facility/company have a written TSCA R&D policy? Yes____ No____

If yes, does the policy reflect record-keeping and notification requirements that became effective 08/04/86? Yes____ No____

Does the facility/company routinely submit *bona fide* inquiries? Yes____ No____

4. Remarks: ______________________________

____

____

____

____

____

____

____

____

____

____

INSPECTION NO. ____________
FACILITY/CITY ____________
INSPECTION DATE ____________

VIII. TSCA §5 RESEARCH & DEVELOPMENT (R&D) (cont.)

C. Specific R&D Chemicals (one chemical per page)

1. Were any R&D chemicals specifically verified for compliance with R&D exemptions? Yes____ No____

a. Name of chemical: ____________

b. Was chemical produced in a quantity over 100 kg/year? Yes____ No____

c. Was recordkeeping complete? Yes____ No____

What type of records? ____________

____

____

d. Were notifications adequate? Yes____ No____

How verified? ____________

____

____

e. Were "technically qualified individuals" supervising use of the chemical(s)? Yes____ No____

f. Were risk reviews adequately documented? Yes____ No____

g. Were "prudent Laboratory practices" documented? Yes____ No____

How documented? ____________

____

h. Were disposition records complete? Yes____ No____

i. Could a reasonable mass balance be accomplished for reviewed chemicals? Yes____ No____

j. Did amounts produced exceed R&D requirements? Yes____ No____

INSPECTION NO. ____________________
FACILITY/CITY ____________________
INSPECTION DATE ____________________

VIII. TSCA §5 RESEARCH & DEVELOPMENT (R&D) (cont.)

k. What was disposition of excess R&D material(s)?

____

____

2. Remarks: ____

____

____

____

____

____

____

____

INSPECTION NO. ____________________
FACILITY/CITY ____________________
INSPECTION DATE ____________________

IX. LOW VOLUME EXEMPTION (LVE) (One LVE per form)

A. Interviewees: (1) ____________________
(2) ____________________

B. General:

1. LVE No: __________ Date of Receipt: ____________________
21-Day Review Date ____________________

2. Chemical: ____________________ CAS No.: ____________________
Other Names: ____________________

3. Use(s): ____________________
____

4. Manufacturing Site(s): ____________________
____

C. Restrictions:

____
____
____
____
____

D. Compliance:

____
____
____

INSPECTION NO. ________________
FACILITY/CITY ________________
INSPECTION DATE ________________

IX. LOW VOLUME EXEMPTION (LVE) (cont.)

E. Production: 1st 12-month period (______to______): ______kg
2nd 12-month period (______to______): ______kg
3rd 12-month period (______to______): ______kg

F. Test Date: Were test data reviewed for completeness? Yes____ No____

Were data complete? Yes____ No____
____Couldn't determine

G. Remarks:

____

____

____

____

____

____

INSPECTION NO. ____________
FACILITY/CITY ____________
INSPECTION DATE ____________

X. POLYMER EXEMPTION (One PE per form)

A. Interviewees: (1) ____________________
(2) ____________________

B. General:

1. PE No.: __________ Date of Receipt: __________
21-Day Review Date: ____________________

2. Chemical Name: __________ CAS No.: __________
Monomer Composition: __________ ___% Residue ___%
(Verified? ________) __________ ___% Residue ___%
__________ ___% Residue ___%

Number Average MW: __________ Verified: ___Yes ___No
Use(s): __________ Annual Production Vol.: ______kg
(Actual): ______kg

Facility/Address of Manufacturer/Importer:

____

____

3. Remarks:

____

____

____

____

____

____

INSPECTION NO. ______________
FACILITY/CITY ______________
INSPECTION DATE ______________

XI. SIGNIFICANT NEW USE RULE (SNUR) (One SNUR Chemical per form)

A. Interviewees: (1) ______________________________
(2) ______________________________

B. General Information

1. SNUR No.: __________ 90-Day Review Date: __________
2. Chemical Name: ______________ CAS No.: ________
Other Names: ______________________________
3. Use at site: ______________________________

C. Production Compliance

1. Date of first commercial manufacture, report or progressing (circle): ______________________________
How verified (records reviewed and dates): ______________
____
____

2. Remarks
____
____
____
____
____
____

Note: The PMN Technical Content (Part V) and 5(e)/5(f) Order (Part VII) forms are to be used as appropriate for any SNUR review.

INSPECTION NO. ____________
FACILITY/CITY ____________
INSPECTION DATE ____________

XII. TSCA §8(a) LEVEL A AND 8(d) COMPLIANCE REVIEW

A. Interviewees: (1) ____________
(2) ____________

B. §8(a) Level A

1. Name of Chemical: ____________
2. CAS Registry Number: ____________
3. Published Reporting Date for PAIR/CAIR: ____________
4. Corporate fiscal year: ____________
5. Was PAIR/CAIR report submitted: Yes____ No____
   Date of Submission: ____________
6. What information on PAIR/CAIR report was verified? ______
   ____
   ____
   ____
   ____
   ____
   ____
   ____
7. What records were reviewed? ____________
   ____
   ____
8. Did records agree with submitted report? ____________
9. Remarks: ____________
   ____
   ____
   ____

INSPECTION NO. ____________________
FACILITY/CITY ____________________
INSPECTION DATE ____________________

XII. TSCA §8(a) LEVEL A AND 8(d) COMPLIANCE REVIEW (cont.)

C. §8(d)

1. Published reporting date for 8(d): ____________________
2. Was 8(d) report submitted? Yes____ No____
   Date of Submission: ____________________
3. Studies submitted (by title): ____________________
   ____
   ____
4. Remarks: ____________________
   ____
   ____
   ____
   ____

INSPECTION NO. ______________
FACILITY/CITY ______________
INSPECTION DATE ______________

XIII. TSCA §8(c) and 8(e) COMPLIANCE REVIEW

A. Interviewees: (1) ______________
(2) ______________

B. §8(c)

1. Did facility have a §8(c) file? Yes____ No____

Location of file: ______________

Contents: (1) Allegations: Yes____ No____

If yes, how many? ______________

(Attach list of chemical(s), processes and effects)

(2) Copy of the 8(c) regulations? Yes____ No____

(3) Copy of company or facility 8(c) policy? Yes____ No____

2. If allegations were on file, did they appear to represent unknown effects? Yes____ No____

Remarks: ______________

____

3. Were recorded allegations filed correctly and completely? Yes____ No____

Remarks: ______________

____

4. Other records (OSHA, incident files, lawsuits) reviewed for allegations and findings? ______________

____

____

____

INSPECTION NO. ____________________
FACILITY/CITY ____________________
INSPECTION DATE ____________________

XIII. TSCA §8(c) and 8(e) COMPLIANCE REVIEW (cont.)

5. Were company officials generally knowledgeable of 8(c) requirements? Yes____ No____

Remarks: ____

____

____

6. Had there been any apparent attempts at employee outreach? Yes____ No____

Remarks: ____

____

7. Were fact sheets and other information left with plant officials? Yes____ No____

C. §8(e)

1. Did the facility or company have a §8(e) policy? Yes____ No____

Did the facility have an 8(e) file? Yes____ No____

Location of file: ____

Has the facility or company made any TSCA §8(e) submittals to the Agency? Yes____ No____

List: ____

____

Were all 8(e) submissions filed within 15 days? Yes____ No____

How verified: ____

____

INSPECTION NO. ____________
FACILITY/CITY ____________
INSPECTION DATE ____________

XIII. TSCA §8(c) and 8(e) COMPLIANCE REVIEW (cont.)

2. Were company officials generally knowledgeable of 8(e) requirements? Yes____ No____
Remarks: ____________
____
____

3. Were other spills or releases reported to EPA State authority or the Coast Guard in a timely manner? Yes____ No____
Remarks: ____________
____
____

4. Have any civil lawsuits been filed against the facility with respect to health or environmental effects? Yes____ No____
Remarks: ____________
____
____

APPENDIX L

PESTICIDE (FIFRA) INSPECTION CHECKLIST

INTERVIEW/RECORDS

1. Are pesticides used at the facility? Yes____ No____

   a. Circle general types used:

      Algacides Insecticides Fungicides Herbicides Rodenticides
      Other ____

2. Are any restricted use pesticides used at this facility? Yes____ No____

3. Are pesticides applied by facility personnel? Yes____ No____

4. Are pesticides handlers certified? Yes____ No____

   a. Circle type of certification:

      EPA State DOD Other ________________________________

   b. Are pesticide handlers authorized for restricted use pesticides? Yes____ No____

   c. Are licenses/certificates current (not expired)? Yes____ No____

5. Has the facility pesticide program been inspected before? Yes____ No____

   a. Circle by whom:

      EPA State DOD Other ________________________________

   b. General results ____

      ____

6. Does the facility have application records? Yes____ No____

7. Has the facility filed restricted use pesticide reports? Yes____ No____

8. Does the facility have inventory records? Yes____ No____

9. Are target pests indicated on application records? Yes____ No____

   a. Are the pesticides used registered for use against the target pest? Yes____ No____

Appendix L (cont.)

10. Are pesticide handlers' training records current? Yes____ No____

    a. Types of training ____

    ____

STORAGE

1. Is the storage area located on a flood plain? Yes____ No____
2. Is the storage area fenced? Yes____ No____
3. Is the storage area kept locked? Yes____ No____
4. Are pesticides stored under cover? Yes____ No____
5. Is the area well ventilated? Yes____ No____
6. Is the area posted with pesticide or chemical warning signs (i.e., DANGER - POISON)? Yes____ No____
7. Are pesticides separated by type? Yes____ No____
8. Are the pesticides properly labeled? Yes____ No____
9. Are pesticides stored in other than original containers? Yes____ No____

    a. Explain, if yes. ____

    ____

MIXING/LOADING

1. Is there a mixing/loading area? Yes____ No____
2. Is the mixing/loading equipment functional? Yes____ No____
3. Does the equipment help reduce the handlers exposure to pesticide? Yes____ No____
4. Are label directions followed? Yes____ No____
5. Is protective clothing worn by handlers? Yes____ No____
6. Does protective clothing look used? Yes____ No____
7. Is there a mechanism for rinsing containers? Yes____ No____

Appendix L (cont.)

8. How is rinse liquid disposed of? ______________________________

____

9. Is spray equipment cleaned between applications? Yes____ No____

a. How is rinse liquid disposed of? ______________________________

____

CONTAINER DISPOSAL

1. Are label directions followed? Yes____ No____

2. Are empty containers triple rinsed? Yes____ No____

3. Are containers offered for scrap or recycle? Yes____ No____

4. Are containers punctured or crushed to help prevent improper reuse? Yes____ No____

5. Are drums given away for burn barrels, etc.? Yes____ No____

6. Is there a container disposal site at the facility? Yes____ No____

7. Is the site fenced and locked? Yes____ No____

8. Are there pesticide or chemical warning signs posted? Yes____ No____

WORKER PROTECTION STANDARDS

1. Does responsible party keep application records? Yes____ No____

2. Does responsible party know when workers re-enter fields? Yes____ No____

3. Does responsible party warn workers and/or post fields? Yes____ No____

4. Is responsible party informed by applicator when re-entry restrictions apply? Yes____ No____

5. Does responsible party understand current worker protection standards? Yes____ No____

6. Does applicator notify responsible party when using RUPs? Yes____ No____

7. Does applicator post fields when using RUPs? Yes____ No____

APPLICATION OBSERVATION

1. Is spray turned on/off outside of the target field? Yes____ No____
2. Is drift of pesticide mist visible off of the target field? Yes____ No____
3. Is the application pattern recorded? Yes____ No____
4. Are weather measurements taken? Recorded? Yes____ No____
5. Are measures taken to ensure safety of field workers? Yes____ No____
6. Is the application planned to minimize drift to houses, schools, cars, etc.? Yes____ No____

APPENDIX M

WATER SUPPLY CHECKLIST

Date of Inspection ____________________

Community ____ Noncommunity ____

1. Basic Information

Supply Name ________________________ I.D. Number ________________
County ____________________________ Phone __________________
Establishment ________________________ Pop. Served ______________
No. of Service Connections ____________________________________
Period of Operation: 12 month ____________ Seasonal ___________
If Seasonal: From ______________________ To ___________________

2. Surface - Other community system ____ Wells ____ Spring Surface ____

3. Other community system name ____________________________________

4. Wells (source of information) ____________________ Well log (attached)

Year installed _______ Casing Diameter _________ in. Depth _______ft.
Distance to potential contamination ____________ ft. Source ________
Controlled access to well? Yes____ No____
If yes, distance ____
Comments: ____

Well Details:

Well house	Yes____	No____	Well seal	Yes____	No____
Heated, lighted	Yes____	No____	Water level device	Yes____	No____
Casing above grade	Yes____	No____	Grouted	Yes____	No____
Subject to flooding	Yes____	No____	Casing vent	Yes____	No____

Pump Details:

Brand and Model _________________ Horsepower _________________
Capacity ____________________ gpm at ____________________ ft. head

Type: (Circle)

Submersible
Vertical turbine
Deep well jet
Shallow well jet
Shallow well centrifugal

Pump removal provision
Pump to waste piping
Capacity adequate
Sample tap

Comments ____

____

Appendix M (cont.)

5. Other Source ____________ Spring ____________ Surface source

Security (signs, fences, etc.) ____________
Minimum available flow ______ gpm ______ Measured ______ Estimate
Sources of contamination ____________
Source area ownership ____________

Springs

Fencing Yes____ No____ Screened Overflow Yes____ No____
Surface run-off ditch Yes____ No____ Hatch and curbing Yes____ No____
Springbox Yes____ No____ Bottom drain Yes____ No____

Comments: ____________

____

Surface Source

Impoundment Yes____ No____ Spillway Yes____ No____
Diversion dam Yes____ No____ Intake screens Yes____ No____
Infiltration gallery Yes____ No____ Drain Yes____ No____

Source name: ____________

Comments: ____________

6. Storage

General: Volume ___gallons Type: ___Reservoir ___Hydro-pneumatic

Separate inlet/outlet Yes____ No____ Drain to daylight Yes____ No____
Hatch Yes____ No____ Flap valve Yes____ No____
Water level indicator Yes____ No____ Booster pump Yes____ No____

Reservoir: Material ____________

Overflow Yes____ No____
Screened vent Yes____ No____
Covered Yes____ No____

Hydro-pneumatic tank: Operating range ____________ - ____________

Appendix M (cont.)

7. Distribution System

Types of piping ____________________

Adequate pressure (20) Yes____ No____
Flushing program Yes____ No____

8. Chlorination: Continuous chlorination? Yes____ No____

Sodium hypochlorite	Yes____	No____	Proportional to flow	Yes____	No____
Calcium hypochlorite	Yes____	No____	DPD chlorine test kit	Yes____	No____
Gas Chlorine	Yes____	No____	Booster pump	Yes____	No____

Type of chlorinator: ____________________
Contact time provided by: ____________________
Volume of contact chamber: ____________________ gallons (A)
Estimated maximum system flow: ____________________ (B)
Contact time - A/B -: ____________________ minutes
Comments: ____________________
____

9. Monitoring: Type of system (check)

_____ Groundwater
_____ Surface water
_____ Purchase from other water system

Parameter	Required Frequency	Sampling Current? Yes	Sampling Current? No	Met MCLs? Yes	Met MCLs? No
Coliform bacteria	________	___	___	___	___
Turbidity	________	___	___	___	___
Inorganics (nitrate)	________	___	___	___	___
Radiologic contaminants	________	___	___	___	___
Organics	________	___	___	___	___
Other	________	___	___	___	___

Comments: ____________________
____

APPENDIX N

UNDERGROUND INJECTION CONTROL (UIC) CHECKLIST

Table N-1
UIC INSPECTION CHECKLIST

Regulatory Authority to Conduct Inspections

- Safe Drinking Water Act §1445
- 40 CFR §144.1(c)
- 40 CFR §144.51(i)
- RCRA §3007(a) (Class I wells only)

I. Type of UIC Program

_____________ EPA Administered (40 CFR Parts 146 & 147 applicable)
_____________ State Administered (Applicable State Regulations)

II. Type of Well (40 CFR 146.5)

________ Class I (see Parts IV, VA)
________ Class II (see Parts IV, VB)
________ Class III (see Parts IV, VC)
________ Class IV (see Parts IV, VD)
________ Class V (see Parts IV, VE)

III. Operation Authority

________ Rule
________ Permit

IV. General Requirements [must comply with 146.65 (as of July 26, 1988)]

<u>Construction</u>

(1) Depth to base of USDW ________________________________

(2) Depth to injection zone ________________________________

(3) If injecting into USDW, has formation been exempted? Yes____ No____

(4) Adequate confining zone between USDW and injection zone? Yes____ No____

(5) Surface casing length, type ________________________________
volume, type of cement ________________________________

(6) Long string casing length, type ________________________________
volume, type of cement ________________________________

Table N-1 (cont.)

(7) Intermediate casing(s) length type: (a) ____________________
volume, type of cement ____________________
(b) ____________________
____

(8) Injection tubing length, type ____________________
packer Yes____ No____
volume, type of cement on packer ____________________

(9) Injection fluid ____________________

Corrosive ________ Noncorrosive ________

(10) Injection pressure ____________________

(11) Field verification of injection pressure Yes____ No____

Pressure ________

(12) Injection pressure limit? ____________________

(13) Annular pressure ____________________
[Exceeds injection pressure (Class I)] Yes____ No____

(14) Annular fluid ____________________

Types of logs run, date and interval tested: (Must comply with 146.66)

____
____
____
____
____
____

(15) Formation data:

Fluid pressure ____________________
Temperature (Class I) ____________________
Fracture pressure ____________________
Physical characteristics ____________________
Chemical characteristics ____________________

Table N-1 (cont.)

(16) Construction complies with Permit or Rule Yes____ No____

If not, specify ________________________________

(17) Facility operations match permit/rule requirements Yes____ No____

If not, specify ________________________________

(18) EPA notified of any discrepancies in operations Yes____ No____

(19) Emergency procedures adequate Yes____ No____

(20) High and low pressure shutoffs on both pumps and source tanks Yes____ No____

(21) Number and location of injection wells are as described in inventory and/or permit conditions Yes____ No____

(22) All information required is available and current Yes____ No____

(23) Information is retained for required period Yes____ No____

(24) Sampling and analysis data are complete Yes____ No____

(25) EPA notified of any well failures and/or corrective actions Yes____ No____

(26) Plugging and abandonment plan on file Yes____ No____

(27) Financial assurance current and on file Yes____ No____

V. Operating, Monitoring, Reporting Requirements

A. Class I Requirements:

(1) Injection pressure exceeds maximum (except during stimulation) Yes____ No____

(2) Injection between outermost casing and well bore Yes____ No____

Table N-1 (cont.)

(3) Continuous monitoring of:

a.	Injection pressure	Yes____	No____
b.	Flow rate	Yes____	No____
c.	Volume	Yes____	No____
d.	Annulus pressure (between tubing and long string)	Yes____	No____
e.	All monitoring equipment operational [automatic alarms in accordance with 146.67(f)]	Yes____	No____
f.	Temperature of injected fluids	Yes____	No____

(4) Sample injected fluid frequently enough to be representative Yes____ No____

(5) Testing and monitoring requirements (146.68)

- Waste analysis plan prepared Yes____ No____
  - Complete in accordance with 146.68, 148.5, and 268.7 Yes____ No____
- Hydrogeologic compatibility Yes____ No____
- Compatibility of well materials Yes____ No____
- Mechanical integrity
  - Long string, injection tubing, and annular seal pressure tested annually (or whenever well workover completed) Yes____ No____

Long string	Pass ____	Fail ____
Injection tubing	Pass ____	Fail ____
Annular seal	Pass ____	Fail ____

If any were failed, were workovers completed and the well retested? Yes____ No____

Table N-1 (cont.)

- Bottom-hole cement tested with radioactive tracer survey annually Yes____ No____
  Pass____ Fail____

- Temperature, noise or other logs every 5 years to test for fluid movement Yes____ No____
  Specify________________________________
  Pass____ Fail____

- Casing inspection logs every 5 years
  Yes____ No____
  Pass____ Fail____

- Other tests, specify________________________________

• Ambient Monitoring

  - Develop monitoring program with, at a minimum, monitoring of pressure build-up in the injection zone and, during shut-in, pressure fall off tested

    Yes____ No____

  - Other monitoring prescribed by the Director, in accordance with 146.69(e)(2) or (f)

    Yes____ No____
    Specify________________________________
    ____
    ____
    ____

(6) Reporting requirements 146.69

• Quarterly reports, including at a minimum:

  - Maximum injection pressure
  - Description of events
    Exceeding operating parameters
    Triggering alarms, required by 146.67(f)
  - Total volume of fluid injected

Table N-1 (cont.)

- Changes in annular volume
- Physical, chemical and other characteristics of injected fluid
- Results of monitoring under 146.68

• Reporting within 30 days, or with the next quarterly report, whichever is later, the results of:

  - Mechanical integrity tests
  - Any other test prescribed by the Director
  - Any well workover

• Closure plan

  - Facility must prepare, maintain, and comply with a closure plan, in accordance with 146.71

• Post closure

  - Prepare, maintain, and comply with a plan for post closure care, in compliance with 146.72

• Financial responsibility

  - Demonstrate and maintain financial responsibility, in accordance with 146.73

• Restrictions on injection of wastes

  - Injection must comply with restrictions in Parts 148 and 268

• Restricted from disposal:

  - Spent solvent wastes in 261.31 numbered F001-F005, unless waste is a solvent-water mixture or solvent-containing sludge containing less than 1% total F001 through F005, listed in Table A (as of August 8, 1988)

Table N-1 (cont.)

- All spent F001 through F005 wastes containing less than 1% F001 through F005, listed in Table A (effective August 8, 1990).

- Dioxin-containing wastes, specified as F020-F023, and F026-F028 (effective August 8, 1988)

The above does not apply if the waste is treated to meet standards of 268.41, an exemption is granted, an extension of the effective date has been granted, or a treatability variance has been granted under 268.44.

Extension or exemption petitions in response to 148.20 Yes____ No____

Waste analysis plan in compliance with 148.5 and 268.7 Yes____ No____

Operating record in compliance with 268.7 (i.e., notifications and certifications for wastes accepted)

B. Class II Requirements:

(1) Injection pressure exceeds maximum Yes____ No____

(2) Injection pressure exceeds confining zone maximum adjacent to USDW Yes____ No____

(3) If operating above fracture pressure: pressure, location, and number of wells affected by injection (attach map)

(4) Injection between outermost casing and well bore Yes____ No____

(5) Representative sample of injection fluid Yes____ No____

(6) Observation of pressure, flow rate and cumulative volume at the following frequency:

a. Brine disposal (II D) weekly Yes____ No____

Table N-1 (cont.)

b.	Enhanced recovery (II R) monthly	Yes____	No____
c.	Hydrocarbon (II H) daily	Yes____	No____
d.	Cyclic steam daily	Yes____	No____

(7) Recording of one observation of pressure, flow rate, and cummulative volume at least once every 30 days — Yes____ No____

(8) Mechanical integrity test every 5 years — Yes____ No____

(9) Manifold monitoring (for II R or II H)? — Yes____ No____

If yes, demonstration approval by Director for alternate monitoring — Yes____ No____

(10) Maintain records until next permit review — Yes____ No____

(11) All monitoring equipment operational — Yes____ No____

C. Class III Requirements:

(1) Formation data (Substitute for IV 15)

a. If naturally water-bearing:

1. Fluid pressure ______________________________
2. Fracture pressure ______________________________
3. Physical characteristics ______________________
4. Chemical characteristics ______________________

b. If non water-bearing:

1. Fracture pressure ______________________________

c. If formation is a USDW, monitoring wells must be located in the injection formation and in any USDW's above the injection formation to detect migration of injected fluids, process by-products or formation fluids outside the injection zone

Table N-1 (cont.)

1. Are appropriate wells located to monitor injection operation Yes____ No____

2. If area is subject to subdence or catestrophic collapse, are wells located so they will not be physically affected? Yes____ No____

d. If injection wells penetrate a USDW and in an area subject to subsidence or catastrophic collapse:

1. Are these monitoring wells completed into the USDW? Yes____ No____

2. Are the monitoring wells capable of detecting the movement of injected fluids and by-products into the USDW? Yes____ No____

3. Are the wells located outside the physical influence of subsidence or catastrophic collapse? Yes____ No____

e. What is the frequency of monitoring wells under c and d above?____________________

f. Were the following points evaluated in the determination of monitoring frequency?

1. Population relying on USDW Yes____ No____

2. Population affected by injection Yes____ No____

Table N-1 (cont.)

	3.	Proximity of injection to points of drinking water withdrawal	Yes____	No____
	4.	Operating pressures	Yes____	No____
	5.	Nature and volume of injected fluid	Yes____	No____
	6.	Injection well density	Yes____	No____
(2)		Injection pressure exceeds maximum	Yes____	No____
(3)		Injection between outermost casing and well bore	Yes____	No____
(4)		Injection fluid sampled frequently enough to be representative	Yes____	No____
(5)		Monitoring of injection pressure semi-monthly and either:	Yes____	No____
	a.	Flow rate	Yes____	No____
	b.	Volume	Yes____	No____
	c.	Metering and daily recording of:	Yes____	No____
		1. injected volume	Yes____	No____
		2. produced fluid	Yes____	No____
(6)		MIT at least once every 5 years for salt solution mining	Yes____	No____
(7)		Monitoring the fluid volume in the injection zone semimonthly	Yes____	No____
(8)		Monitoring the appropriate parameters chosen to measure water quality in the monitoring wells semimonthly (see 12c above)	Yes____	No____
(9)		Quarterly monitoring of wells (see 12d above)	Yes____	No____

Table N-1 (cont.)

(10) Manifold monitoring? Yes____ No____

(11) Individual well monitoring? Yes____ No____

(12) Facility received approval for manifold monitoring? Yes____ No____

(13) Quarterly reports to Director? including: Yes____ No____

a. MIT Yes____ No____
b. Other tests (specify below) Yes____ No____
c. Reported by project/field Yes____ No____
d. Individual wells Yes____ No____

____

____

D. Class IV Requirements:

Class IV wells are banned and have no inspection requirements other than plugging and abandonment or continued monitoring according to individual State/EPA requirements

(1) Date plugged and abandoned ______________________

(2) Other available information ______________________

____

____

____

____

____

____

Table N-1 (cont.)

E. Class V Requirements:

No monitoring requirements unless permit has been issued by a delegated State.

If State issued permit, specify requirements and compliance/ noncompliance

____

____

____

____

____

Table N-2

ADDITIONAL UIC INSPECTION CHECKLIST*

____/___/____ Date of inspection

____/___/____ Date of last inspection

DESCRIPTION OF CORROSION PREVENTION/MONITORING SYSTEM:

____ Corrosion loop
____ Weight loss coupons
____ Electrical resistance probes
____ Polarization resistance Probes
____ Logs-type________________
____ Cathodic protection
____ Soil potential survey
____ Other (please describe)

____

____

DATE OF LAST CORROSION EVALUATION BY OPERATOR:

Type
____ Visual
____ Other
(describe briefly)

____

____

RESULTS:

____ OK
Corrosion of:
____ Casing; depth ______.
____ Tubing; depth ______.
____ Packer

* *From "Underground Injection Control Inspection Manual," prepared by Engineering Enterprises, Inc. for EPA, February 1988*

Table N-2 (cont.)

____ Other (indicate component ______________________________
____

Injection fluid released Yes ____ No ____

Contaminated USDW Yes ____ No ____

CASING MATERIAL:

____ Steel

____ Stainless steel

____ Monel

____ Titanium

____ Other; specify ______________________________

TUBING MATERIAL:

____ Steel

____ Stainless steel

____ Fibercast

____ Fiberglass

____ Other ______________________________

PACKER TYPE AND MATERIAL

____ Tension

____ Compression

____ Material: Steel ___ Other ___ specify ____________________

____ Special protection (please indicate). Note that some packers, especially tension packers, have rubber pads or special coatings to prevent contact with injection fluids.

WASTE CHARACTERISTICS:

pH = __________

____ Dissolved oxygen (concentration) _____ mg/l

____ Hydrogen sulfide, H_2S (concentration) ______________ mg/l

Table N-2 (cont.)

____ Carbon dioxide, CO_2 (concentration) ______ mg/l
____ Amenable to biological degradation
____ Acidic
____ Basic
____ Most recent sample analysis (attached) indicates no significant changes

EVALUATION OF THE CASING/TUBING/PACKER MATERIALS TO RESIST CORROSION:

(By consulting the tables in page _____ of the manual, a preliminary evaluation can be made. The inspector may also use different criteria for evaluation; however, he/she should indicate the reason for the decision.)

______ Adequate

______ Inadequate

Criteria used: ____

____

____

____

Pressure Gauges

	Yes	No	N/A
1. Is Bourdon tube gauge protected from corrosion and freezing?			
2. Is pressure reading relatively constant? (absence of rapid pointer movement due to pulsating pressure or pipeline vibration)			
3. Are gauge materials suitable for the media monitored?			
4. Is a pressure transducer properly installed?			

5. Date gauge last calibrated: ________________________________

Table N-2 (cont.)

6. Method of calibration: ____
____

Pressure Recorders

1. Are pressure recorders properly installed (e.g., chart protected from weather, etc.)?

2. Are pressure recorders operational (e.g., ink, charts moving, etc.)?

3. Is back-up gauge provided?

4. Do back-up pressure and recorded pressure agree?

FLOW MEASUREMENT - GENERAL

Yes No N/A (1) (a) Primary flow measuring device is properly installed and maintained.

Yes No N/A (b) Is there a straight length of pipe before and after the flowmeter of at least 5 to 20 diameters? This depends on the type of flowmeter and the ratio of pipe diameter to throat diameter. Also, the introduction of straightening vanes may reduce this requirement.

Yes No N/A (c) If a magnetic flowmeter is used, check for electric noise in its proximity and that the unit is properly grounded.

Yes No N/A (d) Is the full-pipe requirement met?

Yes No N/A (2) Flow records are properly kept.

Yes No N/A (a) Records of flow measurement are recorded in a bound numbered log book.

Table N-2 (cont.)

Yes	No	N/A		(b) All charts are maintained in a file.
Yes	No	N/A		(c) All calibration data is entered in the log book.
Yes	No	N/A	(3)	Sharp drops or increases in flow values are accounted for.
Yes	No	N/A	(4)	Actual flow is measured.
Yes	No	N/A	(5)	Secondary instruments (totalizers, records, etc.) are properly operated and maintained.
Yes	No	N/A	(6)	Appropriate spare parts are stocked.

Electrical noise can sometimes be detected by erratic operation of the flowmeter's output. Another indication is the flowmeter location in the proximity of large motors, power lines, welding machines, and other high electrical field generating devices.

1. Type of flowmeter used: ______________________

2. Note on diagram flowmeter placement in the system. Observe the direction of flow, the vertical height relationship of the source, outfall, and measuring meter. Give all dimensions in pipe diameters.

3. Is meter installed correctly?

   (a) If magnetic flowmeter, it should be installed in an ascending column, to reduce air bubbles and assure full pipe flow.

   (b) If differential pressure meter such as venturi, it should be installed in a horizontal plane so that high pressure tap is on the inlet of flow and taps are horizontal sloping slightly downward with facilities for cleaning taps.

Table N-2 (cont.)

4. Flow range to be measured: ____________________

Yes No N/A 5. Flow measurement equipment adequate to handle expected ranges of flow values.

6. What are the most common problems that the operator has had with the flowmeter?

7. Flowmeter flow rate: ______ mgd; Totalizer flow rate: _____ mgd; Error ______%

8. Permit project flow: ____________________________

Yes No N/A 9. Flow totalizer is properly calibrated.

10. Frequency of routine inspection by trained operator _____/month.

11. Frequency of maintenance inspections by facility personnel: _____/year.

12. Frequency of flowmeter calibration: ____________

13. Indicator of correct operation:

redundant flowmeters _____ auxiliary flowmeters _____ pressure readings _____ other __________ power usage of pumps _____

14. Indicators of proper Quality Assurance:

redundant flowmeters _____ frequent calibrations _____ other ________________________________

APPENDIX O

COMMUNITY RIGHT-TO-KNOW CHECKLIST

Table O-1

EPCRTKA CHECKLIST

A. Is the facility handling extremely hazardous substances at levels identified in 40 CFR Part 355 Appendix A or handling mixtures at levels defined in 40 CFR 355.30(e) [40 CFR 355.30(a)]? Yes____ No____

If No, go to C

B. Has the facility owner/operator notified the State emergency response commission, the local emergency planning agency and the local fire department that the facility is regulated by EPCRTKA [40 CFR 355.30(b)]? Yes____ No____

NOTE: In the event no State commission was formed, any report or notification required by either EPCRTKA or the promulgated regulations is to be sent to the Governor of the State.

If No, go to C
If Yes:

Obtain copies of all applicable letters or memos of this action.

1. Was the notification submitted by May 17, 1987 or within 60 days after the facility began handling extremely hazardous substances [40 CFR 355.30(b)]? Yes____ No____

2. Has the facility owner/operator notified the local emergency planning committee of the identity of the facility emergency coordinator and that the person is available to work with the committee on emergency planning activities [40 CFR 355.30(c)]? Yes____ No____

3. Was this notification done by September 17, 1987 or within 30 days of the committee's formation [40 CFR 355.30(c)]? Yes____ No____

Identify the date the local emergency planning committee was formed.

4. If changes have been made at the facility which are relevant to emergency planning, has the facility owner/operator notified the local emergency planning committee of those changes [40 CFR 355.30(d)]? Yes____ No____

Table O-1 (cont.)

C. Has the facility had any release of hazardous substances identified in 40 CFR 302.4(a), Table 302.4 or 302.4(b) at levels defined in 40 CFR 302.5? Yes____ No____

If No, go to D
If Yes:

1. Were the persons within the boundary of the facility the only ones affected? Yes____ No____

2. Is the release a "federally permitted release," as defined in CERCLA, Section 101(10)? Yes____ No____

3. Is the release continuous, as defined in CERCLA, Section 103(f)? Yes____ No____

4. Does CERCLA, Section 101(22) exempt reporting of the release? Yes____ No____

If the answer to all four questions is Yes, the release is not reportable under EPCRTKA, go to D.

If the answer to any question is No, was the release immediately reported to the National Response Center [40 CFR 302.6]?

Yes____ No____

Was an immediate report also made to the local emergency planning committee [40 CFR 355.40(b)]?

Yes____ No____

D. Is the facility owner/operator required by OSHA regulation (Hazard Communication Rules) to prepare Material Safety Data Sheets (MSDS) for hazardous chemicals defined by OSHA? (This includes manufacturing facilities contained within SIC Codes 20 through 39 and non-manufacturing facilities which were required to comply with the OSHA regulation by May 23, 1988.) Yes____ No____

If no, go to E

1. Does the facility have hazardous chemicals in amounts equal to or greater than 10,000 pounds or extremely hazardous substances greater than or equal to 500 pounds (or 55 gallons) or the threshold planning quantity defined in 40 CFR 355, whichever is less? Yes____ No____

Table O-1 (cont.)

a. If Yes, were MSDSs or a list of materials covered by MSDSs submitted to the State emergency response commission, the local emergency planning committee and the local fire department by October 17, 1987 or within 3 months of the facility becoming subject to 40 CFR 370 [40 CFR 370.20(b)(1)(i)]? (See 40 CFR 370.21 for information content reporting requirements.) Yes____ No____

b. If Yes, has the facility owner/operator submitted an inventory of hazardous chemicals and extremely hazardous substances to the State emergency response commission, local emergency planning committee and the local fire department by March 1, 1988 or by March 1 of the first year the facility becomes subject to 40 CFR 370 [40 CFR 370.20(b)(2)(i)]? (See 40 CFR 370.25 for inventory reporting requirements, 370.28 for how to handle mixtures, and 370.40 for the inventory format.)

2. For hazardous chemicals handled at the facility in an amount less than 10,000 pounds, were MSDSs or list of chemicals covered by MSDSs submitted to the above groups by October 17, 1989 or within 2 years and 3 months of the facility becoming subject to 40 CFR 370 [40 CFR 370.20(b)(1)(ii)]. (See 40 CFR 370.21 for information content reporting requirements.) Yes____ No____

If Yes, has the facility owner/operator submitted to the State emergency response commission, the local emergency planning committee and the local fire department an inventory of hazardous chemicals by March 1, 1989 or by March 1 of the first year the facility becomes subject to 40 CFR 370 [40 CFR 370.20(b)(20(ii)]? (See 40 CFR 370.25 for inventory reporting requirements, 370.28 for how to handle mixtures and 370.40 for the inventory format.)
Yes____ No____

NOTE: On March 1, 1990, the levels for inventory reporting of hazardous chemicals becomes any level handled. The levels for extremely hazardous substances remain the same.

E. Determine whether the facility is covered by the Toxic Chemical Reporting requirements in 40 CFR 372.30 for each applicable year by answering the following for any calendar year since and including 1987:

1. The facility has 10 or more full-time employees. Yes____ No____

2. The facility has an operation found in SIC codes 20 through 39.
Yes____ No____

Table O-1 (cont.)

NOTE: See 40 CFR 372.22(b) for further criteria of operation combinations covered.

3. The facility manufactured, imported, processed, or otherwise handled toxic chemicals in excess of the threshold quantities identified in 40 CFR 372.25. (40 CFR 372.65 identifies toxic chemicals covered by this regulation.) Yes____ No____

Continue only if Yes to all three of the above questions.
If No, go to G.

F. Did the facility owner/operator comply with the following reporting requirements (40 CFR 372.30).

NOTE: See 40 CFR 372.38 for exemptions:

1. Was an EPA Form R (EPA Form 9350-1) submitted for each toxic chemical manufactured, imported and/or used in excess of the applicable threshold quantity? [40 CFR 372.30(a)] Yes____ No____

2. Was an EPA Form R submitted for each mixture or trade name product imported, processed, or otherwise used which contains a toxic chemical(s) in excess of the applicable threshold quantity? [40 CFR 372.30(b)] Yes____ No____

3. Was each form for calendar year activities submitted before July 1 of the next calendar year? Yes____ No____

G. Determine if the facility is a supplier of toxic chemicals or mixture [See 40 CFR 372.45(d) through (g) for exemptions.] Yes____ No____

If Yes, continue
If No, end the inspection

1. Did the facility owner/operator provide a written notification that a shipment contains a toxic chemical or that the shipment contains a toxic chemical mixture (40 CFR 372.45)? Yes____ No____

2. Did the notification provide the following:

   a. The chemical or mixture is subject to reporting requirements of EPCRTKA and 40 CFR 372? Yes____ No____

Table O-1 (cont.)

b. Each chemical name and Chemical Abstract Service (CAS) Number? Yes____ No____

c. The weight percent of each chemical in the mixture or trade name product? Yes____ No____

3. Was the notification sent with the first shipment in each calendar year beginning January 1, 1987? Yes____ No____

4. If changes were made to the mixture or trade name product, was a notification provided by the facility owner/operator with the first shipment after the material changed? Yes____ No____

5. If the facility owner/operator discovers new information about the mixture or trade name product, was a new notification sent to each previous recipient within 30 days of the discovery? Yes____ No____

6. If an MSDS was required to be prepared, was the notification either attached to or incorporated into the MSDS? Yes____ No____

APPENDIX P

LABORATORY AUDIT CHECKLISTS

Table P-1

METHOD 1310-EP TOXICITY AND STRUCTURAL INTEGRITY TEST

Checklist

Requirement: 40 CFR 261.24

Reference: SW 846, 2nd ed.

Principle: Sample is pretreated and then continuously extracted with a weak acid for, typically, 24 hours. The extract is then analyzed for specified elemental, pesticide and herbicide constituents.*

Essential Equipment:

___ Does the structural integrity tester conform to specifications?
___ 0.33 kg hammer?
___ Hammer free fall of 6 inches?

___ Does the extractor prevent stratification of the sample and extraction fluid?
___ Does it ensure that all sample surfaces are continuously brought into contact with the extraction fluid?
___ If rotary, does it turn at 29 rpm?

---

* *Separate checklists have been prepared for the EP constituents: As, Ba, Cd, Cr, Pb, Hg, Se, Ag, Endrin, Lindane, Methoxychlor, Toxaphene, 2,4-D and 2,4,5 TP Silvex.*

Element	*Maximum Concentration*
As	*5 mg/L*
Ba	*100*
Cd	*1*
Cr	*5*
Pb	*5*
Hg	*0.2*
Se	*1*
Ag	*5*

Reagents:

___ Is 0.5 molar acetic acid used as the extractant?

___ Is deionized or distilled water which has been monitored for impurities used?

___ Is the acetic acid monitored for impurities?

Procedure:

Wastes Containing Free Liquids

___ Is filter preweighed to the nearest 0.01 g?

___ Is the filter handled so as to prevent damage and contamination?

___ Is the sample preweighed to the filter? How much sample ___________?

___ Is the filter prewetted with sample?

___ Are the filters checked for impurities? How? ____________________

___ If samples do not filter at ambient pressure, is filter pressure properly incremented up to 75 psig or until gas passes before filtration is discontinued?

___ Is filter residue dried at 80 °C in order to determine percent solids?

___ Is a new portion used for the actual extraction?

___ Are percent solids correctly calculated?

___ Is the extract properly preserved, stored and refrigerated?

___ If the solid comprises less than 0.5% of the waste is it discarded and the remainder of the sample analyzed directly?

___ If the solid material in the sample has components larger than 9.5 millimeters or individual surface areas greater than 3.1 square centimeters is the material subjected to a structural integrity test?

___ Is the sample for the structural integrity test properly obtained (cut or cast into a cylinder 3.3 cm diameter x 7.1 cm long)?

___ Is the structural integrity test properly performed (drop tester, 15 times)

___ If so tested, are all constituents passed through a 9.5 mm sieve?

___ If the solid material in the sample has components larger than 9.5 millimeters or individual surface areas greater than 3.1 square centimeters, is the material subjected to a structural integrity test?

___ Is the sample for the structural integrity test properly obtained (cut or cast into a cylinder 3.3 cm diameter x 7.1 cm long)?

___ Is the structural integrity test properly performed (drop tester, 15 times)

___ If so tested, are all constituents passed through a 9.5 mm sieve?

___ If the solid comprises more than 0.5% of the sample, are the appropriate volumes of liquids and extracting solution determined? Formula?

___ Is the amount of distilled water to be added determined correctly?

___ Are pH adjustments performed in accordance with the procedure?*

___ Is the temperature maintained between 20 and 40 °C?

___ At the end of the extraction, is the proper amount of deionized water added to the mixture.

___ After filtration, are the resultant liquids from the initial filtration and extract properly combined?

___ Are items contacting the sample cleaned to prevent contamination of the sample?

Analysis:

Elemental Constituents

___ Is the aqueous liquid portion digested in accordance with SW 846 method 3010?

---

* *The pH is adjusted with acetic acid as follows:*

1. *Initially, after a brief agitation unless the pH is already < or = to 5. Thereafter, if the pH rises above 5.2, it will be adjusted to 4.8 to 5.2 [until the maximum allowable amount (4W grams) of acetic acid has been delivered]*
2. *At 15-minute increments until the pH adjustment <0.5 pH units.*
3. *At 30-minute increments until the pH adjustment <0.5 pH units.*
4. *At 60-minute increments until the pH adjustment <0.5 pH units.*
5. *One final time at 6 hours.*

Attachment: NEIC benchsheets

___ If an organic phase results, is this digested by methods 3030, 3040, or 3050?

___ Are the digestion procedures properly performed?

___ Are atomic absorption methods used to analyze the digests?

___ Is the method of known additions used in each case?

Pesticides and Herbicides

___ Are methods 8080 and 8150 used (SW 846, 2nd ed.)?

___ Are the methods used properly?

Calculation

___ Are concentrations properly calculated in individual samples?

___ If more than one phase, is the overall EP concentration properly calculated from the proportions?

Table P-2

TOTAL NONFILTERABLE RESIDUE (TSS)

Checklist

Requirements: 40 CFR 136, October 26, 1984, pp. 43234-43442

Reference: Standard Methods, 15th edition and the 1979 EPA Methods Manual

Principle: When a solution is filtered using a specified grade of glass fiber filter, the solids remaining on the filter, after drying at 103 to 105 °C, constitute the amount of total nonfilterable residue or TSS in that sample aliquot. Differential weighing and mathematical adjustment for sample volume quantifies the result in mg/L.

Essential Equipment:

___ Drying oven capable of maintaining a temperature between 103 to 105 °C

___ Drying oven make and model: ______________________________

___ Thermometer graduated in one degree increments at the 100 degree range

___ Analytical balance make and model ___________________________

___ Analytical balance with adequate capacity and sensitivity of at least .0001 gram

___ Vacuum system capable of developing 0.5 atmospheres suction

___ Air tight desiccator with adequate capacity and sample segregation

___ Appropriate volumetric sample aliquoting device. Specify ___________

___ Gooch crucibles or aluminum weighing dishers. Specify ___________

___ Filtration apparatus. Specify ________________________________

___ Flat, nonpointed tweezers

Reagents and Supplies:

___ Indicating calcium sulfate or silica gel. Specify ___________________

___ RA 934AH filter media or equivalent? Specify size and type __________

Sampling and Preservation:

___ If the sample is not analyzed within 2 hours of collection, is it kept at 4 °C?

___ Are all samples analyzed within 7 days of collection?

___ Are glass or plastic sample containers used?

Procedure:

Method used? ______________________________

___ Is the filter pre-washed with 3- to 20-mL aliquots of distilled or DI water?

___ Filters properly dried and desiccated? Time spent ______________

___ Is the desiccant unspent (blue, not pinkish blue or pink)?

___ Are filters properly seated, wrinkled side up prior to sample introduction?

___ Is the sample well mixed before aliquoting?

___ Is the sample size or filter size selected to yield 2.5 to 200 mg of deposited residue?

___ Is volumetric glassware properly sized to ensure accurate aliquoting?

___ Is the sample residue post-washed with three 10-mL portions of distilled or deionized water?

___ In conjunction with post-washing, is sample rinsed from dispensing glassware if appropriate? (The same rinses should be used for both.)

___ Are residues dried for a minimum of 1 hour and desiccated until cool?

___ Are the drying cycles repeated to verify weight constancy?

___ Are successive weights during this step brought to either less than 4% of the previous weight or 0.5 mg difference?

___ Are special forceps used to handle filters?

___ Are sample volumes and filter weights properly recorded?

___ Are results calculated correctly?

___ Are precautions taken during sample handling, drying and desiccation to keep extraneous material off the filters?

Required by the 1979 EPA Methods Manual:

___ Is the aliquot of sample selected such that at least 0.0576 mg per square cm of residue is filtered and that total filtration time does not exceed 10 minutes?

___ If a 4.7 cm diameter filter is not used, is the amount of wash water used approximately 2 ml per square cm?

___ The 1979 EPA Manual allows material such as leaves, sticks, fish, and lumps of fecal matter to be excluded or removed from the sample if their inclusion would produce results nonrepresentative of the source.

Records:

___ Are bench records maintained for a period of at least 3 years?

___ Are the date and time of sampling, as well as the individual performing the sampling, recorded?

___ Are the date and time of analysis, the analyst, and the method of analysis properly documented?

Recommended Quality Control:

___ Are filter blanks used to check for problems?

___ Are duplicate samples analyzed? Frequency _______ Range _______

___ Is the balance professionally serviced? Last service date ___________

___ Is the calibration of the balance checked each day of use?

___ Is a balance calibration log maintained?

___ Is the balance presently level and in calibration?

___ Is the balance in an area free from temperature excursions and dust?

___ Has the calibration of the thermometer been verified? Documented? ___

___ Is the oven temperature checked each day of use? Documented? _____

Note: Place check in left hand column if this item is satisfactory. If unsatisfactory, additional comments may be included at the end.